THE MEDIEVAL LYRIC

Modern Languages and Literature

THE MEDIEVAL LYRIC

Peter Dronke

Fellow of Clare Hall, Cambridge, and
University Lecturer in Medieval Latin

Cambridge University Press

Hutchinson & Co. (Publishers) Ltd
3 Fitzroy Square, London W1P 6JD

London Melbourne Sydney Auckland
Wellington Johannesburg and agencies
throughout the world

First published 1968
Second edition 1977
© Peter Dronke 1968, 1977

Published in the U.S.A. and Canada by
the Syndics of the Cambridge University Press,
32 East 57th Street, New York, NY 10022, U.S.A.

Set in Monotype Fournier
Printed in Great Britain by litho at The Anchor Press Ltd
and bound by Wm Brendon & Son Ltd
both of Tiptree, Essex

Hutchinson ISBNs
0 09 132080 1 hard covers   excluding U.S.A. and Canada

Cambridge University Press ISBNs
0 521 21944 2 hard covers ⎫
0 521 29319 7 paperback   ⎭ U.S.A. and Canada only

CONTENTS

Contents

ACKNOWLEDGMENTS

I am grateful to Messrs Allen and Unwin for permission to quote Arthur Waley's translation *The cock has crowed*; and to the following for permission to reproduce modern transcriptions of medieval melodies: to the Diputación Provincial de Barcelona for Higinio Anglés; to Ugo Guanda, Parma, for Giuseppe Vecchi; to Oxford University Press for Anselm Hughes; and to Arno Volk Verlag, Köln, for Heinrich Husmann.

PREFACE

This book is intended as an introduction to medieval lyric, secular and sacred, in both the Romance and the Germanic languages. The period covered is approximately 850 to 1300—from Notker to Dante. The lyrical poetry of these centuries is to a striking degree international. The songs composed in Latin and in a number of vernaculars —Provençal and Catalan, Spanish and Portuguese, French, Italian, German and Dutch and English—can be truly understood only within the framework of a European tradition. This tradition is a unity— though by no means an undifferentiated one. At present, however, no book exists in any language that treats this lyrical tradition as a whole.

To attempt such a book is a risk and an adventure. It would have been relatively easy to compile a handbook, based on the standard histories of the various national literatures, which might give synopses of the life and works of several hundreds of poets—without ever having to court the danger of commitment to even one of their poems. But my aim has been a different and I think more arduous one: in each of six chapters I have tried to present one of the principal lyrical genres current in medieval Europe by discussing in detail a few of the outstanding achievements within it. By way of specific examples I have tried also to suggest what certain kinds of lyric throughout Europe have in common, and where the unique contributions lie. This selective discussion is complemented at the end of the book by a bibliographical guide, arranged by languages, dates and authors, so as to give a more detailed historical orientation.

In the chapters themselves, on the other hand, the emphasis and choice are necessarily personal: after surveying as far as possible a comprehensive range of lyric in the period, I have concentrated only on what seemed to me most alive and creative. My criteria have been poetic rather than musical—though where the melodies of lyrics survive I have tried to take these too into account.[1] The aim throughout has been to give what aid I could towards the understanding and enjoying of the medieval lyrics that I value most, by way of interpretation, critical comment, and an essential minimum of background information.

The poetry here presented is so genuinely varied that I hope to be forgiven if I do not begin with a discussion or definition of the nature of lyric itself. My subject is the contents of the *chansonniers* or *Liederhandschriften* of the Middle Ages, in all their diversity, and by 'lyrical' I shall mean whatever belongs to, or essentially resembles, what is contained in these. Is it too much to hope that the very range of the poetry to be cited and discussed in these pages may add to our understanding of what lyric can be?

A few words about the limitations of this book are perhaps necessary. I cannot claim a specialist knowledge of all the languages of the lyrics treated here. I have tried throughout to use the best available editions, and where possible have sought expert advice on textual cruces and difficulties of sense; but inevitably a certain number of disputed readings, and disputable translations, will remain.[2]

In my translations I have tried whenever I could to give some suggestion of the form of a lyric as well as of its content. None the less

---

1. One further consideration was relevant to my choice of material for discussion: with the exception of one or two brief quotations, perhaps twenty lines in all, I have not included any poetry that has been treated in my earlier study, *Medieval Latin and the Rise of European Love-Lyric* (2nd ed., 2 vols., Oxford 1968).

2. My citations of texts are based on the editions (or occasionally, on the manuscripts) indicated in the notes at the back of the book (pp. 261–4). Notes of a more discursive kind are to be found at the foot of the page in the chapters themselves. I have taken some minor liberties with the punctuation of texts, in the hope of gaining greater lucidity for a modern English reader; for this reason too I have normalised þ and ð to 'th' in my Middle English lyrics. Occasionally I have modified the line-arrangement or look of stanzas without comment. When I have introduced a variant reading or emendation not contained in the cited edition, however, I have always mentioned this explicitly.

In the field of medieval lyric so much is still uncertain, so much controversial, that even in an introductory book such as this I have not been able wholly to avoid the occasional more technical note, to indicate at least by a word why I have chosen a certain reading, why rejected a certain way of construing a line, or where a different view may be found. If in these rapid notes I seem to have touched on weighty problems in too cavalier a fashion, I ask specialists to believe it is not out of disrespect, but simply that to have attempted an adequate discussion of such problems (and of many others I have been aware of but have not signalled explicitly) would have radically changed the scope of this book.

formal considerations always took second place: my first concern throughout was that the meaning of the poetry should emerge as clearly as possible, and that the translations should avoid all stilted and unreal language (as I avoided stilted and unreal poetry in my choice of originals). In my discussions I have quoted as extensively as possible. I should have been happiest had I been able to give a complete text and translation of every lyric—but the book would have been twice as long.

A book that centres on interpretation and appraisal cannot pretend to the authority of a handbook or literary history. At times (with such lyrics, for instance, as the Provençal *Mei amic e mei fiel*, the German 'childhood ballad' by the Wilde Alexander or the English song of the moor-maiden, with Dante's *Così nel mio parlar* or Walther von der Vogelweide's *Ir reinen wîp, ir werden man*) I have proposed interpretations which depart radically from what has been suggested hitherto. Yet I have not been able in this brief compass to justify my divergences from previous scholarship in detail. Such interpretations as I have given do not and cannot make any claim to be definitive: their only claim is to stimulate the reader (perhaps even the specialist reader) to look at some exciting poetry afresh.

There are many other poems where I believe I have tried to formulate an interpretation and an appraisal for the first time, lyrics that may have had their due from palaeographer and philologist, but not yet from lovers of poetry. Here the risk may well be even greater than with the famous but much-debated poems. At all events, if by confronting and then discarding my observations the reader wins a new, or closer, relation to the poetry, the observations will have served their purpose.

I should like to express my warmest thanks to the colleagues and friends who have helped me in the preparation of this book: Mercedes Costa i Paretas, who obtained for me the photograph of the *joglar* and *joglaresa* who appear on the cover of the paperback edition; Friedrich Gennrich, who gave me his advice about melodies and the permission to use some of his own transcriptions; Ian Bent, who has transcribed the melody of Hildegard of Bingen's *Columba aspexit* at my request, and John Stevens, who has made me a new transcription of *Bryd one brere*; and those who have generously read various parts of the book in typescript and made suggestions and corrections: Guido Favati, Ingeborg Glier, Peter King, Charity Meier-Ewert, Olive Sayce, Samuel Stern, and Terence Waldron. Marcelle Thiébaux has most kindly read and commented on the whole book in proof. None of these scholars must be held in any way responsible for the faults that still undoubtedly remain; once or twice, I must confess, I have persisted in an opinion even after being most valuably cautioned. My debt to my wife Ursula, who has read and heard and criticised parts of the book at all stages of its making is, as always, incalculably great.

Cambridge
August 1967   P.D.

I

INTRODUCTION:

PERFORMERS AND PERFORMANCE

The men and women who sang and played in medieval Europe were the heirs of both a Roman and a Germanic musical tradition.

In Rome the vogue for music of every kind seems to have increased enormously from the first century of the Christian era. Writers such as Quintilian and Seneca see in the newfangled music signs of moral as well as of artistic degeneration, and look back nostalgically to a time when music was more serious or more sacred, a time when, after a patrician banquet, the lute would circulate among the guests, who performed songs in praise of heroes and of gods; when dances were not lascivious in character, but ceremonial or religious. Under the Empire, it appears, a more sensual quality came to pervade both vocal and instrumental music, the songs and dances of private feast and public spectacle alike. The musicians were mostly Greeks, whether from Europe, Alexandria, or Asia Minor; the most celebrated dancers, girls from Cadiz (the provocative *puellae Gaditanae* described by Martial and Juvenal), or again from Syria—women such as the *copa* so vividly evoked in a poem that was long attributed to Vergil:

> The Syrian cabaret-hostess, whose hair is bound back by a Grecian
> headband,
> whose quivering thighs sway to the rhythm of castanets,
> dances, intoxicated, voluptuous, in the smoky tavern . . .

Music played a part in every aspect of Roman life. The highest art was considered to be that of the citharode, who sang accompanying himself or herself on the lute. Quintilian gives a precise account of the mode of performance:

> Must not the lute-playing singers (*citharoedi*) attend simultaneously to their memory, to the sound of their voice and to the many inflections, and while striking the chords [with a plectrum] with their right hand, with their left they draw their fingers along them, silence them, and prepare the chords to come; and even their foot does not remain idle but observes the formal regulation of the tempo.

The song was often preceded by an instrumental prelude; more rarely, the soloist sang unaccompanied. The other instrument that was important for lyrical performance was the flute (*tibia*, generally the double flute), which accompanied the actor on the stage. Cicero is reported to have said: 'Those who cannot become lutanists become flautists'. Both the lute and the double flute were used polyphonically. Dances and mimes were performed to the accompaniment of the flute and the *scabellum* (an instrument like a castanet, but played with the foot), or of a small orchestra with percussion instruments. Trumpets, and other brass instruments, were employed for martial music, and played a large part in military life. There was special music for funerals, and funeral-songs (*naeniae*). The first-century records often suggest an excess of music, both in private and public life. In Petronius' fantasy of the banquet of the parvenu Trimalchio, almost everything is done to music—a waiter cannot bring a goblet without bursting into song. Nero made frequent and embarrassing public appearances as a singer. Seneca mentions a concert performed by a huge ensemble of orchestra and choir, a choir in which men and women sang in harmony, singing in three registers (as men and boys were to do later in medieval organum). Many references in Suetonius show the passion of the Roman public, high and low, for musical mime, lyric plays and musical spectacle of every kind. From an anecdote he tells of the Emperor Galba we can see how strikingly a song could become 'popular':

> Galba's arrival [in Rome, A.D. 68] was not altogether well received, as became apparent at the very next show, for, when the players of an Atellane [a farce that often contained elements of topical satire] began the well-known song 'Here comes Onesimus, down from his farm', all the spectators finished it in chorus and mimed it, repeating that particular verse again and again. [No doubt they meant it as an allusion to the churlishness of the Emperor.]

At the same time we must reckon with a rich tradition of popular songs associated with many aspects of the everyday life of the people.

There is a remarkable passage about this in a sermon of St John
Chrysostom, the 'golden-mouthed' preacher who became patriarch of
Constantinople in 397:

> By nature we take such delight in song that even infants clinging at the
> breast, if they are crying and perturbed, can be put to sleep by singing. This
> is how the nurses who carry them in their arms, walking them up and down
> many times and singing them childish ditties, make their eyelids close. So
> too journeymen, driving their yoked oxen in the noonday, often sing as they
> go, making the way less weary by their songs. Not only journeymen but
> wine-growers, treading the winepress, or gathering grapes, or dressing the
> vines, or doing any other piece of work, often do it to a song. And the sailors
> likewise, as they pull the oars. Again, women who are weaving, or dis-
> entangling the threads on their spindle, often sing: sometimes each of them
> sings for herself, at other times they all harmonise a melody together.

This was the living reality of popular lyric in the fourth century,
and a number of later allusions indicate that such traditions lived on in
the early Middle Ages. Many scholars today are so sceptical about this
that if a modern literary historian had suggested what St John suggests
—that for instance the *chanson de toile* (usually thought to be a learned
or aristocratic invention of the late twelfth century) had been current
among the common people ever since late antiquity—he would be dis-
missed as a naive, incurable romantic. But the testimony of St John—
himself an implacable enemy of profane music—cannot be refuted or
ignored.

The musical repertoire of the Christians arose in the Roman world,
and in many ways reflected and continued the Roman traditions: the
range of instruments remains, and the technique of solo singing to
the accompaniment of a *cithara*; the ceremonial and sacred uses of
song, as well as popular songs with their choruses, are converted to
Christian ends. At the same time the erotic songs and dances of the
girls of Spain continued into the Middle Ages, and the entertainers,
mimes and actors went on performing in hall and fairground, market-
square and village green, even when there were no more theatres in
Rome. The Christian moralists, like the Roman ones, could deplore
the players but not eradicate them. In popular entertainment their
techniques and repertoire survive, as is recollected (not in tranquillity,
nor perhaps entirely from hearsay) by the Church Father Lactantius,
for example, in the early fourth century:

> As for the utterly shameless movements of the actors, what do they teach
> and arouse but lust—they whose effeminate bodies, supple enough to ape a

girlish walk and posture, impersonate loose women by unseemly gesturing?
What shall I say of the mime-players, who cultivate the very science of
seduction, who teach adulteries by playing them, and mould reality through
what they act . . . as each young man and woman sees a model for their sex
in those portrayals.

There are literally hundreds of such ecclesiastical condemnations—
not only of acting but of singing and dancing, and in particular of the
erotic element in all of these—from the time of Tertullian (born *c.*
160) to the high Middle Ages and beyond. It seems that Thomas
Aquinas was the first theologian to argue expressly that the entertainer's
profession was not in itself sinful!

From ancient times the Germanic peoples, like those of the Medi-
terranean, had had their own rich traditions of oral poetry and song.
From Tacitus alone (our earliest witness) we know of their songs of
cosmogony, their heroic lays, panegyric songs, genealogical poems,
magical incantations, songs of victory and dirges. Other allusions, in
both Greek and Roman writers of the following centuries, testify to
further lyrical genres in the Germanic repertoire: Alemannic songs of
jubilation (Emperor Julian, *c.* 350); Rhenish lampoons (Ausonius,
c. 370); Merovingian epithalamia and love-songs (Sidonius, fifth
century); a Vandal king's elegy (Procopius, sixth century); Merovingian dance-songs and songs of young girls (Council of Autun, late
sixth century). Behind a legend of the birth of Clovis (457), told in
Latin prose by Gregory of Tours in the late sixth century, we may
surmise a romantic vernacular ballad. Childeric is banished from
France: he has seduced too many of the daughters of the Franks. As he
leaves, he breaks a gold coin with a friend, who says, 'When I send
you this half of the coin, and it fits with yours, then it is safe for you
to come home.' Childeric goes into exile in Thuringia, at the court of
King Bysinus and his wife Basina. It is eight years before the coin
comes and he can return to France. So far this need be no more than a
prose anecdote; but the climax of Gregory's story, and especially the
direct speech, seem to me to reflect a traditional *poetic* shaping of the
narrative. The queen from the court of his exile suddenly realises
Childeric's worth:

> Queen Basina left her husband
> and came to Childeric.
> Anxiously he asked her
> why she had come to him
> from so far away,
> and she answered, it is said:

'I can depend on you;
I know you are very strong;
so I have come to live with you.
But know this: if in lands beyond the sea
I could have found a bolder man than you,
I would have sought him out and lived with him.'
Joyfully he seized her as his wife,
and she conceived and bore a son,
and she named him Clovis.
He was a great man,
and an outstanding fighter.

In an Anglo-Saxon poem, *Widsith* ('the far-wanderer'), which
contains some of the earliest Germanic poetry still extant, we have not
only a poetic compendium of rulers and of peoples, but a portrait of
the Germanic poet, the *scop* himself. The portrait is larger than life:
here the *scop* has an aura that brings him close to Cocteau's myth of
the *poète*. He has about him something of the primordial poet, who is
all-seeing and divine, whether his name is Óthinn or Orphée. His role
is the most poignant on earth and the most glamorous; he is the lone-
liest of men and the most sought after; he is both the servant and the
uncrowned legislator of mankind:

So I have traversed many strange lands
across the wide world, lands where I met with
good and with ill—cut off from my kindred,
my own noble race; I served far and wide.
Thus I can sing, and tell a tale
to the crowd gathered in the mead-hall,
tell how lavish great men were in their kindness to me.
I was with the Huns, and the glorious Goths,
with the Swedes, the Geats, and the southern Danes . . .
I was with the Saracens, and the central Asians,
I was with the Greeks, with the Finns, and with Caesar,
who had wine-flowing cities in his power . . .
And I was with Ermanaric for all that time
that the king of the Goths showed me bounty:
he, lord of cities, gave me a bracelet
in which it was reckoned were a full six hundred
shilling pieces of pure gold.
I presented it to my lord Eadgils,
my protector, when I came home,
to reward the loved prince for the land,
my father's land, that he left to me.

Then Ealhhild, daughter of Eadwine,
royal lady of the court, gave me another.
Her praise has spread across many lands,
whenever I was to proclaim in song
where beneath heaven I knew the best
of gold-clad queens bestowing gifts.
When Scilling and I, with ringing voice,
performed a song before our conquering lord,
the singing in clear harmony with the harp,
many a proud-spirited man,
of great discernment in the art, admitted
he had never heard a better song . . .
As the minstrels among mankind
are fated to walk through many lands,
they say what is needed, they express thanks,
and always, south or north, they meet some man
expert in songs, not slow in giving,
who wants to exalt renown before his courtiers,
to do what is noble till all is gone,
light and life alike; such a one wins praise:
beneath the heavens, fixed high, his glory.

This passage of triumphant hyperbole can serve as a focal point for a number of sober facts relating to the performance of lyric in the Middle Ages.

(1) *The performer's travels*

While no one man could have visited as many nations as Widsith claims, or have lived so long that he could have sung in the presence of both Ermanaric († 375) and the Frankish Theodoric († 534), the medieval poet-musician was essentially a traveller. This is true not only of the less reputable strolling-players and variety-artists, and of the singers and musicians who performed the songs of others, but also of the early Germanic *scop* and of the many later troubadours, trouvères and Minnesinger who composed as well as performed their songs. Some received a steady patronage and so became 'minstrels' in the strict sense of *ministeriales*, permanent members of a noble, royal, or episcopal household. Their services were then required at certain times of the year, as for the greater feasts. At other times, however, these minstrels too would travel to other courts, often with a letter of recommendation from their patron, which would give them a certain social advantage over the travelling musicians of no fixed abode. In the mid-fifth century the Hunnish Emperor Attila has two Gothic

minstrels and a Scythian buffoon performing at his court on the
Danube; in 507 Emperor Theodoric at Ravenna sends a singing
lutanist to Clovis; at the Parisian court of Clovis' son Childebert we
find a Celtic bard Hyvarnion, prized for his composition of songs and
lays. In 764 Cuthbert, abbot of Jarrow and Wearmouth, writes to
Lullus, archbishop of Mainz, asking him to send over two men: one
is an expert glass-blower, the other (Cuthbert is afraid it may sound
frivolous) is a *citharista*:

> It would delight me too to have a lutanist, who could play on the kind
> of lute that we call a *rotta*; for I have one here, and no one to play it. If it is
> no trouble, please send me over such a man as well. I hope you will not
> despise this request or laugh at it.

Clearly it was a small matter for a musician to travel from the
Rhine to the north of England. From Byzantium, where there was a
permanent orchestra attached to the imperial court, an orchestra
employed to play sacred as well as profane music, musicians travel to
the court at Kiev from the late ninth century onwards. From the tenth
century Icelandic scalds travel to Norway, Sweden and Denmark, and
are received in honour there as court poets, and later in the twelfth
century they too at times travel as far as Kiev. From the eleventh
century onwards we know of Byzantine minstrels at the Polish court. In
the twelfth century some of the greatest poets are also the most widely
travelled ones: the troubadour Raimbaut de Vaqueiras goes from
Provence to Italy, to Barcelona, and later follows his friend and patron
the Marquis of Montferrat overseas to Byzantium and Thessalonica;
the Latin Archpoet follows his patron, who is Barbarossa's chancellor,
from Cologne to Vienne to Pavia and Milan. At the close of the twelfth
century Peire Vidal, born in Toulouse, makes voyages to Hungary,
Spain, Italy, Cyprus and Palestine. In 1192 King Béla III of Hungary
sends a *clerc* Elvinus to Paris to learn music—and the chronicler's
phrase, *ad discendam melodiam*, suggests practice rather than theory.
King Manfred of Sicily (1258–66) has seventeen German musicians at
his court in Palermo, while in Castile, at the court of Sancho IV
(1284–95), the palace accounts mention salaries paid to fourteen
Arabic musicians (among them two women), one Jewish and twelve
Christian ones. Such was the internationality of song at every period.

(2) *The performer's and composer's social status*

Widsith is both composer and performer; he is of noble birth, and
received with honour at every court. Even a king could on occasion

assume the role of *scop*, as we see in *Beowulf* when Hrothgar takes his
turn at playing the harp—recounting ancient legends, singing elegies
on historic events, elaborating tales of fantasy (*syllic spell*), and finally
lamenting the passing of his own youthful strength (*Beowulf* 2105 ff.).
So too in the Finnsburg lay recalled within the poem, it is Hildeburg,
herself of royal race, who sings the dirge over her dead son and brother.
A harp was found in the royal ship-burial at Sutton Hoo.

It is likely that from the earliest times the Germanic peoples knew
not only Widsiths but musical entertainers of a humbler kind, not only
a *scop* but a *gleomon* or *spilman*. The distinction between different classes
of singer is difficult to establish philologically, however, as the various
terms are often used loosely and interchangeably, as are words such
as *jongleur* and *ménestrel* in the later Middle Ages. There is no *appel-
lation contrôlée*!

In the twelfth and thirteenth centuries a number of the great
princely patrons of poetry and music composed lyrics themselves:
Guillaume IX of Aquitaine, Thibaut de Champagne, who became King
of Navarre, the Hohenstaufen Emperors Henry VI in Germany and
Frederick II in Sicily, King Alfonso the Wise of Castile and King
Denis of Portugal are outstanding examples. The vast majority of
poets and singers, on the other hand, had to earn their living by their
profession. While a distinction was sometimes drawn between performers and composers, and was sometimes insisted on by the composer, the *trobador*, at the *joglar's* expense, the social boundaries between
the two professions remained fluid. In Provence talented *joglars* of
humble origins—Marcabru, Bernart de Ventadour, Guiraut de Borneil
—become great *trobadors*, welcomed in the highest circles. Arnaut
Daniel and Raimbaut de Vaqueiras, though nobly born, become
professional *joglars* through poverty; the other Arnaut, of Mareuil,
becomes a *joglar* after having been a *clerc*. In Portugal the first outstanding poet whose name we know, Martin Codax, rose from the
ranks of playing to composing. An exceptional performer could be as
proud of his art and as much prized as any composer—in the Russian
chronicle of Hypatios we read that (in 1241) a famous singer Mitusa
thought so highly of himself that he refused to serve Prince Daníil,
and comparable anecdotes are told of singers at earlier courts in
Moslem Spain, though I know of none from northern Europe. There
even the fact that *joglars* tend to have a different type of name from
trobadors is suggestive of social differences: the *joglar* tends to adopt a
'stage-name', a name that is striking, piquant, witty, or self-mocking:
Alegret, Esperdut, Falconet, Brisepot, Mal Quarrel, Quatre-œufs. It is
tempting to think of the name of Widsith's companion Scilling (i.e.

shilling) in this connection and to envisage him as an accompanist and singer of lower status, employed by the distinguished *scop*.

The Minnesinger comprise the widest social range, but whatever their birth they nearly always travel, from court to court or from town to town. The more exalted might employ *joglars*—Ulrich von Lichtenstein required 'many a fiddler to accompany him'—but mostly the German poets acted as their own *joglars*. Some of the principal French trouvères (Gace Brulé, the Chastelain de Couci, Conon de Béthune) were great lords who went to the crusades; but the most gifted and many-sided of all, Adam de la Halle and Rutebeuf, burghers in their background and *clercs* in their education, became impoverished *déclassés*. Being married, they could not hope for great advancement in the clerical world, and they were too bohemian to be accepted by the worthier bourgeoisie.

The wide range of Latin lyrics with profane, topical, satirical or amatory themes, on the other hand, were principally composed, as far as we have evidence, not by a ragged band of bohemians ('the wandering scholars', 'the goliards') but by hard-working, intellectually distinguished professional men. We know five outstanding 'goliard' poets by name: three of these (Hugh Primas, Serlo of Wilton, and Walter of Châtillon) spent the greater part of their lives as professors at some of Europe's leading centres of learning; the other two, Peter of Blois, and Philip, Chancellor of the University of Paris, were among the most prominent administrators of their day. Only the already mentioned 'Archpoet', whose name we do not know, would seem to embody the goliardic myth. His 'confession', with its eloquent plea that the poet's inspiration is bound up with his freedom to live freely, to live dangerously, is perhaps the best-known poem in Medieval Latin. But who was this poet? A knight by birth, he was in fact a court poet, perhaps also a civil servant or minor diplomat, in the service of the Imperial Chancellor, and so almost certainly a member of the circle around Frederick Barbarossa himself. I am convinced that his leitmotif of the wayward, wretched vagabond-poet who is compelled to beg from his patron and his audience contains far less autobiography than literary craft. Each of his poems reveals at a closer look stanza after stanza of deft and brilliant play on both classical and Biblical language, and an intimate knowledge of Roman poetry such as even a Renaissance humanist would have envied. Yet the Archpoet's art is to conceal his art—he makes his verse seem almost effortless, the tone is personal and spontaneous. The Archpoet's picture of the vagabond-poet (whatever element of literal truth it may have contained) has been drawn for the sophisticated entertainment of that international set of diplomats and legislators, high-born scholars and prelates who surrounded the Emperor, whose *lingua franca* was Latin, and among whom the Archpoet probably, by his birth and position, moved as an equal. So too the Sicilian love-poets who surrounded Barbarossa's grandson Frederick II were predominantly courtier-administrators. Those of the Tuscan school, on the other hand, were poets of town rather than court: they tended to come from the educated élite in a wealthy urban milieu. They were seldom travelling poets—unless, like Dante, they had suffered banishment from their own city.

The bracelet that Widsith received from Ermanaric sounds as fabulous as his other claims. But jewellery was indeed one of the more frequent gifts that a patron would give to his poet or singer. The twelfth-century Flemish poet Heinrich von Veldeke describes minstrels being presented with 'precious garments of fur, gold and treasures of every kind, silver and gold vessels, mules and stallions, skins and samite whole and uncut, many a red ring of hammered gold, sable and ermine'. At the other extreme we have Rutebeuf's terrible evocations of poverty, or the jongleur of the *Dit de la maaille*, who does not refuse even a ha'penny (*maaille*), for the ha'pennies mount up soon enough; besides, living in Paris is not dear:

> In Paris with a ha'penny we could buy a large half-pound loaf of bread, or you could have a hefty wench just as you please, or plenty of good coal and wood to cook your meal, or else—there's no denying it—butter or lard, oil or fat enough to make your peas taste good, or a huge ha'penny's worth of wine, a big measure, filled to the top, which would cost twopence anywhere else.

The travelling minstrel had, since Roman times, laboured under certain legal disadvantages, and he might at any time incur the wrath of a fanatic churchman. But it is the bourgeoisie of the rising towns in the twelfth and thirteenth centuries who practise systematic discrimination, by denying *varund volkch* the right of legal appeal, or by limiting them to a quota: thus Strasbourg, around 1200, allows four *ioculatores* and no more.

For the poets and musicians dependent on patronage, therefore, the acquiring of property was their highest material hope. It meant both security and new prestige. Widsith gives his most precious treasure from Ermanaric to his own lord in exchange for land: it is a vassal's act of homage, but also an excellent bargain. In the Domesday Book we find the name of Berdic, the royal *jongleur* (*ioculator regis*), who holds land from the Conqueror, also a *ioculatrix* called Adelinda, who holds land from Earl Roger. In 1246 in Cologne 'Henry the Fiddler and his wife Matilda, lutanist' buy a house in St Severin's Lane. And even today one cannot read without being moved Walther von der Vogelweide's shout of joy (followed swiftly by an irony born of despair) when around 1220 Emperor Frederick II gave him tenure of some land near Würzburg. This came to Walther, the most original and many-sided poet of his age, the artist too proud to let himself be classed as *spilman* or to receive gifts of 'cast-off clothes', after more than a quarter of a century of insecurity at the mercy of diverse patrons:

I have my land—all the world hear me!—I have my land!
Now I am not afraid of frostbite on my toes,
now I'll no longer beg from worthless lords!
The noble king, the gracious king, has shown his care for me—
now summer's air is fresh, winter is warm for me.
Among my neighbours too I am far more highly prized:
they no longer look at me as at a poltergeist!
I was poor too long, through no fault of my own;
I was so full of railing words, my breath became unclean.
The king has made it pure, and has made my song serene.

(3) *The mode of performance*

A medieval soloist could sing unaccompanied, or he could accompany himself (especially on harp or lute), or again he could be accompanied by one or more *joglars*. The *joglar* might be expected to play not only harp or lute, guitar or psaltery, but also bowed instruments such as the viol or rebec, or a small portative organ. The *trobador* Guiraut de Calanson demands of a *joglar* that he be able to play no fewer than nine instruments. By and large, the literary allusions leave the impression that, as in the Roman world, unaccompanied singing was much less common than accompanied, and that more often than not the solo singer accompanied himself.

Widsith and his partner Scilling both sing and play the harp. What is notable is that they seem to perform a duet, whether by singing together or (as I think far likelier) by singing in alternation. So too it was a *pair* of Gothic minstrels who performed at Attila's court. The likelihood that alternate singing was an ancient and widespread Germanic practice is of particular interest in that the outstanding lyrical form of the medieval clerical world, the sequence, is one in which either soloists or two half-choirs repeat each new melodic phrase by singing it alternately. We know, moreover, that many early religious sequences adapt the melodies of prior secular songs. In a far-reaching sense, medieval secular and sacred song can be seen as two strands of a single tradition. I shall explain this more fully in my chapter on the rise of religious lyric (pp. 32 ff.), where I also discuss the musical developments more specifically associated with sacred song: choral hymnody, and polyphony. The choral element in secular entertainment is discussed in the chapter on dance-songs (pp. 186 ff.). Meanwhile, let us look more closely at one of the most fascinating detailed accounts of a soloist's performance, from the Anglo–Norman romance *Horn*, composed around 1170.

A lay had been composed, we are told, about Rigmel, daughter of the king of Britanny, by her brother. Rigmel is in love with Horn, the hero of the poem, who visits the court of Ireland during his banishment under the assumed name Gudmod. The daughter of the Irish king, Lenburc, also falls in love with the handsome visitor, and tries to play the famous lay of Rigmel, though she does not know it completely. Next her brother plays, then the harp is circulated among the assembled company, for 'at that time everyone knew how to play a harp well—the nobler a person was, the better he knew the art'. Gudmod tries to excuse himself from playing, but the others insist:

> Then he takes up the harp, so as to tune it. Heavens, whoever might have seen how he could handle it, how he touched those strings, made them vibrate, sometimes in a single melody, sometimes harmonically, he would have recalled the celestial harmony. This man, more than all others there, caused wonderment. When he had played his themes, he raised the pitch of the strings and made them give out quite different tones from before. Many were utterly amazed at his touch. Then he began to sing the lay of Rigmel, singing loud and clear: the Bretons are expert in such performances. After singing, he made the strings repeat exactly what the voice had uttered. He performed the whole lay, omitting nothing. Dear God, what love his listeners felt for him!

The passage certainly leaves the impression that the instrument here performed the part of the second voice in Widsith's performance, or of the second half-choir in the medieval church, repeating each melodic section once before the melody progresses and changes.

(4) *The performer's repertoire*

Medieval song has three main functions: formal commemoration, entertainment, and cult.

Seigneurial authority presupposes retainers. A ruler maintains around him a body of courtiers and officials; they try to win praise and glory in his eyes, and he in theirs. For praise and glory to be truly won, however, they must be celebrated in some lasting mode. Hence the very nature of a court implies the need for the arts, and in particular for the art of celebration by poetry and song, which has the greatest potentiality of diffusion. The songs of Widsith are essentially celebrations: of the kings and queens he visits; of the deeds present and past that deserve to be remembered; of the ideals by which ruler and ruled aspire to live; and last not least, of the vocation of the *scop* himself, who makes such celebration possible. Widsith can stand as a symbol for the 'official' poetry and song that played so large a part in the life of the courts of medieval Europe—the panegyrics and dirges, the songs that recorded battles, splendid weddings, coronations, great historical moments or moments that have become legend.

In every social group, song appears in its greatest variety when its purpose is entertainment. Tristan, proving himself on arrival at the court of King Mark, sings lays to the harp in Breton, Welsh, Latin and French, and, when pressed, admits to playing six instruments (Gottfried, *Tristan*, lines 3624 ff.). Isolde, at the court in Dublin, entertains her father, King Gurmun, by fiddling an *estampie* (an elaborate kind of dance-song) and a *Leich*[1] (*Tristan*, lines 8062 ff.); she performs French songs about saints; she plays lyre and harp exquisitely; she sings *pastourelle* (see p. 200), *rotrouenge* (a monorhymed song with refrain—Richard Coeur-de-Lion's prison song, discussed below p. 212, is a famous example), *rondeau* and *canzone* (see pp. 190, 140), *refloit* (another song with refrain) and *folate* (a genre about which no information survives). In the fascinating Provençal romance *Flamenca* (lines 583–731), Lord Archambaut, when the King of France brings him Flamenca, his bride, holds a feast to end all feasts, in which the full spectrum of medieval entertainment is displayed. 'After eating, the guests washed their hands once more, but remained in their places and had wine, as was the custom. Then the tablecloths were removed, cushions and fans were brought, and the *joglars* arose, each longing to be heard. Then you could hear chords of many a different tone echoing. Whoever could perform a new tune on the viol, a new *canzone* or *descort* or *lai*,[1] came forward with the greatest eagerness. One played the lay of Chèvrefeuil on the viol, another the lay of Tintagel [two songs from the Tristan cycle], one sang the lay of the perfect lovers, another the lay composed by Yvain.'

Next come instrumentalists, playing on a wide range of string and wind instruments. They are followed by (or perhaps provide background music for) a marionettist, a knife-juggler, tumblers and acro-

---

1. *Leich/lai lyrique*: a composition built of varied stanzas, ABCDEF . . ., with a flexible repetition of strophic patterns within the whole. *Descort*: a lyric in lines and sections of unequal length.

bats. Those who wished could then hear stories of kings, marquises and counts of old. An earlier line suggests that for these 'one *joglar* recites the words and another accompanies'. There are stories from antiquity: the matter of Troy and Thebes, and of Alexander, and ancient love-stories such as those of Hero and Leander, Orpheus and Eurydice; poems recounting the more romantic Biblical episodes: David and Goliath, Samson and Dalilah, Judas Maccabeus, as well as a curious story of 'how Julius Caesar walked the waves all on his own: he did not pray for help to Our Lord—don't imagine that he was afraid!' Next there are all the themes of Arthurian romance; and finally stories and songs seem to come pell-mell—the star of Merlin, the Assassins, Charlemagne's conquest of Germany, 'the whole story of Clovis and Pepin', Lord Lucifer's fall from glory, two *chansons de geste*, a song by the troubadour Marcabru, and lastly the tale of Daedalus and Icarus. Many of these were going on at the same time in different parts of the hall. Then the host, Archambaut, calls for dancing, and two hundred *joglars* form a string orchestra to play the dance-tunes. Such, at least in ideal, was the range of entertainment expected of medieval performers in the best circles. By this I do not mean these were exclusive types of entertainment—there is no single item here that could not equally have been performed at a fair or on a public holiday. But in less refined circles, or on a less grand occasion, the performers' repertoire would have been still wider—the songs, for instance, would include a range of fabliaux, satires, ribald jests, ballads, dialogues of witty repartee and mock-abuse, drinking songs—all that is customarily, though rather one-sidedly, understood to be 'jongleuresque'.

The third great function of medieval song, in religious cult and contemplation, is discussed in some detail in the next chapter. Here I should like only to glance at some of the relations between the secular repertoire and the clerical world. It is only through the *clercs* (not necessarily priests, but whoever had received a clerical education) that any pagan Germanic poetry has been preserved in writing; it is chiefly from secular songs composed in Latin, especially from the ninth to the early twelfth century, that we can infer with some accuracy the characteristics of secular songs in the Romance languages in the centuries before such songs were written down. The frequent attempts to discourage or prevent the clergy from occupying themselves with profane song are eloquent testimonies to how much they continued to do so; it is only through two famous Carolingian prohibitions, for instance, that we know that monks were singing heroic lays (of the Heathobard king Ingeld) and nuns composing love-songs (*winileodas*) in the late eighth century. Wherever a monastery or bishop's court, and later a cathedral school or university, had any pretensions to musical culture, it admitted to a greater or lesser extent songs intended for entertainment and not for cult, songs performed in hall rather than in church or oratory, which were thus far less restricted in their choice of themes.

The earliest musical manuscript, of the late ninth century, from the monastery of Saint-Martial in Limoges, contains a collection of songs of some ninety pages that reflects this widening of the musical repertoire. While there are many hymns celebrating saints and feasts of the church, and a number of penitential lyrics, other songs are included that could not have had any connection with the liturgy: the lyrical lays take themes not only from the Bible (Judith and Holofernes, Dives and Lazarus) but from battles among the sons and grandsons of Charlemagne that were still fresh in the memory—the defeat of Lothair at Fontenay in 841, and of Hugo near Toulouse in 848. There are dirges (*planctus*) in the grand manner, one on Charlemagne himself and one on Duke Eric of Friuli, celebrating the warrior's victories against the 'Huns' and the Avars. Three poems from Boethius' *Consolation of Philosophy* are set to music, including the moving invocation to the 'creator of the starry orb' which calls in question God's interest in mankind. The manuscript includes four lyrics by Gottschalk, the finest Carolingian poet before Notker: not only his formulaic songs of penitence but also his haunting autobiographical song about his exile (discussed below, pp. 34 ff.).

Thus already before 900 we see heroic, elegiac, philosophical and personal themes taking their place alongside religious ones in a monastic musical repertoire. By the twelfth century the Saint-Martial repertoire was to include also dance-songs, love-lyrics, and witty songs satirising both sexual and religious practices. But the compromise with profane song seems to have been made gradually. Thus for instance when Adam of Bremen in the later eleventh century describes the recreations of a great prince of the church, Archbishop Adalbert of Hamburg, he writes:

When reclining at meals, he took delight not so much in food and wine as in witty conversation, or in the stories of kings, or in unusual doctrines of philosophers. But if he dined in private, though it was rare for him to be alone, without guests or royal legates, then he whiled away the time with stories or fantasies, but always of sober language. He rarely admitted lutanists, though sometimes he thought them necessary for alleviating his anxieties.

Pantomime players, however, who tend to amuse most people by their obscene movements, he absolutely debarred from his presence.

One Christmas, around 1066, Adalbert and his clergy even tried to quell the boisterous drinking-songs that the Saxon Duke Magnus and his company 'howled in their cups' (*in poculis ululerent*), by capping them antiphonally with sacred chants. Unfortunately the Duke and his men more than held their own, and Adalbert 'shut himself in his oratory and wept bitterly'.

Some of Adalbert's contemporaries in the church, however, had fewer scruples about profane songs. In the mid-eleventh century the German satirist whom we know only by his *nom de plume* Sextus Amarcius draws a delightful caricature of a wealthy Epicurean prelate:

'Give me sweet food to taste, delectable
sounds for my ears; does not our life pass swiftly?
Why should I say "alas", unprompted by
disease, or boils, or raging pleurisy?
Far be it from me. But come, boy, come, Sir Cupid—
where is a singer or skilled lutanist?
Who can best play oboe and tambourine?
If I'm not soon ravished by Lydian airs
I'll—but no, hasten, my mind burns with song
as spark on hearth or kindling-wood in flame!'
A minstrel was brought in, his fee arranged;
he took his harp out of a leather case,
and people rushed in from the streets and courtyards.
Watching intently, murmuring admiration,
they see the artist run his fingers over
the strings (made of dyed sheep-gut), trying out
the notes, now delicately, now clanging them.
Harmonising the tuneful strings in fifths,
he sang of how the shepherd with his sling
laid great Goliath low; of how the little
Swabian cuckold tricked his wife in turn;
how wise Pythagoras discovered octaves;
and how the nightingale sings with flawless voice.

I imagine the performance taking place in a room that opened on to the central *cortile* of the house or palace where the aesthete was staying, so that men and women could enter the *cortile* from the street and look in, and enjoy the tunes, even though the words of the lyrics were in

Latin. By a remarkable coincidence we still have the words of three of
the four lyrics in this programme: the fabliau of the 'snow-child',
which shows the macabre trick that the little Swabian (*Suevulus*) plays
on the wife who had deceived him, the didactic song about Pythagoras,
and the lyrical praise of the voice of the nightingale, are three songs
found in close proximity to each other in the famous Latin collection
known as the Cambridge Songs. (It is at least possible that the collection once also contained the fourth song, about David and Goliath,
on one of the leaves that are missing today.) In its surviving form this
is a collection of forty-nine songs, largely from Germany, a few from
France and Italy, that was copied by an Anglo–Saxon, around 1050,
into a large anthology of Christian Latin poetry. (Once again the
international aspect of medieval lyric is striking.) The range of these
forty-nine songs shows us in little the lyrical repertoire of secular as
well as clerical medieval Europe.

The songs of cult are here represented by half a dozen straightforward hymns and sequences; the songs of official celebration by some
ten lyrics—on the coronations and on the deaths of Holy Roman Emperors and other rulers, on a bishop's accession to his see, or on a
queen's recovery from illness; one of the 'official' songs, a panegyric
on Emperor Otto III, includes a swift, vivid account of a battle that
brings it closer to heroic lay. The songs of entertainment embrace the
widest range: a few, like the Pythagoras sequence, are didactic, a few,
like the ode to the nightingale, are reflections on the nature and power
of music. Moments of high tragedy and emotion from Statius' epic,
and one from Vergil's (*O lux Dardaniae . . .*), and Horace's ode on
Neobule, the girl deprived of her beloved, are here set down for lyrical
performance. In a lighter vein there are a spring song, a racily told
miracle-legend, and no fewer than seven narrative songs concerned
either, like vernacular fabliaux, with deceptions, or else with jests at
the expense of clergy. Finally, there are seven love-songs (four of them
partly erased by a later self-appointed censor). They in their turn
adumbrate a wide range of medieval love-lyric: there are two songs of
women longing for their lover (one is discussed below, p. 92), a
learnedly playful song of farewell to a boy, a saucy dance-song with
a solo part for a woman and refrains for a chorus (discussed below,
p. 190), a fragment of a *romance*,[1] and two lyrical love-dialogues, one
sensual and exhilarating, the other full of a tension between divine and
human love, and containing protestations of courtliness and love-
service.

1. In medieval French, a song in monorhymed stanzas with refrain, generally with a
simple narrative love-theme.

If I have laboured the width and diversity of this repertoire, it is because I believe that the vital historical importance of the Cambridge collection lies in this. While this specific group of songs reflects the musical entertainment of a particular milieu and time, probably that of a Rhenish prelate with worldly tastes, or of a humanistically inclined cathedral school, in the early eleventh century, if we compare it with any of the larger lyrical repertoires, Latin or vernacular, from the twelfth century down to the Renaissance, the similarity in the whole range of lyrical modes and genres is so striking that we can conclude that already around the year 1000 practically all the basic types of medieval and Renaissance lyric had evolved. Nor is there any need to suppose that these developments had occurred only in an exclusive clerical milieu: on the contrary, in secular lyric at least the *clercs* must have been quite as much indebted to vernacular poets and singers as the other way round. We can see the unity of the clerical and courtly traditions symbolised in what Gottfried tells us of Isolde: it was a priest, 'himself a skilled, artistic performer on every kind of stringed instrument, and master of many languages', who had taught Isolde the arts of music and song before she learnt the ultimate refinements in these arts from the courtly visitor, Tristan (7704 ff.). Here *clerc* and courtier stand side by side as experts in lyric. The songs performed for a clerical and a noble audience shade off almost imperceptibly into the songs performed for a popular one, and popular songs themselves continually absorb the influence of more sophisticated art-songs.

The lyrical repertoire that was largely shared by all medieval Europe, and which we can trace back in its essential features and in many points of detail to not long after the year 1000, is thus the product of ancient and scarcely separable traditions of courtly, clerical and popular song. We can only infer the richness and many-sidedness of these traditions from the fragmentary written evidence that survives. But the inference is certain enough, in my opinion, for us to reject any suggestion that the birth of secular vernacular lyric in western Europe was a sudden event, that took place (as many people still believe) at the end of the eleventh century. Such a false assumption, if entertained, cries out for false explanations: this 'birth' of vernacular song appears mysterious, so it must be due, in some mysterious way, to an outside cause: it must have been the crusades in the East, or new contacts with Arabic poets and singers in Spain, that made the duller-witted European poet articulate for the first time and made him start singing in his native tongue. Yet we shall soon see that a French poet composed a lyrical masterpiece around 860, a song that was assuredly not the only French song of its age, and that in the same ninth century there was already so vigorous a tradition of profane lyric in the Romance vernacular in Spain that it inspired Arabic poets to compose strophic songs for the first time in their literary history.

2

THE RISE OF RELIGIOUS LYRIC

(1) *Beginnings*

In the mid-ninth century we see for the first time the emergence of a
fully fledged lyrical stanzaic form in a handful of Latin songs by Gottschalk, a monk at Fulda. These are set in the stylised mould of penitential hymns, yet there is a strong undercurrent of the poet's own fears
and griefs, and in one song at least the transformation into a personal
testimony is complete. At the time of Gottschalk's death (869) another
and greater poet, a monk at Saint-Gall called Notker, nicknamed
Balbulus (the little stammerer), was composing a *Liber Hymnorum*, in
which he brought one of the most remarkable medieval lyrical forms,
the sequence, to its poetic summit. Thus the first heights of achievement in our extant repertoire of medieval European lyric occur in the
religious mode, in the second generation after Charlemagne, more than
two and a half centuries before secular and vernacular lyrics survive in
any abundance. That there were achievements of comparable stature
at still earlier times, and in profane and vernacular as well as in sacred
Latin song, I have little doubt; but through the accidents of preservation, in a world where the lettered were predominantly the clergy,
these have not survived.

Latin hymody, on the other hand, can be traced back as far as the
fourth century. Hilarius, a bishop of Poitiers († 367/8), is the first
western poet we know who, imitating a tradition already current in
the Greek church, composed a *Liber Hymnorum*, for use by a con-
gregation. It was in a range of classical metres, and was accorded great
respect in the early Middle Ages, but today only three fragments
remain. The truly dramatic entry of hymns into western Christendom

is associated not with Hilarius but with his younger contemporary Ambrose († 397), and with Ambrose's city Milan. St Augustine gives a memorable description of that moment (*Confessions* IX 7):

Not long ago the church at Milan had begun an ardent ceremony of consolation and exhortation, in which the voices and hearts of the assembled people sang in unison. A year before, or not much longer, Justine, the mother of the young emperor Valentinian, was persecuting your true servant Ambrose, spurred on by the heresy to which the Arians had seduced her. The devoted populace kept watch in the church, ready to die with their bishop. . . . Then it was decided to sing hymns and psalms, as was the custom in the East, so that the people should not lose their morale through restless anxiety; and the practice has survived to this day, and been imitated in many, indeed almost all, Christian communities throughout the world.

The hymns that Ambrose himself composed had enormous popular appeal. Lucid and concise, written in lapidary quatrains, they combine unadorned exhortation with telling paradoxes and images. The surface of these hymns is serene, the favourite images are those of light; only rarely is a passionate emotion shown, as in the hymn to St Agnes, when the young girl, commanded to burn torches to a pagan god, cries out:

Hic ignis extinguit fidem,	This is a fire that quenches faith,
haec flamma lumen eripit!	this flame obliterates the light!
Hic, hic ferite, ut profluo	Strike here, oh here, that with a stream
cruore restinguam focos!	of blood I may put out these fires!

The 'Ambrosian quatrain' became the commonest of all Latin hymnic strophic forms. With Ambrose it is still purely classical in its metre (the iambic dimeter)—there is no regularity in the occurrence of stressed syllables. In the following centuries the stresses become increasingly regularised, the classical quantities become less important; rhyme, which occurs sporadically in Ambrose's songs, increases and develops its own patterns.

A number of scholars also attribute to St Ambrose the *Exsultet*, a fourth-century prose-poem that plays with the imagery of light almost symphonically, the praises of light mounting until they embrace even the world of darkness, the 'blessed night', which is transfigured and made radiant by Christ overcoming death:

O vere beata nox, quae exspoliavit Aegyptios, ditavit Hebraeos! Nox, in qua terrenis caelestia, humanis divina iunguntur.

Oh truly blessed night, that plundered the Egyptians, enriched the

B

Hebrews! Night, in which heavenly things are joined to earthly ones, divine to human.

The image itself exemplifies this union of divine and human elements: it is an image transformed into *figura*, interpreted, that is, as the fulfilment of a human moment in a divine pattern. In this pattern the Egyptians become the powers of night, the deliverance of the Hebrews, to let them attain their promised land, becomes the deliverance of mankind, freeing them from their captive night to let them attain heaven. Earth is no longer dark, it is radiant with the divine promise. Such figural interrelations, especially between persons and events of the old Law and of the new, affirmed not only with symbolic ingenuity but with a passionate conviction of their truth, were to play a large part in medieval religious lyric. In this the influence of the *Exsultet*, through its use in the liturgical celebration of the Easter vigil, can hardly be exaggerated.

So, too, through their widespread association with liturgy and processional, the hymns to the cross of Venantius Fortunatus († *c.* 609) were to become a part of the heritage of all medieval Europe: *Salve, festa dies*, which sees the renewal of the world's life in spring as an expression of the divine rebirth at Easter; *Vexilla regis prodeunt*, the classic vision of the cross as a banner of the triumph of life over death, as the gleaming tree from which the divine king reigns (this image too is seen as a *figura*, the fulfilment of a prophecy of David); and again the *Pange, lingua*, where such paradoxes are taken further into contrasts worked out within the imagery itself—the cradle-cloth wrapping Christ's body at birth fading into his burial-shroud; the blood and water flowing from his corpse turning into a cosmic river; the noble tree (identified by *figura* with the fatal tree of the paradise-garden), endowed with human emotion, becoming a suffering and reluctant executioner. These songs had a richness of thought and imagery hitherto unknown in the western Christian tradition. In form they were still wholly classical: in the Ovidian couplet, the quantitative Ambrosian quatrain, and in the case of the *Pange, lingua*, in the ancient and much-loved trochaic tetrameter, another measure that was to form the basis of many experiments with accentual verse in the following centuries.

By the time of Charlemagne we have a considerable range of such 'rhythmi' or poems in accentual metres. Yet nothing of what survives, even of the resonant rhythmic experiments in Ireland, is truly comparable in its form to Gottschalk's lyrical strophes. The masterpiece, both in form and content, is the song *Ut quid iubes*, *pusiole* (the melody is given below, p. 236). Gottschalk, persecuted at his own monastery, Fulda, lives on the island Reichenau, where he feels himself an exile, and a young boy asks him for a 'pretty song' (*carmen dulce*). The poet refuses: his melancholy is too great:

> Magis mihi, miserule,
> flere libet, puerule—
> plus plorare   quam cantare
> carmen tale   iubes quale,
> amor care.
> O cur iubes canere?

Poor little lad, I would sooner weep, sooner lament than sing such a song as you, dearly beloved, demand. Oh, why do you ask me to sing?

Such a refusal is of course a *topos*, an old-established literary mannerism. It can never be wholly serious, because it belies itself: in the moment of denying his song, the poet sings. Here too, despite the luxuriant notes of grief—*plus plorare quam cantare*—that sound almost self-pitying, there is playfulness: in the extravagant diminutives by which the poet addresses his petitioner—*divine tyruncule* ('divine little pupil'), *superne clientule* ('sublime little protégé')—and in the poet's final excuse: a song was demanded in Babylon of the captive little folk (*plebecula!*), Israel. But they 'hanged their harps on the willows', for they could not sing there. Therefore, they did not have to—a delightfully easy Q.E.D.! Gottschalk applies the *figura*, by a daring piece of irony, not to a New Testament scene but to himself. And once more there is the plangent refrain, *O cur iubes canere?*

Then comes the wonderful peripety: protest and refusal to sing turn into praise of God, the refrain into a joyous affirmation. As a counter to the six stanzas sung *à contre-cœur*, the poet juxtaposes six in which he prays with overflowing heart—'this I sing spontaneously', *hoc cano ultronee*. As a prayer it is too selfish to be holy—praise and penitence are interspersed with very insistent earthly hopes—but this is what makes the prayer uniquely Gottschalk's own:

> Exul ego diuscule
> hoc in mari sum, domine:
> annos nempe   duos fere
> nosti fore—   sed iam iamque
> miserere!
> Hoc rogo humillime.

I have been an exile, Lord, a little long upon this sea—indeed it will be almost two years, you know; but now, now take pity! This I ask most humbly.

At last, in the coda of the song, we see the poet arrive through his prayer at a measure of serenity—even here, *de profundis*, it is possible to sing in praise. It is almost as if he comes to realise this only after it has happened. Then the last words recall the opening: Gottschalk remembers the boy's plea for a 'pretty song'; *this*, he now seems to say jubilantly, is the true *carmen dulce*—the divine praises are sweet even in the bitterness of banishment.

The impulse to such a poem probably did not arise wholly within the world of learned Latin verse. Exile is one of the most frequent and moving themes of Germanic poetry, and Gottschalk may well have remembered certain elegiac moments in his native tongue. Yet he was able to re-create such a moment out of his own experience in an unparalleled form, in strophes that are essentially akin to those of later lyric virtuosi, not only medieval, but even Renaissance or Romantic lyrical poets. In the midst of his many exclamations of penitence and misery (prompted at least in part by a living fear of predestined damnation, as his theological writings show), Gottschalk had sensed the exhilaration of a torrent of rhyme, in which personal anguish was resolved into the ceremonial of litany:

Porrige dextram,	Hold out your right hand,
erige vernam,	raise up your slave,
exue multam,	strip him of his great
postulo, culpam,	guilt, I beseech you,
corrige vitam,	give his life order,
tu, male tritam.	his badly-worn life.
Tolle ruborem,	Dispel his blushes,
mitte pudorem,	send him true modesty,
pelle pavorem,	drive out his fear;
funde nitorem,	rain down your brightness,
velle rigorem	batter his stiffness
daque vigorem.	and give him strength.

The writing of poems entirely in these short adonic lines was familiar from late antiquity, especially from Boethius, but there is something hectic, or else light-headed, about such rhyming as Gottschalk adds to the metre. It is by way of these stanzas that Gottschalk found his way to *Ut quid iubes*, where formal control is perfect. Through that control, moreover, the individuality of thought emerged more freely—the frantic but anonymous *orante* receives an unmistakable human face.

What of the beginnings of religious lyric in the vernaculars? Perhaps it is misleading to speak of beginnings—wherever myth and cult have existed, there have been religious songs. In the second half of the seventh century the unlettered Caedmon, according to Bede's famous story, was miraculously inspired to sing 'the beginnings of creation', and his song survives, nine alliterative lines reflecting on the opening of *Genesis* with awkward, touching solemnity. In a Bavarian manuscript of the early ninth century we find the fragment of a vernacular creation hymn, the so-called 'Wessobrunn Prayer', that even in a few lines conveys a magical grandeur:

Dat gafregin ih mit firahim firiuuizzo meista,
dat ero ni uuas noh ufhimil,
noh paum [nohheinig] noh pereg ni uuas,
ni [sterro] nohheinig noh sunna ni scein,
noh mano ni liuhta, noh der mareo seo.
Do dar niuuiht ni uuas enteo ni uuenteo,
enti do uuas der eino almahtico cot,
manno miltisto, enti dar uuarun auh manake mit inan
cootlihhe geista. enti cot heilac . . .

I learnt among mankind this greatest of wonders:
there was no earth, nor sky above,
not a [single] tree, nor yet a mountain,
not a single [star] shone, nor the sun,
nor did the moon gleam, nor the glorious sea.
Then there was nothing there, at any turn or corner,
and yet there was the one almighty God,
most gracious of men, and with him too there were many
blessed spirits. And holy God . . .

The prayer begins as a meditation on the primordial chaos, and here the words of a more ancient, pagan Germanic cosmological poem gleam through—words that lie behind both this German fragment and a stanza in the Norse 'sibyl's prophecy' (*Völuspá*) of the world's beginning and end:

Vara sandr né sær né svalar unnir,
iörð fannz æva né upphiminn,
gap var ginnunga, en gras hvergi.

There was neither sand nor sea, nor cool waves,
there was no earth, nor sky above,
there was a gaping void, but nowhere grass.

Striking too is how in the Norse as in the German the exalted but distant enumeration for one moment takes on a human note: for a moment it is not the immense cosmos, but something with which man has a living relation, something that he himself would miss—the glorious sea, the grass. Juxtaposed to this vision in the German is another, such as we know from many early Christian mosaics: a God with human countenance (to whom the old alliterative panegyric formula *manno miltisto*, 'most gracious of men', could be applied), encircled by his divine city of souls. How was the poet going to combine and reconcile these visions? The tantalising final phrase leaves the scope of his design uncertain: did he go on to an extended narrative such as the war in heaven? Or, as I prefer to think, did he confine himself to a canticle, choosing the most direct bridge to the theme of creation ('And holy God [filled the void with life]') and ending with hymnic praise?

The first known composition in German which has a lyrical strophic form is a majestic hymn to the Logos by the Alsatian monk Otfrid of Weissenburg. It is the prologue to one section of a larger work, a poetic elaboration on the Gospel narratives, completed between 863 and 871. Otfrid, like his predecessor, meditates on the void before creation; but for him there is no primordial mosaic of a *civitas dei* to set beside it, only, as his refrain insists with hammer-like blows, the Father and the Word:

Er máno ríhti thia náht,	Before the moon ruled over night,
ioh uurti ouh súnna so glát	or the sun became so bright,
ódo ouh hímil, so er gibót,	or the sky was ever painted
mit stérron gimálot:	thick with stars, as he commanded,
So uuas er io mit ímo sar,	*The Word was with him constantly,*
mit ímo uuóraht er iʒ thar:	*with him wrought all that was to be:*
so uuás ses io gidátun,	*whatever they created*
sie iʒ allaʒ sáman rietun.	*they both had contemplated.*

The poem is a complex formal structure of exactly a hundred short lines—the number itself a divine emblem—articulated into stanzas of rhymed couplets, the five central stanzas carrying the four-lined refrain. It is difficult to explain the genesis of such a form; it has affinities to one variety of the sequence, the most remarkable of the lyrical genres perfected in the ninth century, the genesis of which confronts us with even more daunting problems.[1]

1. The sequence is a composition based on the principle of progressive repetition of syllabically and musically parallel versicles (half-strophes). In the earliest period we can distinguish (1) the 'classical' type, in which the versicles progress AA BB CC DD ... (often with a prelude or coda lacking parallelism); (2) the 'archaic' or 'da capo' type, in which a whole *cursus* (series of versicles) is repeated within the sequence; (3) a much rarer type, a 'repetitionless' sequence, which is attested from Notker onwards. The oldest datable sequence is of the 'archaic' type. As none of the 'archaic' sequences show a connection with a liturgical Alleluia, or show any trace of having grown out of earlier

(2) *The early sequence*

The earliest surviving sequence that we can date with some certainty, the *Rex caeli*, was composed in the first half of the ninth century. However, it already shows us a very highly developed stage in the genre. Its structural achievement is breathtaking: thought and melody alike are guided effortlessly through symmetries as intricate as any to be found in medieval poetry. We know, moreover, that even at this early date this sequence was set and sung polyphonically. To envisage the tradition out of which the *Rex caeli* could have grown, we must resort to conjecture. It is likely, for instance, that some of the far less accomplished sequences that survive in ninth century manuscripts represent or reflect an earlier, eighth century stage of the genre. Again, the fact that a number of early sequences have melodies with secular, not sacred titles—'A sequence based on the lament of the captive boy', 'The troubled girl', 'The old woman Berta', or 'The lament of Berta's maid' (*Prosa de planctu pueri capti, Puella turbata, Berta vetula, Planctus Bertanae*)—indicates that even earlier, secular songs had been composed in the demanding sequence form. We still possess profane Latin sequences from the late tenth century onwards, and it is probably a pure accident that none from the earliest period have survived. The existence of sequences with titles such as those I have noted points to intimate links between the earliest sequence composition and the world of vernacular song, and this is confirmed by the lyrics copied in a remarkable manuscript from the Lorraine region in the last third of the ninth century—four songs written down by three different hands. There are two Latin sequences of the complex type that specialists have called the 'archaic' or '*da capo*' sequence; a German heroic, though deeply Christian, panegyric on the young Frankish king Ludwig and his victory against the Vikings at Saucourt. This song, like Otfrid's hymn, has structural affinities to the archaic sequence. The same hand as added the German song on Ludwig (perhaps in 882) had previously copied here a poetic masterpiece in French, the song of St Eulalia. This composition again is in a strict *da capo* sequence form, which it shares with one of the two Latin sequences, likewise devoted to Eulalia. One might think it would be easy to speak of the French as simply a copy from the Latin model. But quite apart from our having

liturgical compositions, the widely held view that the sequence originated in the liturgy and was first developed out of Alleluia melodies is at the very least questionable. The evidence briefly indicated below suggests to me that at its beginnings the sequence was linked with secular and vernacular song at least as much as with a sacred Latin tradition; for a fuller documentation I refer the reader to my article 'The Beginnings of the Sequence', *Beiträge zur Geschichte der deutschen Sprache und Literatur* 87, Tübingen 1965, 43–73.

no evidence of the priority of the Latin song, the two could hardly be
more unlike in content and in treatment. The Latin lyric uses Eulalia's
name only as a pretext for an ode on the power of music; the French
recalls Eulalia's story, freely inventing a number of details that heighten
its drama, yet telling it with a matchless composure that includes pity
but looks beyond it to serenity:

> Buona pulcella fut Eulalia,
> Bel auret corps, bellezour anima . . .

1. Eulalia was a peerless girl,
   lovely in body, more lovely in soul . . .

4. Not gold nor silver,
   expensive dresses,
   royal threats or
   royal entreaties,

5. Nothing would ever
   force her to yield:
   the girl would never
   cease to love God.

6. For this she was brought
   before Maximian,
   who in those days
   was the pagan king . . .

10. They flung her quickly
    to burn in the flame,
    but she was flawless:
    she came to no harm.

11. The pagan king would not
    believe what he saw—
    he commanded her head
    cut off with a sword.

12. The young maiden heard
    and did not contradict:
    longing to leave the world,
    she calls upon Christ.

13. In the shape of a dove she flew to heaven . . .

This first testimony of French poetry has some of the finest qualities
of Germanic lays such as *Finnsburg* or *Hamthismál*, which also could
treat violent narrative in a lyrical mode: in particular it has the vivid
allusiveness which can swiftly evoke a whole story and interweave the
evocation with a re-creation of the story's climactic moments. Something of this survives in the Romance languages in the best ballads.
But the *Eulalia* has something more: it treats the moments of brutality,
like those of spiritual ardour, with a kind of elegant reticence, even
fastidiousness; the encounters become a ritual, the ordeal as it were a
ballet; after this it seems the most natural thing in the world that Eulalia
should fly to heaven in the shape of a dove (note that it is not just her
soul that flies, nor is she simply *like* a dove). In short, this poem shows
something of that same particularly French sensibility which we shall
meet again in later lyric—in the songs, for instance, of *Aucassin et
Nicolette*—a sensibility that cannot quite be characterised by such

concepts as naivety, or fantasy, or realism, for it takes us into a special region which is all of these and beyond them.

We cannot tell how long before the manuscript the French *Eulalia* sequence was composed—quite possibly it belongs in or near that same rich decade, the 860s, which included much of the work of Otfrid and of Gottschalk—not to mention the vast metaphysical prose-poem of Scotus Eriugena—and in which one of the greatest of medieval poets, Notker, composed his cycle of sequences.

To do justice to the beauties and the complexities of this cycle Notker's editor, Wolfram von den Steinen, needed more than six hundred pages. It is a group of forty sequences, arranged liturgically for every part of the Church year, beginning at Christmas; there are many subtle interrelations and echoes within the whole. In the present context, however, it is perhaps best to isolate one poem and offer some comments on the distinctive qualities of its achievement. I shall choose the final sequence, intended to be sung on the feasts of holy women, poetically perhaps the most arresting of all, and one of the very few which has not yet, it seems to me, received a fully satisfying interpretation. It is a strict 'classical' sequence—that is, apart from the two-line prelude, each pair of the rhymeless half-stanzas, sung to the same melody, shows an exact syllabic parallelism. I try to bring this out as far as possible in my translation:

1. A ladder stretching up to heaven,
        circled by torments—

2. At whose foot an attentive dragon
        stands on guard, forever awake,

3. So that no one can climb even
        to the first rung and not be torn—

4. The ascent of the ladder barred
        by an Ethiop, brandishing
    a drawn sword, threatening death,

5. While over the topmost rung
        leans a young man, radiant,
    a golden bough in his hand—

6. This is the ladder the love of Christ
        made so free for women
    that, treading down the dragon
    and striding past the Ethiop's sword,

7. By way of torments of every kind
        they can reach heaven's summit
    and take the golden laurel
    from the hand of the strength-giving king.

8. What good did it do you,
        impious serpent,
    once to have deceived a woman,

9. Since a virgin brought forth
        God incarnate,
    only-begotten of the Father:

10. He who took your spoils away
        and pierces your jaw with a hook

11. To make of it an open gate
        for Eve's race, whom you long to hold.

12. So now you can see girls
    defeating you, envious one,

13. And married women now
    bearing sons who please God.

14. Now you groan at the loyalty
    of widows to their dead husbands,

15. You who once seduced a girl
    to disloyalty towards her creator.

16. Now you can see women made captains
    in the war that is waged against you,

17. Women who spur on their sons
    bravely to conquer all your tortures.

18. Even courtesans, your vessels,
    are purified by God,

19. Transmuted into a burnished
    temple for him alone.

20. For these graces let us now
    glorify him together,
    both the sinners and those who are just,

21. Him who strengthens those who stand
    and gives his right hand to the fallen
    that at least after crimes we may rise.[1]

The astonishing opening sentence begins with a deliberate dreamlike abruptness in the prelude (1), and then builds a single arc over six half-stanzas (2–7), unfolding a single image. This image is a fusion of two dreams recorded by Perpetua, a young married woman in Carthage in the year A.D. 203, during her weeks in prison, while she waited for death in the arena. In the one dream she faces the ordeal of the ladder, and as she reaches the top an angel rewards her with an apple-bough; in another, she wrestles naked with an Ethiopian in the the amphitheatre, and at last overthrows him. The reason for Notker's alterations, and for his conjunction of the two visions, does not emerge fully until stanzas 10–11, which are the focal point of the poem. God among his challenges to Job had said: 'Can you pierce Leviathan's jaw with a hook?' In the tradition of Christian *figura* this became one of the divine *impossibilia* fulfilled by Christ: in the harrowing of hell that hook became the cross, set in the mouth of the monster, so that all who

1. I give the opening of the Latin text (Ed. W. von den Steinen II, p. 90):

Scalam ad caelos subrectam
tormentis cinctam—

Cuius ima draco servare
cautus invigilat iugiter,

Ne quis eius vel primum gradum
possit insaucius scandere—

Cuius ascensus extracto
Aethiops gladio
vetat exitium minitans,

Cuius supremis innixus
iuvenis splendidus
ramum aureolum retinet—

Hanc ergo scalam ita Christi
amor feminis fecit perviam,
ut dracone conculcato
et Aethiopis gladio transito

Per omne genus tormentorum
caeli apicem queant capere
et de manu confortantis
regis auream lauream sumere.

had been swallowed up could emerge. But Notker enriches the old *figura* by a new stream of associative imagery: the cross is not only the hook that opens the serpent's jaws, it is also the ladder of torments that stretches up to heaven. It was Christ who, in the harrowing of hell, first passed the Ethiop, the threat of death, and at the same time trod the dragon down. That is the secret of Notker's union of the two dreams: through the associations ladder—cross—hook he evokes what is both an encounter with death and a heavenly ascent, both in Christ's harrowing and in the lives of the women here celebrated. That, too, is why Perpetua's angel with the apple-branch is transformed by Notker, first into the radiant young man with the golden bough and then into the divine king offering a laurel-crown: Christ in the harrowing fulfils the classical as well as the Hebrew *figurae*—he is the 'true Aeneas', who holds the golden bough by which the underworld can be faced unharmed, and the true god of light (*splendidus*), Apollo of the golden laurel, who confers immortality. The branch is metamorphosed into the crown. Having won these insignia through his ordeal in the underworld, he can give them—the same protection and the same victory against seemingly impossible odds—to all who face that ordeal. Even Job, by being himself released through the harrowing, now knows that the impossible challenge can be fulfilled.

Thus the four brief lines of stanzas 10–11 modify and give a new dimension to all that goes before. They also motivate the praises of women in the stanzas that follow. These are another of Notker's innovations. Previously only virgin martyrs, apart from Mary, had been celebrated in sacred song. Now, Notker seems to say, not only the martyr heroines but women in all their womanly capacities can triumph in that encounter and ordeal by which the divine is attained: through the harrowing of hell, in which they were achieved archetypally, they lost their impossible fearfulness. Every woman's life can become a vindication of Eve, a bruising of the serpent's head; even the lives of courtesans—for Christ did not reject them. With the last stanza Notker universalises his theme: Perpetua's dreams become an image of every Christian's anguish and aspiration, as the concluding lines implicitly take up the opening image once more. Those who stand and fall and are helped up again—they are whoever dares to climb the ladder stretching to heaven: the Perpetuas of this world, or Everyman.

The sequence ends not in petition but in joyful thanks. Where Gottschalk had pined at the distance between the human and the divine, Notker, here as in all his sequences, celebrates their oneness. As von den Steinen showed, Notker's poetry is never a quest, he never prays *for* anything; prayer for him is objectless, it is nothing but a realisation, again and again, of the bonds between earth and heaven in which all his thought moved. This above all is what makes his sequences distinctive: it lies behind the subtle interrelations in Notker's thought and imagery, and gives the *Liber Hymnorum* its incomparable concentration and unity, complex though ultimately simple, a poetic *Kunst der Fuge.*

(3) *The eleventh century*

Notker died in 912. The century and a half following his death are a golden age for Latin religious lyric in its *musical* aspects. Both monodic and polyphonic composition become increasingly sophisticated. Sequences become more and more abundant throughout this period, especially at the established musical centres such as Saint-Gall and Saint-Martial, but also in England. Gradually syllabic parallelism in the sequence is embellished by regular stresses and rhymes, giving more obvious—and less subtle—harmonies than any that the ninth century had known. Alongside the sequences were composed *tropes,* that is, poetic and musical amplifications of liturgical texts, some of which, probably under the influence of vigorous popular oral traditions of drama and dramatic song, become lyrical dialogues. And the liturgical texts themselves are given ever more splendid musical settings. Towards the end of this period the experiments with lyrical strophes that were begun by Gottschalk are renewed, and especially at Saint-Martial we see the vogue of *conductus*: strophic compositions more elaborate than in the older hymnody, secular as well as sacred, for one or more voices.

None the less these hundred and fifty years, for all their musical vitality, have left us virtually no religious poetry comparable in stature to that of the later ninth century. Poetically, religious lyric seems to gain new strength around the mid-eleventh century, at first through isolated men of genius such as Hermann the Lame at Reichenau († 1054) and Peter Damian in Italy († 1072); then, in the early twelfth century, Abelard in France inaugurates a new period of great richness for the religious lyric, poetically as well as musically, a richness that several of the vernaculars share with the Latin tradition—first Germany, then, from the time of St Francis († 1226), Italy, and in the course of the thirteenth century the Iberian peninsula and England. Only in Provençal and Old French poetry does sacred lyric seem to be almost a trickle beside the great stream of secular song.

Hermann of Reichenau, a pioneer in mathematics, astronomy, historiography and musical theory, brought to the sequence a baroque flamboyance of language and imagery. Occasionally the agglomeration of rare words, many of them Greek, may seem precious, but in a sequence such as that on Mary Magdalen the effect can be stunning. The poem is dominated by the twofold image Babylon–Jerusalem. It opens with three stanzas of ornate invocation, in which the image of the heavenly Jerusalem is already implicit: the angelic 'choir of super-celestial lutanists' (*supercaelestium chorus citharoedorum*), the heavenly dance of maidens playing the tambourine (*tympanistriarum*), and all Christendom, are called upon to celebrate the Magdalen. The whole of *Jerusalem caelestis* must rejoice with the prostitute, the woman who had known Babylon:

4. Quae septeno
    dudum daemone plena
        vesania
        cursitaverat
        pestilentiosa,

5. Per andronas
    lubricas Babylonis,
        cuius gaudet
        Bel gymnasiis
        anathematicis,

6. Et ubi occursant
        daemonia
        onocentauri,
    dracones praevolucres
        struthioque
        simul collusitant,

7. Absonius ululae
        lugubres
        et elegizant,
    et Sirenae delubris
        voluptatis
        coantiphonizant,

8. Pilosi et saltitant,
    lamia catulos lactat,
        foveam torvus
        struit ericius,
        ibix et corvus
    cum onocrotalo
        horrisonum una
        discriminant,

9. Basiliscus sibilat
    cerastes et imperitat—
        genus id multa
    minax, incarcerans,
        exterricula
    quaeque dirissima
    morsibus, experta
        est Maria!

She who for a long time, filled with a sevenfold demon, had raced about in pestilential madness,
    through the seductive chambers of men at Babylon, whose god Baal rejoices in damnable naked sports,
    where demonic onocentaurs charge, dragons surpassing swift and ostrich dally together,
    discordantly lugubrious screech-owls elegize, and in the sanctuaries of voluptuousness sirens chant echoing antiphons,
    where satyrs leap, the lamia suckles her brood, a fierce hedgehog builds a lair, and ibis and raven vie with pelican in horrendous noise,
    where basilisk hisses and cerastes reigns—the whole menacing, incarcerating brood, nightmares each most savage in attack—Mary experienced them all!

The spectacular, nightmarish vision of Babylon in some of its detail
echoes and transforms a prophecy of Isaiah (XXXIV, 11 ff.):' Pelican
and hedgehog will possess Jerusalem; ibis and raven will dwell in her;
her measure will be taken for annihilation, a plummet sounded for her
destruction. . . . Thorns and nettles will grow in her palaces, and the
briar on her battlements. . . .' Isaiah's is a vision of a land drained of
life, a Jerusalem laid waste by divine vengeance. Hermann creates
something very different, he gives his vision a new and fervid life: in
the cavorting of his beasts and monsters he sees not only violence and
ugliness but an element of fantastic play (dracones praevolucres
struthioque *collusitant*); beyond the discords he suggests a new sensual
harmony (Sirenae . . . *coantiphonizant*)—both words appear to be
coinages, and are given special weight by being placed each at the
close of its half-stanza. Isaiah's 'waste land' has been transmuted into a
brilliant complex image of desperate sexual excitement. The echoes lend
the image a further significance: this Babylon is what Jerusalem on
earth could at any time become.

The polarity of the Babylon–Jerusalem image is sustained: Mary,
'divinely touched by the memory of Jerusalem, her beloved mother',
goes to wash Christ's feet, and is thereby freed from the Babylonian
monsters (*bestiis de Babylonicis*). The event is first told with calm
simplicity, then integrated into the pattern of images by a remarkable
use of ambiguity:

> 15. verbum eius audiens
> et intime soli vacans,
> theoriae arcem Sion
> felix conscendit,

> 16. Cui Iesus
> architectus
> stratum tetragonum
> dans aequilaterum
> totum crystallis luminosum
> sternit igneis carbunculis,

> 17. fundans saphyris
> caeruleis
> miris candidatam
> et unionibus,
> iaspidibus, et propugnatam
> munit gemmeis turriculis.

Listening to Christ's word, and devoting herself to the sun within, she
rises joyfully to Jerusalem, citadel of contemplation,

furnished by Christ the architect with a tetragonal, equilateral couch,
all luminous with crystal, studded with fiery rubies,

he who sets the radiant white one in marvellous caerulean sapphires,
pearls and jaspers, and safeguards her he has defended with jewelled
minarets.

'Jerusalem, citadel of contemplation' is both the celestial city and the celestial bride. As Mary Magdalen achieves this state, she becomes city and bride together. In the half-stanzas 16 and 17, and in the pair that follow, this rich double meaning is sustained: the couch and jewels are gifts showered by Christ on the city he has chosen and on the woman he has chosen: *Cui*, at the opening of 16, is both 'to which' and 'to whom'. The city of luxury finds its perfect counterpart in the heavenly city of gems, the prostitute her counterpart in the woman on whom the divine lover lavishes all his wealth. So too in the conclusion of the sequence Hermann, invoking the Magdalen's intercession for mankind, expresses this by another ambivalent image: recalling the opening, where angels and celestial maidens were dancing and playing on instruments, he asks that we, 'dancing with you in the crown of the kingdom (*corona . . . tripudiantes*), may praise the god of gods on the cymbals of jubilation, together with the angels in Jerusalem'. *Corona* may refer both to the final figure of the dance and to the crown of the elect in heaven; *tripudiantes* can still carry associations of the dancing-girls of Babylon; the concluding vision, in effect, is one of earthly and heavenly beings alike dancing in the divine garland: Babylon is transmuted into Jerusalem in this dance, as it had been transmuted within, in the heart of the Magdalen.

Hermann's most outstanding sequence has Notker's tightness of structure, but in its lyrical conception there is also much that is new: an exuberance of imagery, a poet's power to transform Biblical matter freely to his own mood and purposes, and a richness of language that goes beyond encrusted ornamentation to a keen sense of poetic ambiguities. One further accomplishment of Hermann's is artistically important: Notker's Perpetua sequence had quite distinctly a visionary part, thought out entirely as a group of images, and then a conceptual or didactic part—even though the two were superbly linked at the close by the recurrence of the opening ladder-image, now growing once more out of the conceptual structure itself. Hermann's Magdalen sequence by contrast is entirely seamless: from start to finish it is dominated by its images, every moment is thought out visually as well as conceptually.

We can at times perceive an imaginative intensity comparable to Hermann's in songs of his younger contemporary in Italy, Peter Damian: in horrific visions of the torments of the damned and the Day of Judgment—'dragons huge as architraves are opening wide their throats'—or again in the intellectual paradoxes that unfold a paradise in which 'the flesh, transformed to spirit, and the mind perceive alike'. Damian's thought and imagination tended to be governed by extremes, the exultant heights alternating with a sense of the abyss: a moving passage in one of his less known hymns has a ring of experience about it that makes it far more than a platonising commonplace:

> Saepe divino   igne cor accenditur,
> Seque transcendens   mens in alta rapitur—
> Sed genuinae   corruptelae labitur
> Pondere pressa.
>
> Lux inaccessa   micat ut per rimulas,
> Cui mens intenta   sitienter inhiat,
> Cuius obtutus   ecce carnis obvians
> Umbra retundit.

Often the heart is kindled by divine fire, the mind, transcending itself, is caught up into the heights, but slides away, pressed back by the weight of its inborn rottenness.

Light unattainable gleams as through crevices, the mind, intent on it, gapes at it thirstily, and suddenly the body's shadow beats the mind's vision back.

Here the poet uses one of the early Carolingian strophic forms, which was probably invented by his compatriot Paulinus of Aquileia († 802). In what is perhaps his finest poem, the song on St Vincent, Damian reverts to another, but far more sophisticated, Carolingian form and melody, that of a ninth-century *da capo* sequence to St Mauritius, turning it into a remarkable strophic composition. Once more there are the clashing extremes, here the saint's tortures on earth and victorious bliss in heaven; they alternate with extravagant vehemence throughout, but at one moment they are seen almost as aspects of each other:

> Fame corpus maceratum   The body worn away by hunger
>   Cernitur   can be seen
> Velut epulis nutritum   nourished as it were by banquets,
>   Sumptuosis   sumptuous,
>   Ac cibis regalibus.   feasted on royal foods.

Two near-contemporary vernacular songs deserve to be mentioned alongside Hermann and Peter Damian. Shortly before 1065 Ezzo, a priest at Bamberg, composed 'a festive and mighty chorale', which was sung in the course of a vast German pilgrimage to the Holy Sepulchre that year. The thoughts themselves do not break new poetic ground:

each stanza dwells on one of the beliefs about creation, fall and redemption that all Christians shared. Yet in the finest of these stanzas I think we can see a very rare poetic power:

Do sih Adam do beviel,	At the time that Adam fell
do was naht unde vinster.	there was night and darkness,
do skinen her in werlte	there shone into the world
die sternen be ir ziten,	stars at the times ordained,
die vil luzel liehtes paren,	stars that shed very little light,
so berhte so sie waren;	whatever their own brightness:
wanda sie beskatwota	they were overshadowed then
diu nebilvinster naht,	by the mist-darkened night
tiu von demo tievele chom,	coming forth from Satan
in des gewalt wir waron, ·	in whose power we were,
unz uns erskein der gotis sun,	until the son of God shone out,
ware sunno von den himelun.	true sun from the heavens.

It is, we might almost say, Notker's power of unfolding a complex of thoughts and images in an unbroken, arc-like sentence: to achieve so subtle an articulation, so far-reaching a cohesion of syntax, thoughts and images is no small achievement in the vernacular of Ezzo's time. Between the two pillars at either end of the stanza—'naht unde vinster' and 'ware sunno'—a whole world-picture is harmoniously, swiftly but unhurriedly, ordered.

By contrast the stanza before the final doxology, where Ezzo again aims at a grand effect, seems to me to succeed less well:[1]

O crux salvatoris,	O crux salvatoris,
tu unser segelgerte bist.	you are the mast-tree of our ship,
tisiu werlt elliu ist taz mere,	the whole world is the sea,
min trehtin segel unte vere,	my Lord both sail and boatman,
diu rehten werh unser segelseil,	right action is the sail-rope
diu rihtent uns ti vart	that guides us on our homeward
heim.	course,
der segel ist ter ware geloubo,	the sail of true belief
der hilfet uns ter wole zuo . . .	helps us there unfailingly . . .

The surface of the language appears as tranquil and lucid as ever, but here we find images, allegoresis and didactic phrases juxtaposed in staccato fashion, and even (in the twofold appearance of the sail, as

---

1. This stanza survives only in the later, expanded Vorau version of the song, and its belonging to the original *Ezzolied* has been challenged (though I think not conclusively).

both *trehtin* and *ware geloubo*) somewhat confusingly. Ezzo has not yet learnt, like his Latin contemporary Hermann, to let the images speak for themselves, to unite them by other than external bonds.

Compared with Ezzo's song, the finest of the handful of early religious lyrics that survive in Provençal, very near to it in time of composition, has all the appearance of a delightful miniature. It occurs in one of the most many-sided musical manuscripts from Saint-Martial in Limoges, and shares its melody with a stereotyped Latin Christmas-hymn (see below, p. 237). The vernacular song, however, is in my opinion a wholly independent piece. It begins with the jongleur's summons to his audience to hear a new song, and also to learn it for themselves:

> Mei amic e mei fiel,   My friends, my faithful company,
> laisat estar lo gazel: let your trifling ditties be:
> aprendet u so noel   now learn a new melody,
>   *de virgine Maria.*   *about the maiden Mary.*

The word *gazel*, which occurs only here, is still problematic: it has been interpreted, among other ways, both as 'gossip' (*jaser*, *gazouiller*) and as a borrowing of the Arabic *ghazal*, a term for a lyrical genre consisting chiefly of love-songs. If this should be the true derivation, it would be far the earliest of the rare instances in which an Arabic literary term became used north of the Pyrenees. At all events, the jongleur is contrasting the sphere of profane sound with the 'new sound' (*so noel*) of sacred song. He is echoing the Psalmist: *Cantate Domino canticum novum!* His song tells of the annunciation, and the blessings it brought to the world. Suddenly, without explanation, we hear two new voices:

> 'Non perdrai virginitat,   'I'll not lose my virginity,
> tos temps aurai chastitat,   I'll always keep my chastity,
> si cum es profetizat,   according to the prophecy
>   *pois [er] virgo Maria.*'   *I'll still be maiden Mary.*'

> 'Eu soi l'angels Gabriel,   'I am the angel Gabriel,
> aport vos salut fiel: the greeting that I bring is loyal:
> Deus [descen] de sus deu cel   God is coming down from heaven
>   *in te, virgo Maria.*'   *into you, maiden Mary.*'

It is not necessary to suppose that stanzas of narrative transition have been lost. The song is a lyrical dialogue, in which Mary and Gabriel have parts alongside the narrator. It is probable, in my view, that these parts were acted as well as sung, that a young man and woman mimed the sacred courtship here as in many of the dance-songs that portrayed the lover wooing his lass (see below, pp. 197 ff.). The language has the same overtones: the girl covering her excited fear and self-doubt at the man's advances by determined little speeches declaring she will keep her innocence; the man's protestations that he is honourable and loyal—*aport vos salut fiel*; and the girl giving herself at last with the same determination, filled with secret joy, with which she had first resisted:

> 'si cum tu o dit, o crei: 'as you have said it, I believe:
> a lui me do e m'autrei, I surrender to him, myself I give,
>   *ego virgo Maria.*' *I, the maiden Mary.*'

At the end the narrator sums up the story, and then invites his audience to participate: 'from now on, with each new verse, repeat anew the refrain *de virgine Maria*'. It is a little gem among religious lyrics, and perhaps also the first surviving fully vernacular play.

Mei amic was written down at Saint-Martial in the years 1096–9, nearly two and a half centuries after Gottschalk's experiments with lyrical stanzas. For the study of religious lyric in these centuries the Latin material is relatively limited, the vernacular pitifully scant. None the less what survives can I think show us an astonishing range of form, language and mood, and of imaginative conception. At times we can find great technical brilliance—in the choice of vocabulary, in the innovation of sophisticated formal patterns and of new uses of rhyme; we can find a flexible, many-sided use of imagery and symbolism, new ways of treating the old-established figural relationships, a highly individual employment of associative imagery, a conscious, delicate balance of symbolism in far-reaching patterns. We can hear some unmistakably personal notes sounded even in what we might expect to be the most objective of lyrical modes, we can perceive poets sensitively aware, in their use of sacred language, of nuances of emotion drawn from areas of profane experience. All this it is important to bear in mind when we approach 'the Renaissance of the twelfth century'.

(4) *Twelfth-century France*

Towards 1100 northern France becomes increasingly the intellectual centre of Europe. While many learned and influential schools had emerged, each with its special interests, it is above all those of Chartres and Paris that have captured the imagination of posterity. Paris in the

early twelfth century was dominated by the personality of Abelard, its
most spectacular poet as well as philosopher and theologian—and its
most romantic legend. The love-songs that he composed for Héloïse
have not survived, songs that, in her own words, 'were so lovely in
words and tune, and so often sung, that the name of Abelard was on
everybody's lips, and even the unlearned could not forget him, being
charmed by his melodies'. However, we still have two sacred song-
cycles that he wrote in the 1130s, after the tragic separation from his
beloved. The larger is a complete *Liber Hymnorum*, adapted to the
hours of the divine office and the major feasts of the church year,
composed at Héloïse's wish for the use of her convent of the Paraclete.
Abelard's covering letter shows his fine critical understanding of the
older hymnic tradition, and many of his songs are deliberately cast in a
traditional mould. But at times he gives his powers of innovation
scope: for Easter he writes an exuberant series of rondeaux—our first
examples of the lyrical strophe with internal refrain, which Abelard
may even have invented:

> Da Mariae timpanum:
> *Resurrexit Dominus!*
> Hebraeos ad canticum
>   Cantans provocet,
> Holocausta carminum
> Jacob immolet!

> Subvertens Aegyptios
> *Resurrexit Dominus,*
> Rubri maris alveos
>   Replens hostibus,
> Quos involvit obrutos
> Undis pelagus!

Give a tambourine to Mary: Christ has risen! By her singing let her excite
the Jews to song, let Jacob offer holocausts of songs!

Overthrowing the Egyptians, Christ has risen—filling the depths of the
Red Sea with his enemies, ocean that laps the sunken in its waves.

In the brilliant opening image Abelard fuses two Biblical moments:
Mary, the sister of Moses, who with her tambourine joyously led a song
celebrating the Israelites' deliverance from the Egyptians (Exodus XV),
becomes Mary Magdalen, heralding the new deliverance brought about
by the resurrection. Jacob, by an established *figura*, is the Jewish race,
the nation who denies that Christ arose. If Jacob were to respond by
answering Mary's song, this would be truly a sacrifice, fulfilling what
was figured in the ancient holocausts and surpassing them.

The second strophe takes up the *figura* from the *Exsultet* discussed above (p. 34), but in the last two lines gives it a new double edge. The 'ocean' can mean the Red Sea once more; but it also means the risen Christ, an ocean embracing the sunken, embracing his enemies, in quite another sense, a 'true ocean' of which the Red Sea is only a *figura*. This interpretation is no modern supersubtlety: it is guaranteed by the most ancient part of the Good Friday liturgy, in which the Red Sea, opened at the divine command, figures Christ's body, opened with a a lance by his persecutors.

The next rondeau in the Easter series brings other *figurae* of the resurrection: David slaying Goliath, Samson carrying off the enemy gates, the lion-cub brought to life on the third day (as the bestiaries claimed) by the roar of his father's voice. Or again, in Abelard's hymns to the cross, the crucifixion is evoked in *figurae* of superb conciseness: Christ becomes the serpent impaled by Moses that cures the serpent-bites of those who gaze on it:

> Serpens erectus
> Serpentum morsus
> Conspectu sanat—

the cross becomes the wood Moses plunged into the waters of Mara to sweeten them:

> Lignum amaras
> Indulcat aquas
> Eis immissum.

Such figural imagery was to be the common currency of twelfth century Latin hymnody. It is used with great virtuosity in sequences of Adam of St Victor, with great intensity in hymns of Walter of Châtillon; but in the effortless creation of forms, in verve and a sense of intellectual play the finest of Abelard's hymns are perhaps unequalled of their kind.

Abelard's shorter lyrical cycle is a completely individual conception: a group of six *planctus*, in which Old Testament personages, men and women, are brought to life and lament their tragic fates. Formally, these laments take their departure once more from the archaic *da capo* sequence, which is adapted to the dramatic needs of each context with fine inventive freedom. Abelard's melodic structures, like his stanzaic, are so sensitive to each transition and nuance of meaning and emotion that one is led to think of Monteverdi's artistic aims sooner than those of a medieval religious composer. While the germ of each *planctus* is latent in a Biblical episode, Abelard brings to his sources a sensibility that not only extends but at times profoundly alters their human significance.

This is what happens, for instance, in the first lament, inspired by the story of Dinah and Sichem (Genesis XXXIV). The Biblical account tells us nothing about Dinah's feelings; the treacherous action of her brothers, who by a fraud murder her fiancé Sichem and the whole of his tribe, is seen as brave; Jacob's misgivings are seen as cowardly. For Abelard, by contrast, the episode is the tragedy of a woman who has lost her only beloved; who argues that true love excuses what the conventions call 'immorality'; who loathes her brothers, seeing that their talk of 'family honour' was a mere pretext for sadism and injustice. Addressing her dead lover, she sings:

> You who were impelled to take me,
> being taken by my beauty,
> among judges is there any
> who would not have shown you mercy?

> Only you judged otherwise, my brothers,
>   Simeon and Levi,
> you whose sense of duty covered
>   excessive cruelty,

> Who took revenge alike on blameless men
>   and him who caused the hurt;
> you have troubled our father's mind—
>   for this you have my hate!

> Where love is the moving force
> and reparation is made,
> no judgment in all the world
> could fail to extenuate! . . .

> Alas for me, alas for you,
>   my pitiful one—
> your fall has brought so fine
> a nation down.

It is almost impossible to read this *planctus* without recalling certain moments in Abelard's own life, told explicitly in his long letter on the 'story of his misfortunes': the cold seduction of Héloïse, followed so swiftly by his deep love for her, his offer to her uncle of reparation and marriage, accepted by Héloïse's relatives and then betrayed, in Abelard's mutilation as in Sichem's circumcision and murder. The other *planctus* too contain words and moments that can be paralleled, though less overtly, in the letters of Abelard and Héloïse. It would be inept, however, to regard these songs (as many scholars incline) as a kind of

veiled *journal intime*. The musical notation shows that they were from
the beginning intended for performance (though only highly skilled
soloists could have met their technical demands). So it is not 'private
poetry'—yet in the particular choice of Biblical personae we can sense
a private as well as an artistic commitment. Once more it may be
illuminating to recall Monteverdi, who late in life transforms his
lament of Ariadne into a lament of the Virgin over the dead Christ.
Through his artistry he attains a region of imagination where erotic
and spiritual desolation fructify each other.

From the time of Abelard, Paris became Europe's most notable
musical centre, which it remained for at least a century. It was there,
at Notre Dame, that decisive new developments occurred in polyphonic music, under two outstanding musical directors, Leoninus and
Perotinus. A melody could have a second voice written for it already
in Carolingian times (e.g. the *Rex caeli* discussed above); at Saint-
Martial there were increasing attempts to give this second voice a
rhythmic independence of the main melody; but it was the achievement of Leoninus, in a vast range of liturgical music, to accomplish the
complete melodic independence of the upper voice (*duplum*) from the
lower (*tenor*), and to work out new rhythmic patterns, as when he
subordinates the rhythm of the *tenor*, which carries the main melody,
to that of the *duplum*. Leoninus' compilation, the *Magnus Liber Organi*,
was influential not only in liturgical music but in lyrical composition
of every kind, Latin and vernacular. His successor Perotinus went on
to compose for three and four separate voices, and to prepare the way
for, or even himself to perfect, the motet, which around 1200 emerged
as an independent musical genre. Very soon there were motets for
three and four voices, double and triple motets, secular as well as
sacred, and gradually the motet gave rise to a new wealth of polyphony
all over Europe.

The finest poet associated with the musical school of Notre Dame
was Philip the Chancellor, who ruled the university of Paris in a
stormy period from 1218 until his death in 1236. Philip's hymns are
full of brilliant conceits: when the Magdalen pours her perfume and her
tears upon Christ's feet, 'heaven sheds its dew on earth, earth rains on
heaven . . . the patient anoints her doctor, that through the ointment
she may be cured'; when the Virgin makes her complaints against the
Cross, the Cross answers 'You gave him to me mortal, I have returned
him immortal'. But behind the conceits, impelling them, is a passionate
rather than ingenious mind. Often in Philip's poetry the boundary
fades that separates sacred song from invective of religious intensity.
The famous

Dic, Christi veritas,   Tell me, you truth of Christ,
dic, cara raritas,   tell me, dear rareness,
dic, rara caritas,   tell me, rare dearness,
ubi nunc habitas?   where are you now?

with its taut yet serene polyphonic setting (a part of which is printed
below, p. 242), is a perfervid attack on the Church's worldly riches and
lovelessness. A curse on simoniac bishops, uniting elements of prayer,
satire and apocalypse, rings out like a thunderclap:

Vide, deus ultionum,
vide, videns omnia,
quod spelunca vispillonum
facta est Ecclesia;
quod in templum Salemonis
venit rex Babylonis
et excelsum sibi tronum
posuit in medio;
sed arrepto gladio
scelus hoc ulciscere!
Veni, iudex gentium,
kathedras vendentium
columbas evertere!

Behold, God of vengeance, behold, you that behold all, how despoilers of
the dead have made the Church their den—how into Solomon's temple the
king of Babylon has come, and there set up his towering throne! Draw your
sword, avenge this shame! Come, judge of nations, overthrow the seats of
those who are selling doves! (Cf. Matthew XXI, 12–13; Mark XI, 15–17.)

In songs of a Provençal poet, a contemporary of Philip's, Peire
Cardenal, who received a clerical education but became a troubadour,
satire and invective likewise take on a religious quality; they are expressed not through raillery but through visions of remarkable
originality and power. Peire has a haunting lyrical fable about the
world of his time (he had lived through the terrible persecution of the
Albigensians):

There was a town, I know not which,
where a shower of rain fell, such
that all on whom it rained went mad.
Only one man escaped—he had
been lying in his house asleep.

> After the shower, he got up
> and went outside, into the crowd,
> and all were crazed in what they did:
> one wore a tucker, one was bare,
> another spitting in the air,
> one threw a stick and one a stone,
> another ripped his tunic down,
> one was striking, one jostling,
> another thought he was a king . . .
>
> They watch that sane man standing calmly,
> and marvel at his lunacy:
> they see he acts quite differently
> from them, and, knowing themselves wise,
> he is demented in their eyes.
> One cuffs his cheeks and one his neck—
> helpless, he trips, tries to turn back
> out of the crowd that pushes and pulls,
> he takes their blows, arises, falls,
> arises, falls, and with great leaps
> flees home again, and so escapes,
> muddy and beaten and half-dead.
> Escape is all that made him glad . . .

It is not necessary to see in this an explicit allegory of the passion of Christ: Peire himself simply says the city of madmen is the world, flooded with greed and arrogant malice, persecuting one who loves God; yet by his evocation he compels us to see a glimpse of Christ in the face of any human being who is hunted. In another startling vision-like song (*Un sirventes novel*) Peire imagines himself as mankind's advocate on the Day of Judgment, arguing before the court of heaven that no one whatsoever should be condemned to hell. Here, behind the skilful wit of the poet's logic, we can again see an intensely religious plea against religious fanaticism and persecution.

(5) *Italy and the Franciscans*

In Italy meanwhile religious lyric proliferated in movements of popular devotion. The beginnings of these movements can be traced to the early thirteenth century; before that, our testimonies are scarce: apart from a rhythmic narrative of the life of St Alexius, only two brilliant and distinctive religious poems in the borderland between lyric and narrative, composed around 1200 or a little earlier. One, the *Ritmo cassinese*, is a dialogue, full of subtle and humorous interplay, between a Western man and a visitant from the East, who leads his groping interlocutor, a little as Diotima led Socrates, to the notion of a more-than-human life. The poet exploits his sense of the enigmatic delightfully throughout—even in the concluding lines, in which the Westerner acknowledges

> et em quella forma bui gaudete   and in the way that you rejoice
> angeli de celu sete!   you are an angel of the skies!

an ambiguity remains: they do not to my mind completely define the nature of the mentor (though many scholars would disagree). Has he been describing the perfect life on earth or in heaven? Is he prophet or desert father, magus or heavenly habitant? All is left open. The poet has taken us, like his own Western neophyte, on a way of discovery whose end is wonderment.

The other poem is the 'Jewish–Italian elegy', part of a long Hebrew tradition of ritual *planctus* that goes back ultimately at least as far as the lamentations of Jeremiah, but this time composed in the Italian vernacular, among the Jewish community in Rome. It moves from bitter mourning over the loss of Zion, the exile and captivity, to a savage prayer to God for Zion's renewal, through the crushing of all her enemies; between these moments, unifying them, is the story of a brother and sister sold separately into slavery, who are coupled in a brothel by their owners, recognise each other, and, dying in grief and shame, win back their lost nobility. The sensational story-matter (an ancient Near Eastern *koinê* best known through the Greek romances) is treated with unsurpassed imaginative tact, and at the moment of recognition—

> Sister and brother, to what point have we come?—

we see the tragic moment as the focus and epitome both of the threnodies and of the desperate pleas, in short, as an overwhelming symbol of the course of Jewish history.

The future of religious lyric in Italy, however, lay not with poems such as these but with the popular songs of the many lay orders and confraternities which gathered strength in the generation after St Francis (1182–1226). These groups (Disciplinati or flagellants, Laudesi, Serviti and others) adopted a characteristic lyrical form, the *lauda*, perhaps from profane dance-songs current at the time (see the discussion below, p. 191). In Italy it was a Franciscan poet, Jacopone da Todi, who brought the *lauda* to its perfection. The links between the Franciscan order and religious lyric had been established by the saint himself, who invited his followers to become 'God's jongleurs',

and who towards the end of his own life composed the 'Praises of
Creatures' or 'Canticle of the Sun'. This is not a *lauda*, but a vernacular
psalm, a 'Laudate Dominum' that echoes especially Psalm 148 and the
song of the children in the fiery furnace (Daniel III, 57–88). Like these
in the Latin Vulgate, it is in versicles of rhythmic prose rich in
assonance and rhyme, and like these too its musical setting was almost
certainly plain-chant. But in content Francis makes important innovations. Where the Biblical psalm and canticle call upon created
things themselves to praise God, here the God whom 'no man is
worthy to name' is praised in and through his creations. Where the
Biblical texts simply enumerate, Francis limits his choice (sun, moon
and stars, the four elements, and death), and individualises: these are
our brothers and sisters, each has a human physiognomy, a share in
human life as well as in divine:

> Be praised, my Lord, through sister Water,
> who is very useful, and modest, and precious and chaste.

> Be praised, my Lord, through brother Fire,
> through whom you irradiate the night;
> and he is fair and joyous and robust and brave . . .

Above all, St Francis' song is no simple, joyful litany like the
Biblical ones: it has a darker, even despairing side. God cannot be
praised in all mankind as he can in the elemental world—only in those
who (in Blake's words, like those of Francis) 'suffer and forgive'.
Francis calls down beatitudes on these, yet cannot do so without
stating the terrible corollary, 'Woe to those who die in mortal sin!'.
Between beatitude and fulmination comes the bitter-sweet acceptance
of 'our sister, Bodily Death'—she too is a source of divine praise.
Then a final beatitude leads into the closing invocation, addressed
(now for the first time) to all mankind: 'Praise and bless my Lord and
thank him, and serve him with great humility'—the jubilant psalmist
and the preacher conscious of sin and death are both present at the
end. The undertow of litany has enabled the poet to channel the
beauty and the terror of his universe into a single unbroken stream.

Jacopone († 1306) is a more flamboyant, more overtly passionate
poet, both in his satirical impulse (see below, p. 215) and in his mystical.
Whether he leaps up to the redeeming Christ with ecstatic longing—

> Oh sweet love,
> you that have murdered Love,
> I beg you to kill me with love!

or takes the way of unknowing towards the '*infigurabil luce*'—

> Willing, the soul unwills,
> for its own will has gone,
> and now it wills to see
> this loveliness alone:
> not demanding now,
> not longing to possess,
> no impulse of its own
> in such sweet possessiveness.
> This so lofty height
> is built in nothingness . . .

there is always the exuberant energy with which he can obectify even
the seemingly innermost limits of religious experience. In one song, a
dialogue, in alternate stanzas of affirmation and negation, each followed
by the refrain

Fugo la croce che
   me devura,
la sua calura non posso portare—
	I am fleeing the cross that
	   devours me,
	I cannot endure its fieriness—

Jacopone depicts the extremes of joy and pain that contemplation of
the cross can arouse:

'Frate, eo sì trovo la croce
   fiorita,
de soi pensieri me sonno
   vestita;
non ce trovai ancora
   ferita,
'nante m'è ioia lo suo delettare.'
	'Brother, I find such flowering in
	   the cross
	that I have dressed in its forget-
	   me-nots;
	it has no wound I have yet come
	   across,
	rather, my joy is its delightfulness.'

'Ed eo la trovo piena de
   sagitte
ch'escon del lato, nel cor me s'ò
   fitte:
lo balestrieri en vèr me l'ha
   ritte,
onn' arme c'aio me fa
   perforare.'
	'And I find it full of arrows that
	   dart
	out of its flank; they are fixed
	   in my heart:
	the archer has aimed them at me
	   and they spurt
	through each piece of armour that
	   I possess.'

The translation can scarcely suggest the effect of the headlong, often dactylic rhythm, the rich rhyming, or the witty ambiguity in *pensieri* ('pansies, for thoughts').[1]

The achieving of such striking ways of expression entails, perhaps inevitably, a certain loss of inwardness. Jacopone often courts the danger of replacing thought by intensity, and intensity by theatricality. In the most famous of his *laude*, *Donna de paradiso*, he runs this gauntlet bravely: he moves into a fully dramatic form (it is one of the earliest dramatic *laude* that survives), and stakes everything on theatrical truth.

There is a part for a messenger (whose opening words 'Lady of paradise, your dear son is seized, the blessed Jesus Christ!' become the refrain), parts for the Virgin, Christ, and the crowd. Basically there are two scenes—one in which the messenger reports each new indignity and torment inflicted on Christ, the other enacting the last words exchanged between Mary and her son. They are linked by the lament of the Virgin, who is the central figure. Her utterances stand out from the rest: her pathetic appeals to Pilate (we do not even know whether he is present to hear them)—'I can show you how wrongly he is accused. . . . Perhaps even this moment you have changed your mind . . .'; her helpless but calm reply to Christ's reproachful 'Mother, why have you come?'

Figlio, che m'aio anvito,	My son, I have good cause,
figlio, pate e marito!	my son, father and husband!
Figlio, chi t'ha ferito?	My son, who has struck you?
Figlio, chi t'ha spogliato?	My son, who has stripped you?

Her aching physical desire to die with him ('in one grave . . . choked together . . . embracing'), and her final outburst of luxuriant mourning:

Figlio bianco e biondo,	My son, white and golden,
figlio volto iocondo,	my son, blissful face,
figlio, per che t'ha 'l mondo,	my son, why has the world,
figlio, così sprezzato?	my son, despised you so?

1. The arrows would seem to be a metaphor for the force of love, terrifying in its violence, that radiates from the cross, as if the lance that pierced Christ's side had turned into darts of love and remorse that strike the beholder. The archer may, as Franca Ageno suggests, signify Christ himself. Certainly the stanza seems to imply that the arrows are released by an archer *who is on the cross*. But while I know of no instance of the crucified Christ as archer, it is noteworthy that a small archer figure, whose significance is still uncertain, appears on the eighth century Ruthwell Cross. Could some such figure in a representation of the cross in Italy underlie Jacopone's image?

Jacopone has here used his prodigious powers of expression to
attain a special effect: a fusion through tension between the language of
harsh colloquialism and that of sweet lyrical incantation, between the
sorrow of an Umbrian carpenter's wife at the death of her beloved but
unsuccessful son and the sorrow of the Donna de Paradiso, that
greater role of whose existence we are reminded at each return of the
refrain. The human familiarity and 'realism' of many phrases and
details is evident ('Mamma, ove si' venuta? . . .' 'Figlio, chi t'ha
ferito?')—but they are integrated with the unashamed tirades:

> O figlio, figlio, figlio,
> figlio, amoroso giglio . . .   (lily of love)

which for the carpenter's wife represent uncontrollable emotion, but
for Jacopone the artist a kind of surrealism: wail passes into ritual, the
longing bride of the Song of Songs is superimposed on the hysterical
contadina.

It is this complexity of effect that here guarantees the dramatic truth
of the conception—for it is never merely dramatic, it never plays on
human feelings alone. The Carmina Burana passion play (*c.* 1200) had
used three laments of the Virgin, two in Latin, one in German. But
compared with Jacopone's these seem one-sided—the Latin ones
because of their sheer virtuosity, a language so polished that it lacks
the pungency of living speech; the German because, though direct
and touching, it aims at expressing nothing beyond the naive emotion.

Jacopone is perhaps most widely known as the reputed author of
the *Stabat mater*—yet it seems to me that the Latin song lacks precisely
those qualities that most distinguish the Italian poet. Out of two
thoughts—'The mother watched the crucifixion sorrowing', and 'Let
me mourn with you'—the anonymous Latin poet constructs a chain
of sixty lines that varies these thoughts by near-synonyms:

> Stabat mater dolorosa   O quam tristis et afflicta
> iuxta crucem lacrimosa,   fuit illa benedicta
>   dum pendebat filius;   mater unigeniti,
> cuius animam gementem   que merebat et dolebat,
> contristantem et dolentem   et tremebat, dum videbat
>   pertransivit gladius.   nati penas incliti . . .

The mother stood grieving, tearful, beside the cross, while her son was
hanging; a sword pierced her groaning soul, saddened and suffering.
Oh how sad and afflicted was that blessed mother of an only child, who

mourned and sorrowed and trembled, while she saw the torments of her illustrious son . . .

Even if we are hypnotised by the rich rhyming in the Latin, a literal translation reveals how verbose and repetitious the content is. In all their variations, both the grief of the mother, and the singer's plea to share it (*fac, ut tecum lugeam*), are expressed one-sidedly; a purely human poignancy prevails. At the close the singer's plea to the Virgin for his own safety on the Day of Judgment—*per te, virgo, sim defensus/in die iudicii*—seems petty and selfish compared with the passionate concern of St Francis himself, as of Peire Cardenal, for the whole of mankind at that moment. So too in the equally famous *Dies irae*, attributed to St Francis' disciple and biographer Thomas of Celano, the repeated cries 'Don't let *me* burn in the fire' belittle the genuine grandeur of the opening stanzas, and appear ignoble in the light of his master's canticle. It seems that, with one or two shining exceptions (above all Jacopone himself, and in England John Pecham [† 1292]), the 'jongleurs of God' became a race of lesser men, poets who fell all too easily into the nets of obsession and sentimentality suspended below the tightrope which the saint had walked unerringly.

(6) *Early English lyrics*

The combination of simple and spectacular expression that we find in Jacopone is also characteristic of the finest religious lyrics in Middle English. Before the thirteenth century, little survives. A few verses by the hermit St Godric († 1170) are our earliest testimony—a childlike invocation to the Virgin, and one to Saint Nicolas:

> Sainte Nicholaes, godes druth,   4: champion[1]
> tymbre us faire scone hous!   4: lovely
> At thi burth, at thi bare,   6: bearing
> Sainte Nicholaes, bring us wel thare!

The image is freshly conceived, and at one with the disarming modesty of the language: Godric's image of heaven is not the bejewelled golden Jerusalem designed by the divine architect, but a plain man's house, beautiful but small enough to be built by one carpenter, a saint with whom he has a special bond. When Godric has a vision of his sister reaching heaven, the Latin life of the hermit gives it utterly conventional hagiographic trappings: two angels, preceded by the Virgin Mary, bring the woman's soul to the altar of Godric's oratory,

1. The number preceding the gloss indicates the place in the line of the Middle English word glossed.

where she sings a hymn of thanksgiving. Godric's own rendering of
his sister's words is less pretentious and far more beautiful:

> Crist and sainte Marie
>   swa on scamel me iledde   1–3: so on a crutch[1]
> that ic on this erthe ne silde   7: should
>   wid mine bare fote itrede.

Godric can dispense with angels: it is Christ himself who, with
Mary, guides his sister (a real woman, bare-footed, not a mere soul)
on the heavenward journey; the crutch, sign of the cripple's infirmity
on earth, now becomes an instrument of freedom—she can take the
road to heaven by leaps and bounds, her foot never touching ground.
Any day one might have seen on the village street a woman on
crutches, supported in the first moments by a friend on either side,
then finding her freedom of movement—but it take's a poet's eye to
see the latent possibilities of meaning.

The thirteenth-century lyrics are for the most part anonymous. To
the earlier decades of the century belongs the quatrain at once elegiac
and radiant:

> Nou goth sonne under wod—
> me reweth, Marie, thi faire rode.   6: face
> Nou goth sonne under tre—
> me reweth, Marie, thi sone and the.

The sun grew dark at the moment of Christ's death; the death of the
divine Sun was re-enacted in nature, the physical sun showed compassion for the other by dying at the same moment as he. This conceit
had become traditional in Christian hymnody. So for instance Walter
of Châtillon writes

> Sol eclypsim patitur
> dum sol verus moritur;

(the sun suffers an eclipse as the true sun dies). What is new and
creative in the English quatrain is to begin *now*: a particular moment at
nightfall, as the sun sinks behind a wood, can bring to mind the sunset
of Good Friday, and the setting of the greater Sun that it reflects. Any
sunset—even the one at this moment—can become the historic and
the omnitemporal moment; any tree—or this tree—can become the
tree of the cross. But the poet particularises further: the forest sunset
evokes not the crucifixion itself but the image of Mary watching; it

1. The normal meaning of *scamellum* in Medieval Latin.

evokes a surge of pity for a lovely woman's face that has lost its beauty by weeping too much. The author of the *Stabat mater* exclaims 'Oh how sad and afflicted she was!', but he cannot *imagine* it. The English poet does not have to say to Mary 'Let me mourn with you'—his compassionate insight shows itself, without need of protestations. In four moments of vision—the sun among the trees, the beautiful face ravaged, the sun beneath one particular tree, the mother with her dead son—he has seen everything, and said all that needs saying.

The sufferings of Christ and of Mary at the crucifixion loom large in thirteenth century religious lyric, especially in England, where a devotional movement inspired by meditation on Christ's passion and on the joys and sorrows of the Virgin can be traced back at least as far as the *Meditationes* of John of Fécamp († 1078). This movement, given new force by the Cistercians in the twelfth century and the Franciscans in the thirteenth, became widespread in all Europe, but its deepest roots seem to have been in England. It is probably no mere accident of preservation that in medieval European vernacular lyric England alone shows a striking preponderance of sacred lyrics over profane.

At times we can observe the vernacular lyric growing out of the Latin meditation: where John of Fécamp wrote 'Candet nudatum pectus, rubet cruentum latus, tensa arent viscera, decora languent lumina, regia pallent ora, procera rigent brachia, crura dependent marmorea, et rigat terebratos pedes beati sanguinis unda',[1] the vernacular poet sings

> Whyt was hys nakede brest
>   and red of blod hys syde,
> bleyc was his fair andlet,   1: pale, 5: countenance
>   his wunden depe and wide;
> starke weren his armes
>   i-streht upon the rode;   1: stretched, 4: cross
> on fif stedes on his body   3: places
>   the stremes ran on blode.

Compared with this, the Latin makes a lifeless, almost mechanical impression. It is too symmetrical, it is determined to leave nothing out. The English poet selects, and varies his syntactic pattern, though indeed through his dominant opening syllables—whyt, bleyc, starke —and through the force of his alliteration, he imposes a rhythm of his own. But most important is that he is more specific at the close:

1. The naked breast shows white, the bleeding flank grows red, the tense reins wither, the lovely eyes languish, the royal face grows pale, the long arms grow stiff, the marble legs hang down, and a wave of blessed blood drenches the perforated feet.

C

where John speaks of 'a wave of blessed blood', the poet ignores the non-visual 'blessed', but *sees* five places on the body from which streams of blood run out. It may be objected that these are nothing but the traditional five wounds. And so they are. But the poet does not use the formulistic concept 'five wounds'(which would have prevented him from seeing)—he looks, and sees afresh.

So too in another contemporary song of the passion, every detail is newly visualised and brought to life:

> Hey a-pon a dune
> as al folke hit se may,
> a mile wythute the tune
> abute the mid-day,
> the rode was op a-reride;   5: raised
> his frendis werin al of-ferde, 5: afraid
> thei clungin so the cley.   2–5: shrivelled like (parched) clay
> The rod stonit in ston,   3: stands
> Mari hir-selfe al-hon;   3: alone
> hir songe was way-le-way.

It is not only specific, it brings to the divine moment the living immediacy of everyday, the sense of shameful publicity, the colloquialism with which any man might taunt his friends for cowardice, the wordless wail that would spring to the lips of any woman who had been left alone.

In the finest early English lyrics, even very complex thoughts and images can be unfolded with the same vivid and personal lucidity. A Latin poet had worked out an elaborate conceit about the Virgin at the cross: her sorrows then were only the labour-pains she had not felt at the nativity, but had to feel before the rebirth, the resurrection, could take place:

Now harsh Natura, seizing the time, demands her rights, now sharpens her pains: now she extorts with usury the moans Mary had denied her before giving birth.... The new birth of Christ from the closed sepulchre preserves the form of the virgin birth; there he proceeded, here arose, in both he comes forth through a seal preserved intact.[1]

Intellectually it is admirable, but a little difficult, a little pedantic or

1. Tempus nacta trux Natura   Christi novus hic natalis
     nunc exposcit sua iura,   formam partus virginalis
       nunc dolores acuit;   clauso servat tumulo;
     nunc extorquet cum usura   hinc processit, hinc surrexit,
     gemitus quos paritura   hinc et inde Christus exit
       Naturae detinuit . . .   intacto signaculo.

dry. The English poet, adapting these stanzas, performs an astonishing feat: suddenly all is direct and passionately alive:

In that blisful bearnes buirde	3–5: child's blissful birth
wrong wes wroht to wommone wirde,	5–6: women's lot
ah Kinde craved nou the riht.	1: but
Then thu loch ah nou thu wep,	3: laughed
thi wa was waken that thenne slep—	2–4: woe awakened
childing-pine haves the nou picht . . .	1: labour-pains, 5: stabbed
Thi luve sone uprisinge	2–3: dear son's/sun's
was selli liik to his birdinge—	2–3: wondrously like, 6: birth
bitwene two is litel schead—	5: distinction
for, so gleam glides thurt the glas,	5: through
of thi bodi born he was,	
and thurt the hoale thurch he gload.	2–7: through the intact coffin he glided

The goddess Natura (Kinde) is here given a motive: she becomes a jealous rival who thinks 'It's not fair, not natural, that a woman should give birth without pain'. The vividness increases when (unlike the Latin) the Virgin is addressed directly, quite possibly by the gloating 'midwife' Natura herself; the colourless Latin word *gemitus* (moans) becomes the stabbing *childing-pine*. In the later stanza, where the Latin laboriously *explains* the resemblance between Christ's birth and resurrection, the English lets us see it. The poet introduces a new (though traditional) image: the gleam that glides through glass. It is prepared by the word-play in the first line: Christ the sun *is* that gleam. The image of the window unites those of the hymen and the tomb; the divine ray of light glides through window, hymen and tomb, leaving each unscathed. The analogies are not expounded conceptually but perceived in an image.

The English poet's freedom of invention in the thirteenth-century religious lyric could also by-pass learned sources altogether—for instance in a ballad-like song of Judas, for most details of which no parallel has been found. Christ sends Judas to buy food in Jerusalem, giving him thirty pieces of silver, and saying very blandly (*ful milde*) 'You may meet some of your relatives on the way'. The song continues in swift, taut scenes, throwing dialogue in such sharp relief that even 'he said', 'she said' become superfluous:

Imette wid his soster, the swikele wimon:	1: Met, 6: deceitful
'Iudas, thou were wurthe me stende the wid ston!	5–6: one should stone
Iudas, thou were wurthe me stende the wid ston—	
For the false prophete that thou bilevest upon.'	

The 'sister' is of course Judas' mistress, in a euphemism sanctioned
not only by the Song of Songs and all its poetic imitations but also, as
a passage in *Piers Plowman* (B V 651) tells us, by a deception current
in everyday life. Her harsh teasing provokes in Judas nothing but
panicky fear of his master: will that mind-reader not guess her thoughts
and take revenge on them both? Reassuring him lovingly, she leads
him to the top of a cliff, where he lies, her arms around him; then as
he sleeps she takes his money and runs away. By this she thinks she
has drawn her lover away from Christ: he will not dare to go back to
his employer now. Judas awakes and flies into a mad rage: he is in an
impasse, afraid to lose honour and employment with Christ, and afraid
to lose his mistress. At that moment Pilate comes in—he is presented as
a 'rich Jew', a caricature of a money-lender. When Judas names his fee
for betraying Christ, he is so astonished at its smallness (thirty silver
coins for a piece of espionage!) that he probes further—'You mean
you want gold?' But Judas wants the exact amount he has lost, nothing
else: only thus, he imagines, will he not be found out when Christ asks
for a reckoning. In a flash the scene changes to the Last Supper:
Christ's opening words ring terrifyingly, but Judas controls himself
and tries to brazen it out:

> 'Wou sitte ye, postles, ant wi nule ye ete?—   1: How, 7: will not
> Ic am iboust ant isold today for oure mete.'   3: bought
> Up stod him Iudas: 'Lord, am i that?
> I nas never o the stude ther me the evel spec.'

Christ does not answer. He does not need to, for Judas in his
excitement has given himself away. His non-sequitur 'I was never in a
place where anyone spoke evil of you' is the very thing that Christ
knows to be false. In a moment Judas will remember: he had had his
answer at the outset of his errand, in the apparently nonchalant but
deeply ironic 'You *may* meet some of your relatives'. Peter gets up
and brags how he would fight to protect Christ, even against a
thousand knights. As the Gospel narrative shows, Peter is no physical
coward: he can draw his sword on Pilate's soldiers, though (like the
Judas of this ballad) he cannot stand up to the taunts of a girl. With
Christ's crushing answer:

> 'Stille thou be, Peter! Wel i the icnowe:
> Thou wolt fursake me thrien ar the coc him crowe'   5–6: three times
>   before

the poem comes to a subdued close. The two deserters are left standing, with no more to say.

Seldom in medieval poetry has such dramatic compression been achieved in lyrical form. A notable Middle English scholar, George Kane, has recently written that this poem 'apart from the attraction of the antique, has little to recommend it'. I would say it has everything to recommend it—*except* 'the attraction of the antique'. It is one of the most 'modern' of medieval poems: with its swiftly changing tableaux, its terse, explosive use of dialogue, its sharp moments of tension and climax, one could well call it the first masterpiece of expressionism.

There are still other ranges of achievement in the early Middle English religious lyric, which it is difficult to convey in brief compass. Perhaps three short songs can at least signal three streams of tradition that were to flow copiously in England until the end of the Middle Ages. One is the contemplation of mortality and death:

Wen the turuf is thi tour	3: turf
and thi put is thi bour,	3: pit
thi wel and thi wite throte	2: skin
ssulen wormes to note.	1–4: shall profit worms
Wat helpit the thenne	2: helps
al the worlde wunne?	4: bliss

Cognate with such reflections are the lyrical dialogues between body and soul, in which the body is constantly reminded of its corruptibility, the wistful elegies on the theme of *Ubi sunt*—'Where are Paris and Elayne? . . .'—and later, the dances of death. Often in all these, as in the lines just cited, there are the light, aphoristic touches, and the flickers of sardonic humour, that tend to distinguish the English mortality lyrics both from the shrill agonies of the Italian penitential movement and from that horrified fascination with death associated— not always unjustly—with the Gothic in northern Europe.

Then there is a stream of joyful personal devotion to the Virgin Mary, not as a sufferer at the crucifixion but as a romantic heroine in her own right. Perhaps its most perfect expression is in a stanza in a fourteenth-century manuscript:

At a sprynge-wel under a thorn	
ther was bote of bale, a lytel here a-forn;	3–5: remedy for ills
ther by-syde stant a mayde	
full of love y-bounde.	
Ho-so wol seche true love,	1, 3: Whosoever, seek
yn hyr yt schal be founde.	

It was at a fountain, beside a thornbush, that, according to some of the early Christian apocryphal writings, the angel's annunciation to Mary took place. This is the moment of the incarnation, the 'bote of bale' for all mankind. It is to a fountain, too, that girls in the *romances* and dance-songs of medieval Europe often come to meet, or dream about, their beloved. The poet is aware of both associations: impalpably he makes the bridge that joins the omnitemporal moment to the particular one. The annunciation took place 'a little while ago'; but still a maiden is standing at that fountain, rapt in the fullness of love. It is at once the Virgin, whose true love can absorb all human love, and any girl made beautiful by loving. The image is left unbroken, hence enigmatic: this girl opens the gate of poetic imagination behind which 'heavenly things are joined to earthly ones, divine to human'.

Finally, there is a stream of lyrical poetry filled with mystical aspiration towards union with Christ:

Gold and al this werdis wyn	5–6: world's joy
is nouth but Cristis rode.	2: nought
I wolde ben clad in Cristes skyn	
that ran so longe on blode,	6: blood
and gon t'is herte and taken myn in—	2–4: go to his, 9: lodging
there is a fulsum fode!	4: abundant
Than gef I litel of kith or kyn,	2–3: I would give (care)
for ther is alle gode.	

It is in songs of this stream that we encounter some of the most striking images in the English religious lyric, whether as here they are new creations—the cross compounded of the world's gold and felicity, the shape-changing into the torn skin of Christ—or traditional images re-lived—such as Christ the knight who meets his death jousting for mankind, the bridegroom enticing his bride to the wedding-night, the vintner bespattered by the grapes he has trodden, the lover rejected by the far-off princess, mankind. Here as in all early English lyric the most distinctive and brilliant achievements lie in the briefest songs, songs that in their sharp but supple language—not yet over-worn or over-familiar—create moments of magnetic vitality and concentration.

(7) *Spain and Portugal*

Thirteenth-century religious lyric on the Iberian peninsula is over-shadowed by the huge collection of *Cantigas de Santa María* by the polymath king Alfonso the Wise of Castile. The *Cantigas* consist of over four hundred songs celebrating the Virgin Mary, written and composed by the king himself and collaborators working on his instructions, in the Galician dialect which was the 'special language' of lyric both in Spain and Portugal. Apart from six surviving melodies by the *trovador* Martin Codax (earlier thirteenth century), the music of the *Cantigas*, preserved in the magnificent manuscripts that were copied for Alfonso, is almost our only evidence of how lyrics on the peninsula were sung. In Alfonso's reign, as in that of his father and grandfather, the Castilian court was brilliant and cosmopolitan: here Castilian and Galician poets, musicians and scholars mingled with Arabic and Jewish ones, and with the numerous Provençal and Italian troubadours who came as visitors. It was a civilised milieu, in which differences of race and religion were relatively unimportant. So too the miniatures of the fullest manuscript of the *Cantigas* show Moorish, Jewish and Christian performers side by side, singing, dancing, and playing more than thirty kinds of instrument. To me it seems certain that these performers, whatever their religion, had some share also in the composition of the songs, both words and music. A number of scholars would violently disagree, and would limit the creative role in the lyric strictly to the Christians at the court. But where in all medieval Europe was there ever such a demarcation between composers and performers?

Some forty of the *Cantigas* are purely lyrical 'songs of praise' (*cantigas de loor*). Of the others, the great majority are lyrical narratives, 'songs of miracles' (*cantigas de miragres*)—miracles accomplished by the Virgin Mary. These draw in part on the rich fund of popular miracle-legends that had begun to be written down in the eleventh century and drawn together into collections in several countries in the twelfth. But Alfonso also makes use of local oral traditions, and even, he claims, of his own experience—he often explicitly distinguishes wonders he has read about from those he has heard and those he has seen. The miracles are told in a light, relaxed ballad fashion, the stanzas linked by their final rhymes with a refrain that was sung and danced after each by the assembled company. These songs were far more than a court entertainment: their greatest appeal must have been during popular festivities on the Church's holy-days. Often there is a delightfully pagan quality both in the story and the way it is told. A pretty nun who is treasurer in her convent (and, like all the heroes and heroines of these legends, deeply devoted to the Virgin) falls in love with a knight and runs away with him. But first she goes to the altar, leaves her keys there, and commends them to the Virgin's keeping:

'Ay, Madre de Deus', enton	'Ah, Mother of God!' she then
diss' ela en ssa razon,	said within her thoughts,
'leixo-vos est' encomenda,	'I'll leave you these to care for,
e a vos de coraçon	and with all my heart
m'acomend'.' E foi-ss',	put myself in your care,' She left,
e non	and not
por ben fazer sa fazenda,	to do what she was meant to do,
con aquel que muit' amar	with the man she loved so much
mais ca si sabia,	more than herself,
e foi gran tenpo durar	and lived for a long time
con el en folia.	with him in foolishness.

The nun bears her lover several children, and in all that time St Mary loyally assumes her shape and performs the convent duties in her stead. At last the nun repents, abandons her knight, and returns, trembling with fear, to her convent. She finds the keys and her habit just where she had left them. Then, 'without the slightest shame', she told the sisters the story; to convince them she even 'had her lover summoned, to come and tell them too'. The sisters (and, we may presume, the contemporary audience) are not in the least shocked— 'By St John, we have never heard anything so beautiful!'—and the song ends with their joyful thanks to the Virgin. In this blithe and complaisant world it seems natural that the Queen of Heaven should abet a pair of lovers 'living in sin'—if they are among her devotees, she will bring them to God's grace in the end. For she is the 'refuge of sinners', idol of that vast majority whom she helps to make a satisfactory compromise between the absolute demands of a jealous God and the more attractive demands of everyday life. In many ages and places a compromise-religion of this type, though in every sense the most popular, goes virtually unrecorded. We glimpse it frequently, however, as a living reality, in the best of the *Cantigas*, which have something of the raciness and light touch of Boccaccio's *novelle*, though not the comprehensive subtlety of Chaucer's tales.

Where Alfonso had shown true friendship and tolerance towards Arabs and Jews, and even founded a centre of studies where they could work with Christians on an equal footing, his younger Catalan contemporary Ramón Lull spent most of his life in passionate attempts at converting Arabs and Jews to Christianity. He too founded a college (through the patronage of his king, Jaime II), but this was intended only for Christian clergy to learn Arabic and Hebrew—not so as to study the philosophy and science of their 'adversaries', but so as to defeat them in their own tongues in arguing about the true religion. None the less, Lull was an immensely gifted visionary, no fanatic;

and beside his many volumes of encyclopaedic range in Latin, Arabic and Catalan, he has left us one or two poems in which he emerges as a living, but also a lovable, human being. The greatest of these is the *Desconhort* (Comfortlessness), an autobiographical reverie of some eight hundred lines, an impassioned dialogue with a hermit who appears before him in a wood and challenges the whole basis of his life. The hermit is a projection of one half of Ramón's mind: he voices all the self-doubt that a sensitive man of such precarious genius must have felt. Ramón feels that his system, his *Art general*, was a true inspiration, a key to the whole of knowledge, human and divine—he is angry and embittered because almost everyone ignores it. Does that mean he was writing for success, not for God's glory? Is he a failure not only as a writer but as a human being, having abandoned wife and children and possessions and laboured thirty years for a mirage? Are the popes and cardinals right who ignore all his schemes for the conversion of Islam? Was the school of languages, which broke up after less than two decades, a futile venture? If God wanted a new apostolate, would he not show it through another Pentecost, by the gift of tongues? Does God indeed want all men to be believers—or rather to show his love at the Judgment even towards unbelievers? At every turn Ramón tries to defend the convictions by which he had lived. At last the hermit lets himself be persuaded, and the two walk together into the future, their confidence shaken but not wholly destroyed.

Little of Ramón's strictly lyrical poetry can stand beside the *Desconhort*—often he uses songs only as a simple means of religious instruction—but in one song, the *Cant de Ramón*, he questions his life and work once more. As at the opening of the *Desconhort*, he speaks in formulaic language of the vanity of his youth, and then he speaks of the new life:

Lo monestir de Miramar	The monastery of Miramar
fiu a frares menors donar	was my foundation, that the Friars
per sarraïns a preïcar.	Minor might preach to Saracens.
Enfre la vinya e·l fenollar	Between the fennel and the vine
amor me pres, fé·m Déus amar	love seized me, made me to love God,
e·nfre sospirs e plors estar . . .	to stay half between sighs and tears . . .
Novell saber hai atrobat;	I have discovered a new science
pot n'hom conèixer veritat	by which mankind can know the truth
e destruir la falsetat.	and do away with falsity:
Sarraïns seran batejat,	Saracens will be baptised,
tartres, jueus e mant errat,	Tartars, Jews, and many who've erred,
per lo saber que Déus m'ha dat.	through the science God has given me.

Ramón's use of the future tense in this stanza shows that even then he still regarded his aspirations as a visionary possibility, however distant. But almost at once his sense of reality harshly returns:

Són hom vell, paubre, menyspreat,	I am an old man, poor, despised,
no hai ajuda d'home nat	I have no help from any alive,
e hai trop gran fait emparat.	I've tried to undertake too much.
Gran res hai de lo món cercat;	I've traversed great parts of the world,
mant bon eximpli hai donat:	I gave it many a valid proof;
poc són conegut e amat.	I am little known and little loved.
Vull morir en pèlag d'amor ...	I want to die in a sea of love ...

The song now moves into prayer—for the world, at which Ramón casts a final troubled glance; for himself and his books (perhaps at least God will take some notice of them!); and at last for his fellow-workers, who may continue his labours to the greater glory of God. It is one of the most remarkable prayers ever written: like Gottschalk's *Ut quid iubes* it is a personal prayer, but it shows a strength and ripeness that Gottschalk lacks. And paradoxically, it is more self-revealing than Gottschalk's song because it is less self-absorbed: in a few stanzas, with such concision that it seems almost casual, this wonderful man has shown us the essence of his life.

(8) *Germany and the Low Countries*

The other heights of personal religious lyric in the thirteenth century occur in Germany and in Brabant. In Germany the objective or hymnic tradition, which we have indicated through major contributions such as those of Otfrid and Ezzo, culminates in the early twelfth century in the 'Song to Mary' from the monastery of Melk. It is a symphony of praises. The material of this poet's imagery is indeed traditional: the old *figurae* of Mary's fertility (the flowering of Aaron's rod, or the sprinkling of Gideon's fleece with heavenly dew), and of her purity (images such as Moses' burning bush), and the many images Mary inherits from the Bride in the Song of Songs (the sealed fountain and enclosed garden, cedar, rose, honeycomb, the diverse perfumes and spices): but in the vernacular all these, even in their simplest use, have a sparkling freshness. The poet, however, is far more than a synthesiser: in his direct and unprecious language he can create an incomparable conceit as simply as if it were the most accepted image, as if it grew spontaneously out of his litanies of praise:

Ein angelsnuor geflohtin ist,	A fishing-line was woven,
dannen dû geborn bist:	out of which you were born:
daz was diu dîn chunnescaft.	that was your ancestry;
der angel was diu gotes chraft,	the hook was the divine energy
dâ der tôt wart ane irworgen:	on which Death was choked:
der von dir wart verborgen,	through you he was revoked,
Sancta Maria.	Sancta Maria.

The concept of the 'line' of David and the old *figura* of the cross, the hook with which Christ pierced Leviathan's jaw, become totally transformed in a new image that is more than the sum of its parts, creating new symbolism even in the moment of explaining allegory. So too in the following stanzas: the explanation of the next image— the flower that grows out of the branch of Jesse's tree—itself turns into a greater image:

Dô gehît ime sô werde	There so gloriously
der himel zuo der erde . . .	heaven and earth marry . . .

A decade or two after the composition of the *Melker Marienlied*, a German woman, Hildegard of Bingen, prodigiously gifted in many directions, scientific, mystical, and poetic, composed a cycle of Latin liturgical lyric—hymns and sequences, antiphons and responses—in which such fusion of images is taken to an unparalleled visionary extreme. In its forms and melodies, as in its poetic techniques, this 'symphony of the harmony of heavenly revelations', as she called it, stands apart from all other religious lyric, Latin or vernacular, of its time. The most spectacular songs in the cycle are the sequences; in their metrical and musical freedom they have analogies with some from the ninth and tenth centuries—some of Notker's, and others of this time, only recently discovered, from Mozarabic Spain. They are totally unlike the regularised strophic sequences of her own time. Even where Hildegard uses parallelism, the symmetry never becomes complete— the half-stanzas both echo and modify each other. And this pattern of echo and modification pervades not only the formal structure—it is the very rhythm of the imagery itself. I shall illustrate by citing Hildegard's sequence *Columba aspexit* (the Latin text and the melody are given below, pp. 238–40), dedicated to St Maximinus (the disciple who is said to have sailed with the three Maries and Lazarus to Provence, and with whose church at Trier Hildegard was closely connected):

1a. The dove peered in
    through the latticed window,
    where before her gaze
    raining, a balm rained down
    from the brightness of Maximinus.

1b. The sun's heat blazed
    and streamed into the darkness
    from which blossomed the gem
    —in the building of the temple—
    of the purest generous heart.

2a. He, the sublime tower
    made of Lebanon's tree,
    made of cypress,
    is decked with jacinth and sardonyx,
    city that no architect's skill can match.

2b. He, the swift hart
    ran up to the fountain
    of purest water
    bubbling from the mightiest stone
    whose moisture made the sweet perfumes flow.

3a. You perfumers
    who live in the gentlest greenness
    of the king's gardens,
    you who mount into the heights
    when you have consummated
    the holy sacrifice among the rams,

3b. Lucent among you
    is this architect, wall of the temple,
    he who longed
    for an eagle's wings as he kissed
    his foster-mother, Wisdom,
    in Ekklesia's glorious fecundity!

4a. Maximinus, you are mountain and valley,
    and in both you appear, a pinnacle,
    where the mountain-goat walked, and the elephant,
    and Wisdom played in her delight.

4b. You are both brave and gentle;
    in the rites and in the sparkling of the altar
    you mount as a smoke of fragrant spices
    to the column of praise

5. Where you plead the cause of your people
    who aspire to the mirror of light
    for which there is praise on high.

This cascade of images (many of which derive ultimately from the
Song of Songs) is not directly concerned with Maximinus himself, but
gives lyrical expression to the relation between mankind, the saint,
and God. The first pair of half-stanzas evoke the divine (dove, sun)
entering what is both the saint's cell and a paradise garden dewy with
balm—and the paradise is the saint's own inward state. In stanza 1b
the ambiguous *gemma*—which is both bud and jewel—heralds the
twofold imagery of heavenly garden and heavenly city that continues
throughout the song, and the fluid syntax allows a further enrichment
of meaning: Maximinus is the fairest flower in the temple, but the
temple is also his own heart.

The saint is the masterpiece of both nature and art: he is formed of
trees (the same trees as make the bridal-bed for the mystic marriage
in the Song of Songs), and of jewels (the same jewels of which in the
Apocalypse the divine city is built). He can drink of the divine fountain
for which the hart thirsts; by two further associations Hildegard links
this fountain with the rock from which Moses made water flow (the
traditional *figura* for the piercing of Christ's side), and with the perfumes of the Song of Songs. So too the perfumers, who prepare the
bride and make her delectable for her lover, are by an ancient *figura*
the prophets who prepare mankind for the incarnation. But Hildegard
infuses the *figura* with a new and far richer meaning: the perfumers
exemplify that twofold movement, that twofold relation with God and
with the rest of mankind, which also epitomises the role of the saint:
they ascend into the divine, and they establish the way to the divine on
earth (by sacrifices, the smoke of which, as a later image recalls, rises
from earth to heaven). So too this saint, in realising the godhead
within him (as the architect realises himself in what he builds), both
aspires to the kiss of Sapientia and mediates with mankind below. He is,
as the bestiary legends have it, an eagle whose wings are set alight by
the divine sun, a mountain-goat that can scale the heights, but also an
elephant who, in the words of *Physiologus*, 'walks in the lowest places';
he returns from the heights to share his joy with men below. For
Wisdom too both played with God in the heights and delighted to be
with the children of men. The upward movement is conveyed once
more by the fragrance rising heavenwards from the altar, the return
by the descent of heavenly light, mirrored to mankind. It is the same
light as streamed into the saint's cell: here, as at first, we see the meeting-

point of human and divine: the highest point of human aspiration, where the divine light comes down to enter and perfect it.

Hildegard's images are traditional; what is new is the alchemy for which she uses them, and which produces a poetic effect profounder than any explication can hope to suggest.

While the repertoire of a number of Minnesinger in the later twelfth and early thirteenth centuries included a small proportion of religious songs, and while some of their crusade songs (see below, p. 139) show unusual elements of religious feeling, there is nothing in any way comparable to the *Melker Marienlied* or to Hildegard's sequences. Even the stanzas to Mary in Walther von der Vogelweide's *Leich* lack something of the concentration and the glow of these. It is in the later thirteenth century that we find a new creativeness in religious lyric, but now in an intimate, not hymnic, mode: in the lyrical interludes in Mechthild of Magdeburg's book of visions, *The Flowing Light of Godhead*, and in an Alemannic poet whom we know only by his nick-name—'the wild (i.e. vagabond) Alexander'—and by the seven notable songs linked with that name, four of which contain religious elements. In the finest of these he creates a wholly personal blend of reminiscence and vision (the melody is given below, p. 245):

> Long ago, when we were children,
> in the time that spanned the years
> when we ran across the meadows,
> over from those, now back to these,
> there, where we at times
> found violets,
> you now see cattle leap for flies.
>
> I remember how we sat
> deep in flowers, and decided
> which girl was the prettiest.
> Our young looks were radiant then
> with the new garland
> for the dance.
> And so the time goes by.
>
> Look, there we ran to find strawberries,
> ran to the beech from the fir-tree,
> over sticks and stones,
> as long as the sun shone.
> Then a forester called out
> through the branches
> 'Come along, children, go home!'

All our hands were stained,
picking strawberries yesterday;
to us it was nothing but play.
Then, again and again, we heard
our shepherd calling
and moaning:
'Children, the forest is full of snakes!'

One child walked in the tall grass,
started, and cried aloud:
'Children, right here there was a snake!
He has bitten our pony—[1]
it will never heal;
it must always
remain poisoned and unwell.'

'Come along then, out of the forest!
If you do not now make haste
it will happen as I say:
if you are not sure to be gone
from the forest while there is day,
you will lose your way
and your joy will become a moan.'

Do you know that five young women
loitered in the meadow-lands
till the king locked up his hall?
Great were their moans and their distress—
for the bailiffs tore
their clothes away,
so that they stood naked, without a dress.[2]

I am convinced that this poem is not fragmentary, as certain scholars have conjectured. Poetically, the finest allegory is closest to pure vision. Instead of conceptualisation, there is a deepening of recognition, in which thoughts grow out of imaginative perception yet still

1. The garbled word *pherierlin* in the unique MS has received several suggested corrections. I have been persuaded by D. Blamires (*Medium Aevum* 45, 1976, 269–75) that the text should read *pherdelin* (pony): Blamires cites in support not only the lines from Genesis in which a snake bites a horse, but several medieval German uses and allegorisations of these lines.

2. I should like to recommend to readers Robert Lowell's recent and delightful English version of this song (*Imitations*, pp. 6–7)—with a caution, however, against one or two misconstructions of the original that it contains (cf. M. Wehrli, *Deutsche Lyrik des Mittelalters*, pp. 435–9): st. 2 'which bunches were prettiest' instead of 'which girl'; 'our childishness was obvious' instead of 'our young looks were radiant'; st. 4 'We came out in spots' (with over-eating of strawberries) instead of 'We got stains' (on our hands, with *picking* strawberries); st. 5 'that snake would go to hell' is based on Kraus's gratuitous emendation of MS *eʒ* to *er*.

remain circumscribed by it. In seven stanzas this poet moves from memories of a particular childhood to the paradigm of a Biblical allegory. The transition is a very subtle and gradual one. He does not explain, but he shows, the passage from innocence to experience, the child's journey from an uncomplicated world into a world filled with dangers and the need to make decisions—the inner journey from Paradise into Fall. At first it is hinted at only very lightly: the land-scape is not quite as enchanted now as then—then one saw only the violets, not the cattle plagued by flies. By degrees danger becomes explicit. The forest is no longer simply a playground. The first warning, that of the forester, conveys little meaning to the children; the shepherd is more insistent and more specific; the unknown voice at the end discloses all. Who are the warners? And in what forest? Clearly the poet does not want us to label and objectify—he wants us to relive the children's own drama of apprehension. The shepherd who warns of snakes evokes certain associations; then one of the children discovers the snake's track for himself, and sees that it has bitten the pony they had brought along. This moment may contain a swift allusion to an enigmatic passage in Genesis (XLIX, 16–17), where Jacob's son Dan is fated to become 'the horned serpent by the wayside, biting the horse's hooves', a passage often interpreted in the Middle Ages as a prophecy of Antichrist, who harries the world as the final doom approaches. Yet once more the poet, in the following stanza, deliberately leaves this sense of doom unexplained. Definition might appear to be reached at last in the closing strophe: the unknown voice (or yet another?) seems to go on to tell the well-known parable, holding up the five foolish virgins as a warning. Yet even here the poet's art is illusion: the story is not quite that of the foolish virgins after all. The fate of these five maidens moves into that of the celestial bride in the Song of Songs (V, 6–7), when she loses her way in the dark in frantic pursuit of her beloved:

> I looked for him and did not find him,
> I called, and he did not answer me.
> The watchmen who patrol the city found me,
> they struck me and wounded me,
> the watchmen of the town walls tore my clothes away.

This is the 'dark night' that the beloved soul *must* endure before the divine lover can enter her garden (VI, 1). Does this mean that the well-meaning voices warning against the dark were wrong? That children, before they know fear, can tread the serpent underfoot as easily as saints? Does the last stanza evoke a vision of foolishness and humiliation before God, or before the world? I think the poet, by his conflation of two visions, the punishment of the foolish virgins and the necessary ordeal of the divine bride, has left the close deliberately ambiguous. The haunting quality of the poem is bound up with this final enigma. It is, we might say, a poem that recollects and recreates a child's first moments of dread as it reaches the limits of childhood, uncertain whether the voices in the mind are angels or demons.

Lyrical poetry of comparable originality and power was composed by two poetesses, Hadewijch of Brabant in the earlier thirteenth century, and Mechthild of Magdeburg in the later. It is to women that we owe some of the highest flights of mystical poetry in the Middle Ages. Where Hildegard's *Symphonia* was, outwardly at least, in the objective liturgical mode, Hadewijch's and Mechthild's poetry is a poetry of meditation; it is their inner colloquy with divine Love, who is a projection of their minds comparable in some ways to Ramón Lull's hermit—but Love (*Die Minne*) is a womanly figure, divinely beautiful and seductive; she is both relentless tyrant and sweet enchantress. Under her spell, these women know and recreate in themselves all the heights and all the abysses, the raptures and the torments of the beloved in the Song of Songs.

Mechthild, and probably Hadewijch also, belonged to a *béguinage*, one of the spiritual communities of women that grew up among the laity, first in the Netherlands, then in France and Germany, in the early thirteenth century. They did not take vows like nuns, and were not wholly cloistered, but cared for the poor and the sick. It is in and for the hours of contemplation of such a group that this astonishing lyrical poetry must have arisen.

In some of her finest poems Hadewijch adapts the 'nature-opening' characteristic of troubadour love-lyric, though she proceeds to develop it in a startlingly different way:

> 1. The birds have long been silent
>   that were blithe here before:
>   their blitheness has departed,
>   they have lost their summer now;
>   they would swiftly sing again
>   if that summer came again,
>   which they have chosen above all
>   and for which they were born:
>   one hears it in their voices then.

2. I'll say no more of birds' laments:
   their joy, their pain, is quickly gone;
   I have more grievous cause to moan:
   Love, to whom we should aspire,
   weighs us down with her noble cares,
   so we chase after false delights
   and Love cannot enfold us then.
   Ah, what has baseness done to us!
   Who shall erase that faithlessness?

3. The mighty ones, whose hand is strong,
   it is on them I still rely,
   who work at all times in Love's bond,
   heedless of pain, grief, tragedy;
   they want to ride through all the land
   that lovers loving by love have found,
   so perfect is their noble heart;
   they know what Love can teach by love,
   how Love exalts lovers by love.

4. Why then should anyone refuse,
   since by loving Love can be won?
   Why not ride, longing, through the storm,
   trusting in the power of Love,
   aspiring to the cult of Love?
   Love's peerlessness will then be seen—
   there, in the brightness of Love's dawn,
   where for Love's sake is shunned no pain
   and no pain caused by Love weighs down.

5. Often I call for help as a lost one,
   but then, when you come close, my dear one,
   with new solace you bear me up
   and with high spirit I ride on,
   sport with my dear so joyously
   as if north and south and east
   and west all lands belonged to me!
   Then suddenly I am dashed down.—
   Oh, what use to tell my pain?

It is a turbulent poem, but with its own coherent strength, both poetically and humanly. The first and last stanzas are linked in thought and enrich each other: the alternation between joy and wretchedness, which for the birds is as 'natural' as the alternation of summer and winter, has its deeper analogy in the soul's experience of *Minne*. At first (stanza 2) it is an analogy that the loving soul wants to deny—in nature such alternations are swift and inescapable, but there is nothing natural, nothing inevitable, about the neglect and betrayal of divine Love in the world. Can it not be fought and vanquished by those who love heroically?

In the third and fourth stanzas Hadewijch envisions such an heroic élite, a chivalry of divine Love. She uses the terms of reference of the most exalted conceptions of human love: these lovers have a *cor gentil* (Hadewijch's 'fine herte'), they want to experience the whole of love, even its sufferings, for they know that the sufferings are inexorably linked with love's ennobling power. Theirs would be a commitment to active longing, regardless of whether love is requited, for such loving seeks no reward outside itself.

Such is Hadewijch's ideal—she longs to be one of these heroic riders. But do they exist? In her moving final stanza Hadewijch returns to reality. A real lover cannot go on without some solace from the beloved. He, or she, cannot ride as a conquering hero, finding invincible strength within himself alone: the real lover is a helpless being, whose moments of elation and of despair depend wholly on the gestures of the beloved. With touching honesty Hadewijch abandons her fantasy of a Britomart of divine love and resigns herself to the love-service of submissiveness, and to a condition from which human beings, in their own way, can no more escape than the birds or the seasons.

Mechthild's poetry is more loosely knit than this: it consists of numerous lyrical interludes, in a rhyming free verse, in her book of meditations. Sometimes they are long, passionate dialogues of the soul with *Minne*, with God, or with the senses; or again they can be as short as two lines, spoken by the divine *Minne*:

> I come to my loved one
> like a dew upon the flowers.

The thoughts are simple but beautifully direct, and time and again the imagery sparkles: as when Mechthild transforms a profane dance-song, that survives among the German stanzas in the Carmina Burana:[1]

1. CB 145a: If the whole world were mine,
from the sea up to the Rhine,
I would renounce it all
if King . . . of England
were to lie in my arms!

The missing name may well have been 'Richard' (Coeur-de-Lion). A corrector in the Codex Buranus has altered the line to read 'the queen of England'; but Mechthild's lines suggest that the original was composed from the woman's viewpoint: 'even if I were empress, I'd rather have him as *my* Emperor'.

If all the world were mine
and were made of flawless gold,
and I were here, as I could wish, for ever—
the noblest of all, loveliest of all,
mightiest empress of all—
this I would hold as nothing
beside my great desire
to see my dear lord Jesus Christ
in his heavenly honour.
Imagine what they suffer who lie waiting for him long!

Or again, when she imagines herself in a forest, and the music of the
nightingales makes her long for the divine Prince to ask her to dance
—then he comes, and suddenly she is afraid:

I cannot dance, my Lord, unless you lead me.
If you want me to leap high,
you yourself must lead the dance and sing.[1]
Then I shall leap into love.
From love into understanding,
from understanding to fruition,
from fruition upwards, past all human sense.
There I shall stay, and, circling more, still dance!

Or when *Minne* invites her into God's wine-cellar:

If you want to come with me into that tavern,
you will have to spend so lavishly—
if you order wine for a thousand marks,
you'll have finished it within an hour . . .

Or in Mechthild's anguished evocations of the 'fatal' quality of her
love. For all its torments, she cannot help her longing—it is her
destiny to sing of love through pain, like the nightingale. The bitter-
sweet cry of Aeschylus' Cassandra, which Mechthild cannot have
known, is recreated spontaneously in a new dimension:

How long shall I remain so parched?
An hour oppresses me too much.

1. Compare the celebrated 'round dance' episode in the *Acts of John* (94 ff.), in which
Christ is the leader in the dance with his disciples, and sings the words that accompany
the dance. It is not certain, however, that Mechthild could have known this episode
directly: until now only allusions to the passage and brief citations from it have come to
light in the Latin tradition.

> A day is a thousand years,
> if you want to be estranged from me.
> If it should become a week,
> I would rather fly to hell—
> indeed I am in it now . . .
>   The nightingale
> cannot help singing,
> for she sparkles with love in her whole being.
> If this were taken from her, she would die . . .

With these highly individual thirteenth-century poets the brief survey of this chapter must close. We have reached an important turning-point in the tradition, a point where religious lyrical poetry has begun to take a very different course from that of hymnody. This distinction between two genres would have been meaningless even half a century earlier. Henceforth the creative achievements in religious lyric occur, almost without exception, in the poetic, not the hymnic, tradition, in the subjective and mystical modes, not in the objective.

3

'CANTIGAS DE AMIGO'

The earliest surviving secular lyrics in a Romance language were discovered in 1948 under remarkable circumstances. It was then that an
Orientalist, Samuel Stern, working on the Arabic and Hebrew strophic
poems composed in Moslem Spain during the eleventh and twelfth
centuries, was able to show that many of these poems concluded with
lines in the Romance dialect of the region. It had become a custom to
end the rhetorically elaborate panegyrics and love-songs composed at
the sophisticated courts of al-Andalus with verses specially appropriate
to the *chanteuse* who performed them. Most often these consisted of a
woman's love-song, which contrasted with the rest of the piece by its
simplicity and directness, at times by its coquettish or provocative wit.

The Arabic or Hebrew poet would take such a Spanish love-song as
his starting-point. Often at least he took over a song that was already
well-known. The technique can best be explained by an illustration.
The Arabic poet al-Tutili († 1126) built a love-song around the
Romance verses:

> Meu 'l-habib enfermo de meu amar—
> quen ad sanar?
> Bi nafsi amante, que sed a meu legar!
>
> My dearest one is sick with love of me—
> who will his doctor be?
> By my love's soul, how he waits, thirstily!   (21)[1]

1. The interpretation of the second and third lines is uncertain. That of the third is
based on the text as given in the anthology (*Jaysh*) of Ibn al-Khatib (1313–74), which
here differs significantly from the other MSS. The *kharjas* cited here are numbered
according to the editions of Stern and Heger (see p. 256).

He uses the metre and rhymes of these verses as the basis for his own
Arabic refrain:

> A stream of tears, heart kindled ardently—
> water and fire can be
> joined only in a great extremity.

This refrain in turn gives the pattern for the second part of each stanza
in the new poem. For instance (I give a somewhat free English version,
so as to give an approximate impression of the rhymes and form):

> I have made a tyrannic lady my lord,
> I stammer her name and can scarce speak the word.
> Marvel that all my justness has incurred
> such great injustice! Ask her why I'm unheard!
> She has destroyed my soul capriciously
> by her timidity—
> and without her there's no good company![1]

A poem of this kind, called a *muwashshah*, consisted of some five
such stanzas, each stanza being followed by the refrain. The last stanza
ended with the adopted lines (the *kharja*, or concluding verses):

> Bondage to her will never let me rest,
> reproachful, arrogant, she holds me fast;
> she has abandoned me, sick and distressed,
> but then she sings, half in love, half in jest:
> 'My dearest one is sick with love of me—
> who will his doctor be?
> By my love's soul, how he waits, thirstily!'

While the *muwashshah* was in classical Arabic or Hebrew, the *kharja*
was always colloquial—whether in Arabic or in a Spanish interspersed
with Arabic words, as was common in the everyday speech of the
bilingual, 'Mozarabic' areas.

The Spanish *kharjas* show a wide range in expression and in quality.
At one end of the scale, poetically, are the seemingly artless exclamations and cries of a girl in love:

Que faray, Mamma?	What shall I do, mother?
Meu 'l-habib est' ad yana!	My lover is at the door! (14)

---

1. The precise syllabic scheme in the original is: refrain 11 4 11, rhyming aaa;
strophes 11 11 11 11 11 4 11, rhyming bbbb aaa, cccc aaa . . .

| Que farayu, o que serad de mibi, habibi? | What shall I do, or what will become of me,   beloved? |
| Non te tolgas de mibi! | Do not withdraw from me!   (16) |

| Aman, aman, ya 'l-malih, gare | Pity me, pity me, handsome one —tell me, |
| por que tu me queris, bi 'llah, matare? | why in God's name would you kill me?   (26) |

| Como si filyol' alyenu, | As if you were a stranger, |
| non mas adormis a meu senu. | you no longer fall asleep on my breast.   (7) |

Are these brief verses fragments from longer lyrics, the rest of which is lost? Not necessarily: as Joseph Bédier showed with regard to the Old French *refrains*, often of precisely similar length and scope, the context to envisage for such lines may well be a dance rather than a longer poem: there they could be built out by repetition, instrumentation and mime, or, in a longer dance-play, each *kharja* or *refrain* could have acted as a focal point for one scene. (See below, p. 198.)

At another extreme among the *kharjas* are some lyrical masterpieces, songs in which a girl's sorrows in love are portrayed as movingly and imaginatively as they have ever been before or since:

Garid vos, ay yermanellas,	Ah tell me, little sisters,
com contenir a meu male!	how to hold my pain!
Sin al-habib non vivireyu—	I'll not live without my beloved—
advolarey demandare.	I shall fly to seek him again. (4)

Here the question of fragmentation scarcely arises: the poetic self-sufficiency of such a quatrain is evident.

While only a few of the *kharjas* reach this impassioned strength, the frankness with which the girl sings of her feelings is characteristic of nearly all. She is an active lover rather than a passive loved one. Thus she importunes her lover:

Meu sidi Ibrahim,	My lord Ibrahim,
ya tu omne dolǧe,	oh my sweet love,
vent' a mib	come to me
de nohte!	at night!
In non, si non queris,	If not, if you don't want to,
yireym' a tib.	I shall come to you.
Gar me a ob	Tell me where
legarte!	to see you! (22)

At times she teases him:

Ya rabb, com vivireyu 　　con este 'l-halaq, ya man qabl an yusallam 　　yuhaddid bi 'l-firaq!	Oh Lord, how shall I bear a life 　　with this deceiver, who, before a girl's even welcomed him, 　　threatens to leave her!　　　　(6)

Or again, she rouses his desire by suggesting a new way of making love:

Tan t'amaray, illa con 　　al-šarti an taġma' halhali ma' 　　qurti!¹	I'll give you such love!—but only 　　if you'll bend my anklets right over to my 　　earrings!　　　　　　　(29)

It is especially in the songs the girl addresses to her confidante, her mother, that we see how complicated her feelings can be:

Non quero tener al-'iqd, ya 　　mamma— a mano hulla li.² Col albo verad fora meu 　　sidi, non querid al-huli.	I don't want to wear a necklace, 　　mother— the dress is enough for me. My lord will see a pure white 　　throat displayed, he won't want jewellery.　　(11)

There is both modesty and pride here, submissiveness and determination. In another, where several details remain problematic,

Alsa-me de min hali— mon hali qad bare! Que faray, ya 'ummi?— Faneq bad lebare!	Take me out of this plight— my state is desperate! Mother, what shall I do?— The falcon is about to snatch!　(27)

the fantasy of the last line (if this attractive reading of the words is right) is wonderfully suggestive of the young girl's indecision between wanting love and being afraid of love, at once lured and threatened.

The sixty-one Romance *kharjas* discovered so far are preserved in *muwashshahs* composed between 1000 and 1150. But the *muwashshah* it-

1. That the majority of words in this *kharja* are Arabic does not, I think, justify the general inference drawn by several scholars, that a lascivious note is essentially Arabic and alien to the Romance songs.
2. The interpretation of this line is uncertain.

self was introduced as a literary genre in Moslem Spain around 900, and there is nothing to suggest that the Romance songs which the earliest *muwashshah* poets must have known were a novelty at that time. It is significant that church councils throughout Europe from the sixth to the ninth centuries protest against the singing not only of amatory or lascivious songs, but specifically against the songs of girls (*puellarum cantica*). From the *kharjas* we can win some notion of what this earlier range of European song was like. And even if certain formal developments within Arabic poetry helped to pave the way for the *muwashshah*, it was undoubtedly the vivacious and flourishing strophic lyric in the Romance vernacular that gave the principal impetus towards the innovation of strophic poetry in Arabic, and later in Hebrew.

Thus the *kharjas* at times represent and at times reflect a type of traditional or popular song—not confined to an aristocratic or learned élite—such as was probably sung in the various Romance *patois* from their beginnings. Their themes are elemental, and, as Theodor Frings showed in his brilliant lecture to the German Academy in 1949, such themes recur in the songs of nearly every epoch and nation. The ranges of thought and mood in the Spanish *kharjas* can already be found in Egyptian collections of love-songs from the late second millennium B.C., and in Chinese songs contemporary with Sappho. At Pompeii, among the ancient *graffiti*, we can find quite artless lovers' messages, including some that seem to be from a woman's viewpoint:

> Romula hic cum Staphylo moratur
> (Romula dallies here with Staphylus)
>
> Serena Isidoru fastidit
> (Serena's getting tired of Isidore)

What prompted these scribbles? Were they to vaunt a love, or jest about it? Were they written up by Romula and Serena themselves, or (perhaps likelier, if we can go by today) by friends who wanted to tease or to provoke them? Another message seems to be more serious and touching:

> Venerusa opto te ut eum bene ames
> (Venerusa, I implore you, love him well!)

Is it a woman's plea to another, who has won her lover away from her? Again on a Pompeian wall we have some fragmentary lines of verse which, though formally crude, are vibrant and alive with wit:

If you felt any stirrings of love in you, mule-driver,
you would drive more swiftly to see love's goal!
I'm in love with a beautiful boy—use the spurs, please go faster!
You're drunk! Go faster! Use the reins and whip!
Bring me to Pompeii, where my sweet love lies!
You are mine . . .

So too, many poets and poetesses of medieval Europe turned to the ancient and universal themes of women's love-songs, and made new poetry out of them in a fascinating variety of ways. In 789 Charlemagne issued a capitulary ordering that 'no abbess should presume to leave her convent without our permission, nor allow those under her to do so . . . and on no account let them dare to write *winileodas*, or send them from the convent'. The *winileodas* (literally, 'songs for a friend', 'cantigas de amigo') from this period have not themselves survived, but one Germanic song in particular, preserved in a tenth-century manuscript, may give us some impression of what they were like. It is the song known as *Wulf and Eadwacer*, one of the summits of Anglo–Saxon poetry:

> To my people it will be like an offering—
> how they'll welcome him if he comes in their midst!
> Our fates are torn apart.
>
> Wulf is on one island, I on another,
> the island a fastness, imprisoned by fens.
> There are cruel men on that island—
> how they'll welcome him if he comes in their midst!
> Our fates are torn apart.
>
> I longed for my Wulf in his wide wanderings,
> when the rains came, and I sat here in tears;
> when the branches of his body embraced me,
> I felt the joy—but the harshness too.
>
> Wulf, my Wulf, I am sick with longing
> for you, with the rareness of your coming,
> the grief of my heart, not the famine I live in.
>
> Do you hear, Eadwacer? Wulf is carrying
> our pitiful cub to the woods!
> How easy to sunder what never was joined—
> our song together!

Though there are many uncertainties about points of detail in this poem, its dominant notes, the woman's fierce longing for her lover

Wulf, her fear for his sake and her contempt for her husband Eadwacer, are unmistakable. Wulf 'in his wide wanderings' has been
outlawed (the choice of name is perfect, the wolf is indeed the essential
outlaw), and he returns secretly to the hostile island where his beloved
waits, knowing

> the place death, considering who thou art,
> If any of my kinsmen find thee here.

In the prelude of the song, of which two lines are repeated as an
irregular refrain, she speaks of his danger with a grim irony. Then
comes a stanza that concisely sketches the narrative setting, with an
allusiveness characteristic of Germanic poetry and reflected at times in
both German and English medieval love-songs. There follows the
essential *winileod*, with its intensity both of joy (the latent image of
the lover entwining his beloved like the branches of a tree, the image
that Chaucer was to develop fully in *Troilus and Criseyde*), and of the
hatefulness (*lað*) of the ever-imminent partings and perils. Finally, in
the woman's outburst to her husband, the dramatic conclusion is
revealed: Wulf has come back to carry off his child into safety (perhaps
fearing that Eadwacer would kill it if he knew who the father was).
As soon as Wulf is out of reach his mistress defiantly tells her husband,
with almost grotesque humour in the implied play on Wulf's name
when she speaks of 'our cub' (*uncerne hwelp*). In the last two lines the
bitterness tinged with irony of the opening returns for a moment, but
only to dissolve in the deep and resplendent recollection of 'our song
together'—the phrase is symbolic of the lovers' oneness, and carries a
passionate conviction of that oneness even in the very moment that
the woman is reflecting on separation.[1]

From the earlier eleventh century, contemporary with the first
surviving *kharjas*, we have a Latin *winileod* of great beauty and sensitiv-
ity, preserved in the 'Cambridge Songs' manuscript (see above, p. 29):

Levis exsurgit Zephirus	Zephyr arises gently
et Sol procedit tepidus:	and the warm Sun proceeds;
iam Terra sinus aperit,	Earth lays bare her bosom,
dulcore suo difluit.	melting with her sweets.
Ver purpuratum exiit,	Spring enters, dressed in crimson,
ornatus suos induit,	puts on her finery,
aspergit terram floribus,	scattering flowers on the earth,
ligna silvarum frondibus.	leaves on every tree.

1. In the original the word 'joined' (*gesomnad*) carries the additional, technical sense
'composed', as of a song.

Struunt lustra quadrupedes et dulces nidos volucres— inter ligna florentia sua decantant gaudia.	Animals build their lairs now and the sweet birds their nests: among the flowering branches they sing their happiness.
Quod oculis dum video et auribus dum audio, heu, pro tantis gaudiis tantis inflor suspiriis.	While I see it with my eyes and hear it with my ears, alas, instead of all those joys I am swollen with as many sighs.
Cum mihi sola sedeo et, hec revolvens, palleo, si forte capud sublevo nec audio nec video.	As I sit all alone, racked with thought and wan, if I should lift my head, then I do not hear, I do not see.
Tu saltim, veris gratia, exaudi, et considera frondes, flores et gramina— nam mea languet anima.	You at least, for the sake of spring, listen, and take in the leaves, the flowers and grass— my soul is languishing.

In its own way this song, like *Wulf and Eadwacer*, is an essentially dramatic creation. It is deeply personal, but in lyric this implies not (or not necessarily) the revelation of private experience, but rather the realisation of a *persona*, that is, the attainment of a certain dramatic objectivity. If the personal element here were only subjective, the result would be less a work of art than an embarrassment: the authenticity lies not in 'the spontaneous overflow of powerful feeling' (which may or may not be present), but in the strength of the imaginative projection.

At the beginning there is a certain 'distanced' effect in the presentation of spring. There is a marked change in diction between the first three stanzas and the rest, and dramatically this rings true: spring is presented by way of personifications, for indeed to the woman speaking spring at this moment is something that she knows but cannot feel. Yet the literary language, for all its remoteness, hints also at what she longs to feel: the gentleness and warmth of Zephirus and Sol, the radiant, sensual generosity of Terra's gesture, the sense of both receiving and giving beauty that the gestures of Ver (again I think a womanly figure, a Botticellian Primavera) imply. Though the setting is seen with a cold, detached eye, there is joy latent in it, a joy that can be fulfilled by participation: she sees it in the creatures, who can 'tame' the flowers and trees, make them into a home, something which is truly theirs.

It is these thoughts that reveal the extent of her loneliness to the woman who speaks them. Loneliness is to know all this but not know it for oneself, to take it in with all one's senses and at the same time be unable truly to hear or see it at all. The paradox is stated with a simplicity that is dramatically perfect—the effect is of discovering this elemental contradiction for oneself for the first time, of discovering it slowly, piecemeal, in the midst of moments of anguish and numbness.

But the song is more than a meditation, it reveals more than a state of mind and feeling. By a brilliant intuitive artistry, the turning-point of the poem is delayed till the opening of the final stanza: suddenly we see that the sorrowing meditation was no mere self-indulgence, that it was all to be directed to another person, to provoke a change of mind and heart in him. She does not say 'for my sake', but 'for spring's sake'; not 'consider me', but 'consider the springtime world around you'. With subtlety and humility she is saying in effect: 'If you have any capacity for love and joy, the leaves and flowers will prompt in you all the thoughts that I have been thinking. And will they not call to you to respond to them—to make the response I cannot make unless you make it with me?' In a single quatrain the song has changed its course —the woman transforms her lament into an invitation to love; her simple parting words portray all her delicacy and complicated indirectness, as well as the passion that lies behind it.

The earliest medieval German women's love-songs, for all their simplicity, are found embedded in a learned context. It is at the end of a girl's Latin letter to a *clerc*, in which a literary, Ciceronian ideal of friendship as well as flirtation and ardent affection seem to be inextricably joined, a letter that was copied as a stylistic model into a Bavarian manuscript of about 1160, that we find the German lines

> Dû bist mîn, ich bin dîn: You are mine, I am yours,
> des solt dû gewis sîn. of this you must be sure.
> dû bist beslozzen You are locked
> in mînem herzen: within my heart,
> verlorn ist daz slüzzelîn: the little key is lost:
> dû muost immer drinne sîn. there you must for ever rest!

Did the learned lady improvise these, or was she quoting a popular *winileod*? We shall probably never know. So too, in the Carmina Burana, we cannot tell whether the haunting German lines

> Gruonet der walt allenthalben. The woods are green on every side.
> wâ ist mîn geselle alsô lange? Where is my love all this while?
> der ist geriten hinnen. He has ridden away.
> owî! wer sol mich minnen? Ah! who will love me now?

are the original of the Latin verses conjoined with them, or a later variation on these, or whether (as I incline to believe) a single poet, composing for a mixed audience of young *clercs* who knew Latin and girls who did not, composed both together, planning them as one song.

Others among the German *winileodas* are composed in a strophic form that has affinities with the quatrains of the *Nibelungenlied* and with traditional German ballad-stanzas:

> Mich dunket niht sô guotes   noch sô lobesam
> sô diu liehte rôse   und diu minne mînes man.
> diu kleinen vogellîn
>   diu singent in dem walde: dêst menegem herzen liep.
> mirn kome mîn holder geselle,   in hân der sumerwünne niet.

> I know nothing so good   or so deserving praise
> as the bright rose   and my dear one's love.
> The little birds,
>   they sing in the woods,   so many a heart feels joy;
> but if my true-love does not come,   I have no summer joy.

Is the delightful naivety of such lines unconscious and spontaneous, or is their author just a little disingenuous, archaising so as to achieve a 'traditional air'? Again, we can only guess. At all events it is easy to see the distance between such lines and the subtle women's songs, in a longer but still similar stanza-form, by Meinloh von Sevelingen, one of the earliest Minnesinger in the twelfth century whom we know by name:

> Mir erwelten mîniu ougen   einen kindeschen man.
> daz nîdent ander frouwen: ich hân in anders niht getân,
> wan obe ich hân gedienet   daz ich diu liebeste bin.
> dar an wil ich kêren   mîn herze und allen den sin.
> swelhiu sînen willen   hie bevor hât getân,
> verlôs si in von schulden,
>   der wil ich nu niht wîzen,   sihe ichs unfroelîchen stân.

> My eyes have chosen for me   a man who's very young.
> Other women are jealous,   yet I've done them no harm—
> only that I was able   to be his dearest one.
> To this I want to bend   my heart and all my will.
> Whoever did his will   till I was his,
> if she lost him deservedly,
>   I shall not reproach her now,   should I see her comfortless.

Meinloh has succeeded in recreating the very turns and temperamental changes of her thoughts—from the gentle mock-innocent self-justification, to the moments of serene acquiescence and ardour, to a petulance that regains composure in sardonically planning an imaginary situation. In half a dozen lines Meinloh achieves a remarkable richness of dramatic texture, and succeeds in giving the illusion that we are watching the inner workings of a woman's mind rather than listening to her making a speech.

In medieval French women's love-songs, by contrast, external narrative elements are more characteristic, and tend to play a more important part, than moments of self-revelation:

Siet soi bele Aye as piez sa male maistre,	Fair Aya sits at her cruel mistress' feet,
sor ses genouls un paile d'Engleterre;	a length of English cloth spread on her knees:
a un fil [fin] i fet coustures belles.	with finest thread she stitches dainty seams.
he he! amors d'autre pais,	*Ah, ah, love from a far-off land,*
mon cuer avez et lie et souspris.	*you have caught my heart and hold it bound.*
Aval la face li courent chaudes lermes,	Down her face runs a stream of burning tears,
q'el est batue et au main et au vespre,	for she is beaten every night and day,
par ce qu'el aime soudoier d'autre terre.	because she loves a soldier from afar.
he he! amors d'autre pais,	*Ah, ah, love from a far-off land,*
mon cuer avez et lie et souspris.	*you have caught my heart and hold it bound!*

The lines used as a refrain are Aya's song, her *winileod*. But here (in contrast, for instance, to the woman's lament in *Wulf and Eadwacer*) they are not the kernel of the lyric; rather they emphasise the objective situation. As in *winileodas* everywhere, the girls and married women of the French songs know the sorrows of love-longing. But their suffering is most often externalised: where in the Spanish and Galician songs the girl's mother is always evoked sympathetically, as the one to whom the girl can admit ardent feelings that otherwise she might have hidden even from herself, in the French songs the mother is cruel, ferrets out the girl's feelings and punishes them (always, of course, to no effect): thus in a thirteenth-century motet for three voices, musically highly sophisticated, that takes up a traditional motif:

Bele Aielis par matin se leva,	Bele Aelis rose when morning came,
en un pre juer ala	went into a field to play,
par deport et par doucour;	full of game, in sheer delight.
lor li menbre d'une amour	Then she calls a love to mind
k'enprise a, si grant	with which so long she's been
piecha.	inflamed:
en souspirant s'escria	sighing, she now exclaimed
'dièus, con vif a grant doulour	'God, how I live in misery
qant on mi bat nuit et jour	since I'm beaten night and day
pour celi qui mon cuer a.	for my sweetheart's sake!
mais com plus mi batera	But the more my mother beats me,
ma mere, plus me fera	the less will she ever take
penser folour.'	my wild thoughts away!'

Similarly in the French songs of the *mal mariée*, the girl is almost invariably beaten by a jealous husband, and revenges herself by taking a lover. The husband, like the mother, is seen as belonging to that 'grown-up' conforming world which no longer lets itself understand youth and joy and love, though indeed the punishments it devises cannot prevent them.

Some of the most individual contributions in the French tradition are to be found among the so-called *chansons de toile*, in which a more extended romantic narrative is developed, largely from the woman's viewpoint. These songs raise a number of problems: to what extent are they really the songs, or the kind of song, that girls sang at their spinning? Are they early or late, archaic or archaising, traditional or literary? A look at one of the most attractive may indicate some tentative answers.

Bele Yolanz en ses chambres seoit,	Fair Yolande sat in her room,
d'un boen samiz une robe cosoit,	sewing a cloak of precious silk—
a son ami trametre la voloit.	she wanted to send it to her love.
en sospirant ceste chancon chantoit	Sighing, she was singing this song:
'dex, tant est douʒ li nons	*'God, how the name of love is*
* d'amors:*	* sweet:*
ja n'en cuidai sentir	*I never thought it would bring*
* dolors.*	* me grief!'*
Bels douz amis, or vos voil envoier	'Fair, gentle lover, I want to send
une robe par mout grant	this cloak now with my great, great
amistie.	love.
por deu vos pri, de moi aiez pitie.'	In God's name I ask, pity me.'
ne pot ester, a la terre	She could not stand, sank to the
s'assiet.	ground.

D

A ces paroles et a ceste raison	At these words and at these thoughts
li siens amis entra en la maison.	her lover came into the house.
cele lo vit, si bassa lo menton,	She saw him, and she hung her head:
ne pot parler, ne li dist o ne non.	she could not speak, not 'yes' or 'no'.
'Ma douce dame, mis m'avez en obli.'	'Sweet lady, you have forgotten me.'
cele l'entent, se li geta un ris,	She heard him, and she laughed aloud;
en sospirant ses bels braz li tendi;	sighing, stretched out her lovely arms;
tant doucement a acoler l'a pris.	so sweetly she embraced him then.
'Bels douz amis, ne vos sai losengier,	'Fair, gentle lover, I cannot lie,
mais de fin cuer vos aim et senz trechier.	I love you with true, perfect heart.
qant vos plaira, si me porrez baisier,	You may kiss me whenever you please;
entre voz braz me voil aler couchier.'	I want to come to lie in your arms.'
Li siens amis entre ses braz la prent,	Her lover takes her in his arms,
en un biau lit s'asient seulement:	together they lie in a fine bed:
bele Yolanz lo baise estroitement,	fair Yolande clings to him with kisses,
a tor francois en mi lo lit l'estent.	and in France's sport she pins him fast.

The scene is set, here as in the other songs of this group, in robustly romantic fashion. Fair Erembors watching the procession of courtiers from her window, Fair Aiglentine sewing in the royal chamber, Fair Yzabel in her high tower, peeping out through the battlements—there is a touch of Hollywood about such openings. But this does not of itself give any sure indication towards the date or literary stage at which these songs developed: it seems to me that such an escapist world could well have been enjoyed by women (and men) in village or palace, in the eleventh and twelfth centuries, and indeed earlier, as easily as in the thirteenth. On the other hand, the openness with which the young women here speak of their passionate feelings need not imply, as an older generation of scholars thought, that these songs are relics of a more archaic, 'pre-courtly' world.[1] Not only can we not trace the first refinements of courtliness back to a fixed time or place,

---

1. Nor for that matter, as Faral suggested in all seriousness, that the songs were too lascivious to have been sung by or among girls at all!

but we must reckon with the co-existence at most times and places of songs in which love is expressed in diverse modes.

In this song of Bele Yolanz certain elements are clearly traditional. First the refrain (which recurs after each stanza), with its age-old insistence that in love joy and sorrow are inseparable: there are dozens of such refrains in Old French lyric that would be virtually interchangeable with this one. Traditional too are a number of other phrases repeated within the song: *en sospirant, bels douz amis, entre voz braz*; to one who is familiar with a range of medieval French poetry, almost half the lines in a song such as this will appear as formulaic. What is distinctive here is the deliberate simplicity and the conscious naivety. The poet achieves a stark, laconic effect by lavish use of asyndeton:

> ne pot ester, a la terre s'assiet . . .
> cele lo vit, si bassa lo menton,
> ne pot parler, ne li dist o ne non.

He shows a fine sense of dramatic economy in the one line he gives the lover:

> 'Ma douce dame, mis m'avez en obli.'

He neatly conveys the flooding confusion of Yolande's feelings by the chiastic

> cele l'entent, se li geta un ris,
> en sospirant ses bels braz li tendi.

The youthful spontaneity with which Yolande offers her body is balanced against the adult wit of the 'curtain-line', in which the poet comments in his own person.

All this may be intuitive art rather than factitious or learned technique. The poet may never have heard of asyndeton or chiasmus; and as Augustine himself, laying the foundations of a Christian rhetoric, admitted, 'we have known many people who without any rhetorical education have been stylistically more accomplished than many who have learnt it all' (*De doctrina christiana*, iv, 3). And while there is sophistication in the effects of naive directness, this again is a sophistication that can be inborn in a gifted poet. It need not be consciously archaising, and it need not be late: it is a characteristic vein especially in French lyric, and I have suggested traces of it already in the earliest surviving French song from the ninth century (see above, p. 40).

The *chansons de toile* create a self-contained, openly romanticised world, but a world whose appeal I think cut across most distinctions of milieu, and may well have lasted far longer than the recorded examples indicate. The qualities and unspoken assumptions of the world of Bele Yolanz emerge strikingly if we contrast a thirteenth-century Sicilian song that superficially might seem to be comparable enough: here too is a love-song shaped by a narrative situation, a song in which the lovers meet and where the woman again has the dominant role. But here everything is specific, contemporary, and painfully real:

—Lévati dalla porta:
lassa, ch'or foss'io morta
lo giorno ch'i' t'amai!
　　Lévati dalla porta,
vatten alla tua via;
ché per te sería morta,
e non te ne encresceria.
Parti, valletto, pàrtiti
per la tua cortesia:
deh, vattene oramai.
　　—Madonna, ste paràule
per dio non me le dire.
Sai che non venni a càsata
per volermene gire.
Lévati, bella, ed aprimi,
e lasciami trasire:
poi me comanderai.
　　—Se me donassi Trapano,
Palermo con Messina,
la mia porta non t'àpriro,
se me fessi regina.
Se lo sente marítamo
o questa ria vicina,
morta distrutta m'hai.
　　—Marítato non sentelo,
ch'el este addormentato,
e le vicine dormeno:
primo sonno è passato.
Se la scurta passàssenci,
sería stretto e ligato.
　　—E tu perché ci stai?
　　—Che la scurta passàssenci,
o vergine Maria,
tutti a pezzi tagliàssenci
en mezzo della via!

'Away now from my door—
oh that I could have died
the day I gave you love!
　　'Away now from my door,
begone, go your own way—
for you I could be dead
and still you would not care.
Leave me, wretched man, leave
if you have any grace—
oh leave, and stay away.'
　　'My lady, in God's name
don't speak such words as these:
you know I've not come here
just to go home again.
Lovely lady, rise,
open and let me in:
I'll be your servant then.'
　　'If you gave me Trapano,
Palermo and Messina,
I'll not open my door for you
though you should make me a queen.
If my husband hears it,
or the bad woman next door,
you'd have me dead and ruined.'
　　'Your husband doesn't hear it,
for he is fast asleep;
the women next door are sleeping—
it's after the first watch.
If the night guard should pass here
I would be caught and bound!'
　　'Why, why then do you stay?'
　　'If the night guard should pass here,
virgin mother of God,
they'd cut us all in pieces
in the middle of the road!'

—Ma non dinanzi a càsama,
ch'io biasmata seria.
E perché non te n'vai?

'But not in front of *my* house,
so that I'd have the shame.
Why, why don't you go home?'

The women in the *chansons de toile* who pine for their lover are hardened offenders, their love is an immutable attitude: the wife is not afraid of her 'mals mariz', she knows no moments when fear makes her uncertain of her love. In the Sicilian song the fears of the lady are piercingly conveyed by her self-accusations and reproaches to the lover, the dramatic outlet of her own moments of panic. There is irony that she herself does not notice in

> Parti, valletto, pàrtiti
> per la tua cortesia . . .

Valletto (unless it could be read purely as an expression of abuse) implies a class distinction between the two—he is of the 'lower orders', she the wife of a respectable burgher; yet even as she addresses him 'valletto', with a kind of pitying disdain, she implores him 'by your courtesy'. He answers insensitively, with even perhaps an ironic retort to 'valletto' in the courtly flourish 'poi me comanderai'. The urban atmosphere, the oppressive nearness of the neighbouring houses, is brought out by her next appeal, by her sense that 'the bad woman next door' could hear him: it is far more vivid and intense than the conventional vague 'slanderers' and 'spies' of so many medieval love-songs. The mounting urgency is conveyed by the way she now cuts across his speeches, breaking into his stanzas instead of answering in a stanza of her own. The sense of danger reaches its climax with the mention of the night watch (a weird echo of the Song of Songs—see p. 80). For the first time he too, kept outside for so long, feels panic. But she at that moment cannot even think of him, only of herself and her respectability, and how she would be compromised by the ugly and violent scene outside her house. The song ends in this moment where terror has magnified reality to the dimension of nightmare. The dramatic pace of the whole, the pungent sense of the real that extends from nuances of detail to the obsessive fantasy at the close, reveal how remote we are from the confines of Bele Yolanz's world.

The greatest flowering of women's songs in medieval Europe occurred in thirteenth-century Portugal. There both the court poet and the *jogral* composed *cantigas de amigo*, which approach in number and often surpass in quality their other love-lyrics, their *cantigas de amor*. Once again there is a transformation of traditional songs and themes; the poets restrict their conventions of matter and manner more than anywhere else in Europe, but within their limits show great sophistication, exploiting the refinements of parallelism and refrain with a subtlety comparable to that of Yeats in the refrain-songs of his final years. The limitations of form here correspond beautifully to those of content: while the extreme use of patterns of repetition allows for little narrative or psychological progression, such lyric can mirror perfectly a gathering intensity of passion, each variation returning more vehemently to the original thought, or again it can be a trance-like expression of a dream or a love where each line lulls the mind in its single vision.

The song that seems to come nearest to a truly dramatic inspiration is one by Mendinho, a *jogral* perhaps from Vigo of whom we know nothing beyond this single lyric that survives under his name:

> I sat in the chapel of Saint Simeon
> and great waves crept around me, came on and on,
>   waiting for my love,
>   waiting for my love!
>
> I stood in the chapel, at the altar-side,
> and the waves crept around me, the great sea tide,
>   waiting for my love,
>   waiting for my love!
>
> And the waves crept around me, waves so great—
> I have no boatman to row my boat,
>   waiting for my love,
>   waiting for my love!
>
> And the waves crept around from the sea below;
> I have no boatman, I cannot row,
>   waiting for my love,
>   waiting for my love!
>
> I have no boatman to row for me—
> my beauty will die in the boundless sea,
>   waiting for my love,
>   waiting for my love!
>
> I have no boatman, I cannot row—
> my beauty will die in the deep sea's flow,
>   waiting for my love,
>   waiting for my love!

At the same time, the intensity and inexorable movement are gathered into a single image, an image larger than life, within which the dramatic possibilities—has her lover abandoned her? has he died at sea? will the little chapel be washed away in the flood?—are held in tension but deliberately not unfolded. But it is the inward symbolic associations rather than the narrative ones that predominate: the sight of the nearing tide makes the girl feel engulfed in the greatness of possible disappointment; the sea is time, is waiting with no way out; the sea is separation.

There is a dramatic quality of a different kind in the elusive transitions within a song by Martin Codax (text and melody, below, p. 244), one of the earliest and most outstanding of the Galician poets, who composed under the patronage of Ferdinand III of Castile:

1. Ah God, if only my love could know
   how much I am alone in Vigo,
       and go about in love.

2. Ah God, if he knew, my dearest one,
   how I am in Vigo, all alone!
       and go about in love.

3. How in Vigo, alone, I stay—
   and near me not a single spy,
       and go about in love.

4. How in Vigo I stay alone,
   with no spies around me, none,
       and go about in love.

5. And I have no spies with me,
   only my eyes, that weep with me,
       and go about in love.

6. And near me now I have no spies
   —only my pair of weeping eyes—
       and go about in love.

Martin Codax implicitly places his lady in a more courtly ambience, where secrecy is important and where love is always endangered by the scandalmonger and the spy, those caricatures (in Provençal the *lauẓenjador* and *gardador*, in Arabic the *nammam* and *raqib*) so often alluded to in both Eastern and Western medieval love-lyric. The poet achieves his effect at first without an image, only by the modulations, loneliness—provocative invitation—grief. Each is given a pair of stanzas, yet the art, here as always in the *cantiga de amigo*, consists in making the formal links between the stanzas more than formal, in making them many-dimensional with meaning. Being alone can mean both loneliness and accessibility; but there are spies more troubling than those of the outer world. Her eyes spy for him, and weep because he is not there; the moment of amorous intrigue cannot be made permanent, and will always throw her back into her solitude; even if the outer world does not see, she will see what she has done and grieve over it—all this may be latent in the tender, lamenting close.

Most of the finest *cantigas de amigo*, however, are songs of a single image and impulse: thus for instance Pero Meogo's brief but magical song:

Ai cervas do monte, vin vos preguntar:
foi-s'o meu amigu' e, se alá tardar,
    que farei, velidas?

Ai cervas do monte, vin vo-lo dizer:
foi-s'o meu amigu'. e querria saber,
    que farei, velidas.

Hinds on the hillside, tell me true,
  my love has gone, and if he lingers there,
    fair ones, what shall I do?

Hinds on the hillside, I'm telling you:
  my love has gone, and I long to know,
    fair ones, what I shall do.

In many of the Galician songs the hinds (*cervas*) are symbolically the confidantes of the girl in love, embodying all that is *farouche* and all that is ardent in her own nature.[1] When she questions the hinds, she is looking for the truth of these qualities in herself. So too when in other songs she asks the sea for news of her beloved, the sea comes to carry the whole meaning of her love, the serenity and the tumult, the dangers, the thoughts of the lover's death and of his safe return. Yet these questionings are not only introspection—they are outgoing impulses, a surge of sympathy with all that is wild and beautiful on earth, as if the love which the girl feels within her had heightened all her senses.

While the range of the Galician *cantigas de amigo* is admittedly confined, it must not be forgotten that it includes some delightful humour:

Heavens, don't worry, my lady mother,
that I am off to San Salvador;
    for, if three pretty girls should go
      that way   today,
  I shall be one, I know.

I want to go today, do you know why:
to say my prayers there, and (to tell no lie)
    if two pretty girls should go
      that way   today,
  I shall be one, I know.

1. These associations seem to me more immediately relevant to the thirteenth-century songs than the folkloristic survival of erotic pagan mimes and rites filled with stag-symbolism—though, as has been argued, these too may well lie behind the Galician deer-songs.

> I have a lover there, dearest mother—
> I'm off to see him, to give him pleasure;
> and if one pretty girl should go
>   that way   today,
> I'll be that one, I know!

Here the poet, Martin Padrozelos, plays lightly with the motif of the pilgrimage, which is one of the commonest in Galician lyric. It is easy to surrender to the wit and charm of such a song: when a girl asks her mother's 'permission' by announcing what she intends to do, when she works around to the truth by way of several fibs, and yet at last lets her mother in on the secret, it is all so familiar, it looks so easy to write, that one can forget what professional art is needed to create something so spontaneous.

The songs of the Galician poets, in their tenderness, playfulness or intensity, in their sheer singable beauty, represent the summit of a long poetic tradition. The finest songs are mostly also the simplest, those in which the poet has put all his concentration and art in the service of the ancient and familiar patterns.

To conclude this chapter, I should like to indicate two songs that in some ways stand apart from those so far discussed and reach poetic heights of a rather different kind. These illustrate a range of lyric in which women have taken the poetic language and conventions of aristocratic and masculine love-lyric as their point of departure, but fused them with that more direct and more overtly physical language of the passions which characterises the oldest surviving *winileodas*. We can see this, for instance, in the songs of the few women poets whose names have come down among those of more than four hundred Provençal troubadours, and of whom the most outstanding was Béatrice, Countess of Die. She composed in the essentially courtly form of the *canso* with *coblas unissonans* (the rhymes remaining identical in all the stanzas), a type in which the language of love seldom went beyond what could be sung without censure in the best circles. Béatrice shows her skilled knowledge of the stylised language, but again and again disrupts it with a startling freedom:

Estat ai en gran consirier
per un cavallier qu'ai agut,
e voill sia totz temps saubut
cum ieu l'ai amat a sobrier.
   Ara vei qu'ieu sui trahida,
quar ieu non li donei m'amor;
don ai estat en grant error
   en leit e quan sui vestida.

I have been in great distress
for a knight for whom I longed;
I want all future times to know
how I loved him to excess.
   Now I see I am betrayed—
he claims I did not give him love—
such was the mistake I made,
   naked in bed, and dressed.

Ben volria mon cavallier
tener un ser en mos bratz nut,
qu'el s'en tengra per errebut
sol c'al lui fesses coseillier;
    quar plus m'en sui abellida
non fis Floris de Blancaflor.
Mon cor eu l'autrei e m'amor,
    mon sen, mos oillz e ma vida.

How I'd long to hold him pressed
naked in my arms one night—
if I could be his pillow once,
would he not know the height of bliss?
    Floris was all to Blanchefleur,
yet not so much as I am his:
I am giving my heart, my love,
    my mind, my life, my eyes.

Bels amics, avinens e bos,
quora·us tenrai en mon poder,
e que jagues ab vos un ser,
e que·us des un bais amoros—
    sapchatz gran talen n'auria
que·us tengues en loc del
       marrit
ab so que m'aguessez plevit
    de far tot so qu'ieu volria.

Fair, gentle lover, gracious knight,
if once I held you as my prize
and lay with you a single night
and gave you a love-laden kiss—
    my greatest longing is for you
to lie there in my husband's
       place,
but only if you promise this:
    to do all I'd want to do.

Here the end of the first stanza contrasts sharply with the dignity of the opening lament. The phrase 'tener . . . en mos bratz nut', so common in troubadour lyric as a man's expression of sexual desire, confronts us with an unexpected force, almost a shock, as a woman's utterance. With the vivid and homely 'lui fesses coseillier' the poetess quite abandons courtly language for a moment, only to return to it with her allusion to the legendary pair of lovers in medieval romance, Floris and Blanchefleur. The second stanza closes on a subdued note, with utter simplicity. Once more, with 'Bels amics, avinens e bos', Béatrice makes a gesture in the direction of conventional troubadour love-language; but the final stanza portrays her physical desire ever more frankly and specifically. She does not dwell on the misfortunes of a *mal mariée*, she shows no trace of coyness or of dissemblance: 'en loc del marrit' is concise and bluntly factual, and the last two lines are a climax of open sensual provocation. By her high-spirited fusion of the worlds of *canso* and *winileod*, Béatrice de Die has created a lyric with a poetic effect quite of its own, both touching and daring.

A daring of a different kind is revealed in a French woman's song[1]

1. The date and provenance of this song is uncertain; it survives only in one late thirteenth-century MS (the 'Chansonnier du Roi'): there it is attributed to Gautier d'Espinau in the text, to Jehan de Nuevile in the table of contents, but it is generally agreed that both attributions are improbable. I think it quite possible that the author was a woman. The question, is the song complete as it stands, is equally difficult. Bédier argued cogently on technical grounds that it is fragmentary; intuitively, I feel it is perfect as it stands, and would only be spoilt by the addition of further stanzas (Bédier postulates one before the first stanza, and two after the third). Or is this a purely subjective and anachronistic judgment?

for her lover who has left for a crusade (cf. below, pp. 127 ff.)—it is a daring that moves into sublime tenderness:

Jherusalem, grant damage me fais,
qui m'as tolu ce que je plus
    amoie.
Sachiez de voir ne vos amerai
    maiz,
quar c'est la rienz dont j'ai plus
    male joie,
et bien souvent en souspir et
    pantais,
si qu'a bien pou que ver Deu ne
    m'irais,
qui m'a osté de grant joie ou
    j'estoie.

Biauz dous amis, con porroiz
    endurer
la grant painne por moi en mer
    salee,
quant rienz qui soit ne porroit
    deviser
la grant dolor qui m'est el cuer
    entree?
Quant me membre del douz viaire
    cler
que soloie baisier et acoler,
granz merveille est que je ne sui
    dervee.

Si m'aïst Dex, ne puis pas
    eschaper;
morir m'estuet, teus est ma
    destinee,
si sai de voir que qui muert por
    amer
trusques a Deu n'a pas c'une
    jornee.
Lasse, mieuz vueil en tel jornee
    entrer
que je puisse mon douz ami
    trover,
que je ne vueill ci remaindre
    esguaree.

Jerusalem, you do me a great wrong
by taking from me that which I loved
    best.
I'll never love you—know this
    for the truth—
for from this thing I have the
    poorest joy:
often I sigh breathless because
    of it,
so that I almost grow incensed with
    God
who has robbed me of the joy in
    which I moved.

Fair, gentle lover, how will you
    endure
your great ache for me, out on the
    salt sea,
since nothing that exists could ever
    tell
the depth of grief that has come
    over me?
When I think of your gentle, spark-
    ling face
that I used often to caress and kiss,
it is a miracle that I'm not
    crazed.

So help me God, there's no way of
    escape:
I have to die, such is my
    destiny—
I truly know that one who dies for
    love
needs but a single day from here to
    God.
Alas, I want to enter such a
    day,
that I may find my sweet love once
    again,
rather than linger on, a lost one,
    here.

The diction has not the originality or range of Béatrice de Die's: a number of phrases ('la grant dolor qui m'est el cuer entree', 'morir m'estuet, teus est ma destinee') belong to the over-confined *koinê* of trouvère love-complaints. Yet by way of this language, with all its limitations, a woman's love is conveyed of a purity and absoluteness that outstrips the other songs here discussed, in a dimension that widens the bounds of *cantigas de amigo*, and which the hint of convention in the language makes if anything more moving, as if she were exerting all the powers of expression known to her. We see these qualities from the woman's first outcry against Jerusalem and God: for her, human love has a grandeur and significance that the most sacred notions of Christendom can scarcely vie with. Insofar as God's claims have thwarted the human claims of her immense longing, she feels compelled to cry out, like Héloïse in her letters, 'O si fas est dicere, crudelem mihi per omnia Deum!'

Where the first and third stanzas show human love taking heaven as its measure, the second is a moment of wholly human tenderness. Where the Countess of Die imagined only her own voluptuous pleasure, this woman, speaking out of the certainty of a love that is shared to the limit, imagines her lover's pain of loss and feels it even more keenly than her own. She thinks of his face as it used to light up in her presence, and of his face as it must be now, *en mer salee* (behind the objective meaning of the crusaders' sea-voyage seem to lie associations of a sea 'distasted with the salt of broken tears'). The last stanza, in which her thoughts turn inward again, gives the conventional desire for ending unhappy love in death an incomparable depth of meaning: the God who at the outset seemed a bitter rival is in the last resort great enough to contain even a limitless human love. The loving woman of the *cantigas de amigo* has here taken on the stature of Rilke's ideal heroines of love-longing: 'they make lament . . . they hurl themselves after the lost one . . . and before them is only God.'

4

TRANSFORMATIONS OF MEDIEVAL

LOVE-LYRIC

(1) *Guillaume and Kürenberc*

The first poet of secular lyric in France whom we know by name is Guillaume of Aquitaine (1071–1127); the first German, Kürenberc, who was composing, perhaps in Austria, perhaps in South Germany, in the mid-twelfth century. From Guillaume we have eleven songs, from Kürenberc little more than a dozen stanzas—yet these are enough to show us that each was a poet of genius, a striking and many-sided personality. The work of each bears a distinctive signature. Guillaume and Kürenberc were followed in France and Germany by many poets who excelled in other ways. But they themselves must not on any account be regarded, as they have often been, as 'predecessors' or 'beginners'. Their names are the first that happen to survive (perhaps just because the individuality of these two seemed as remarkable to the twelfth and thirteenth centuries as it does to us); yet their songs represent not the beginnings of a tradition but summits of achievement in that tradition. Behind them lie centuries of anonymous Romance and Germanic song, of which only brief and fragmentary testimonies survive (see especially above, p. 90). But even if no external evidence remained at all, we could still win some conception of this earlier lost lyrical poetry by close attention to the songs of these two poets.

We know many details of Guillaume's life, nothing at all of Kürenberc's. The French poet at the age of sixteen became a *grand-seigneur*, inheriting the vast duchies of Poitou and Aquitaine. He spent much of his youth preventing their encroachment and trying to enlarge them. At thirty he led a disastrous crusade, which was routed in Asia Minor. He escaped and returned to France, where (except for a brief expedition into Spain, against the Almoravids, six years before his death) he remained, ruling his lands, arbitrating (and provoking) disputes among clergy and laity; he was frequently excommunicated. The anecdotes about him are legion, and the assessment of medieval historians varies: he was renowned for his impiety and for his prodigality, as well as for being 'one of the world's greatest deceivers of women'; 'he was daring, gallant, and full of mirth, outdoing even the strolling players in the gaiety of his entertainments'.

Guillaume's songs cannot be dated with any precision. The most specific is his 'Petit Testament', in which he says farewell to his son and friends, relinquishing his lands, his life of pleasure, knightly prowess and love, in order to go 'into exile', to prepare his soul for dying and being judged. This might have been written on the eve of his crusade, but the occasion could as well have been the journey into Spain or some pilgrimage later in life. Then there are five jesting, ribald songs, and five more serious love-lyrics. It would be naive to follow those scholars who assume that the risqué songs must be the earlier ones, seeing them as the poet's youthful excesses—they could as easily correspond to different moods as different ages, and, perhaps more significantly, to different audiences. While some of Guillaume's songs are intended for a mixed audience of lords and ladies, who laid claim to *corteᵹia*, others are explicitly addressed to his *companhos*—knights and soldiers, a company of men only, whose literary taste can hardly have been over-delicate:

> Comrades, I'll make a song of   true excellence:
> It will contain more folly   than it does sense,
> It will be all compounded   of love, *joi* and *jovens*.
>
> Consider him unworthy   who cannot guess
> Its meaning, or won't learn it   without duress.
> But he who finds he likes it   will hardly love the less!

The humorous, self-confident, egocentric manner is unmistakable. In other songs too Guillaume shows his half (though only half) jesting certainty that he 'wins the flower in this craft' of poetry, that his melodies are 'excellent, though I say it myself', even that people 'improve in worth' through hearing and enjoying his songs. The notion of worth is bound up with that of an élite: those who do not understand such poetry are *vilan*, unworthy and insensible in a social as well as an aesthetic sense; also with the notions of *joi* and *jovens*, the élan and sensibility which are the hallmarks of 'refined' love, and which in Provence come to be almost technical terms.

Yet Guillaume is not prepared to take the poetry of *joi* and *jovens* seriously: he promises a song of this kind, but already his second line warns that he will not keep this promise. Instead of a love-song acceptable (*covinen*) to the well-bred, Guillaume launches into a broad *double entendre*:

> I have two splendid horses,   and can mount either;
> Each has its points, each is a   marvellous charger—
> And yet I cannot keep both,   for they can't stand each other!
>
> If only I could tame them,   as was my plan,
> I'd never change my battle   equipment then,
> For I'd have better riding   than any other man!

The details about the two 'horses' become more circumstantial: one is so proud and wild, she refuses to be combed, the other 'I gave to her lord when she was still a foal'. Here the climax is a grotesque fantasy of a *droit de seigneur*: 'But I insisted that if he keeps her for one year I'd keep her more than a hundred.' Then Guillaume turns to his audience of 'cavallier':

> Noble riders, resolve my   predicament:
> Never has a choice caused such   embarrassment—
> I don't know which to keep now—   Agnes, or Ermensent!

The crowning impudence is to mention the two ladies by name.

The lines turn on an indelicate and rather obvious joke (which certainly need not, as has been argued, be borrowed from a learned Latin source); but in its technique the song is sophisticated. Guillaume has taken his melody and form from a Latin hymn (he had the advantage of being overlord of Saint-Martial in Limoges, which since the tenth century had been perhaps the greatest musical centre in Europe); he has made it even harder for himself by using only one rhyme throughout (which no translation can emulate); yet in this metrical tour de force he maintains a freedom and ease which show complete poetic mastery. To see in such a song the 'beginnings' of troubadour lyric is absurd. Not only the technique belies this, but the content. The effectiveness of Guillaume's jest depends on the difference between what his audience is expecting and what he gives them: his song can be understood only as an arrogantly humorous protest against an existing tradition of songs involving an 'élite' conception of love.

Another of Guillaume's songs is in fact an outright parody of idealised love for an inaccessible lady:

> Who is my love? I can't conceive—
> I've never seen her, I believe . . .
>
> Never have seen, yet love her well:
> She's never done me good or ill;
> I haven't met her, so I feel
>   Quite free of care—
> For I know a better lady still,
>   Surpassing fair!

Many details in this piece ('I know not if I sleep or wake . . . I tremble at the point of death') fill in our conception of the poetry of exalted sentiment at which Guillaume aimed his wit. Eleventh-century Provence must have known a range of idealised love-poetry perhaps more exaggerated in its protestations than it was ever to be again after Guillaume. The hyperboles of eleventh-century Latin panegyrics to great ladies, especially in France, would bear this out.

So too the German poet, Kürenberc, in four deft lines parodies the figure of the lover who so idealises his lady and is so much in awe of her that he does not even think of enjoying her favours:

> 'Late last night I stood   before your bed,
> and I did not dare   to wake you, lady.'
> 'May God hate you   for this for ever!
> After all, I wasn't a wild boar',   the lady said.

Like Guillaume, Kürenberc shows a many-sided delight in creating *personae* of himself. Where Guillaume had with absolute confidence declared himself the finest poet and the supreme lover (*maiestre certa*)—

> For on a pillow I know how to play
>   At every game . . .
> I never lie beside my love at night
> Without her wanting me again next day—

Kürenberc creates a similar effect with more subtle wit, using (as in the quatrain already cited) the device of the *Wechsel* or lyrical dialogue, with alternating speeches of identical length, a convention of great antiquity in Germanic song:

> 'I stood on the battlements   late last night:
> there I heard an exquisite   song from a knight
> down there in the crowds—   it was Kürenberc's tune!
> He must clear out of my land,   or else be mine.'
>
> 'Bring me my horse, quick now,   my armoured coat,
> since for a woman's sake   I must clear out.
> She's putting pressure on me   to revere her—
> she'll have to do without   my love for ever!'

Where in the quatrain the *Wechsel* was used for a dramatic exchange, one speech capping the other, here the speeches do not make contact —the man and woman talk past each other, they remain shut each in their own world of assumptions and inflexible wishes; it is a brilliant use of the traditional form to convey an image of talking at cross purposes.

The theme of the lady who is too eager to own the man she admires, while he longs to retain his pride and freedom, recurs in a different mode in another of Kürenberc's lyrics. Where the *Wechsel* had humorously implied a rough masculine vanity, here with sensitive imagination Kürenberc evokes the theme symbolically, and from the woman's viewpoint:

> I nurtured a falcon   for more than a year.
> When I had him tamed   exactly as I wished
> and had gracefully decked   his feathers with gold,
> he raised himself so high   and flew to other lands.
>
> Since then I've seen that falcon   flying superbly:
> he was wearing silken   fetters on his feet
> and the whole of his plumage   was all red gold.
> May God bring those together   who want each other's love!

The last line, with its wistful, bewildered but generous thought (almost comparable to the last lines of the Marschallin in *Rosenkavalier*) clarifies the complex dramatic meaning latent in what precedes. Each line contributes a nuance to the lady's train of thoughts: there was the self-delusion, of which she is now aware, and yet also her discretion and good taste, and the sense of social superiority that lends an ironic detachment to the fourth line (*er huop sich ûf vil hôhe*), followed perhaps by reluctant admiration, perhaps by deeper irony, in the fifth. Between the next two lines we can perceive her thoughts turning to her falcon's new mistress, who has bought him more blatantly, dressed him more showily, without his yet being aware of the new

fetters; and then we come to the exclamation, in which the figurative
pretences are at last dropped, and which is poignant because it is not
self-pitying.[1]

The extraordinary delicacy and sophistication of Kürenberc's art
has not perhaps been sufficiently recognised. There are a number of
such falcon poems, from different milieux, which bring this out
strikingly by contrast: the much-praised one, near in time to Kürenberc's, that is attributed to Dietmar von Eist, is so much less subtle in
that the lady, watching the falcon in free flight, makes an outright
comparison ('This is what I did too: I chose myself a man . . .'); an
anonymous thirteenth-century Italian sonnet uses the image verbosely
and sentimentally ('Hapless am I, who loved a sparrowhawk,/loved
him so much that I was dying for him . . .'); only perhaps a Serbian
folk-song achieves an effect as telling in its own way as Kürenberc's,
though by incomparably simpler means:

> A falcon is perched on the fortress of Salonica,
> his talons yellow right up to the spur,
> his wings golden right up to the shoulder,
> his beak bloody right up to the eyes.
> The girls of Salonica question him:
> 'In God's name, you grey-green falcon,
> who is it who has yellowed your talons,
> who is it who has gilded your wings,
> who is it who has bloodied your beak?'
> 'Leave me alone, you girls of Salonica!
> It was a good master whom I served,
> and he had daughters three:
> the first was she who yellowed my talons,
> the second, she who gilded my wings,
> and the third was she who bloodied my beak.'

Here too there is a disturbing, enigmatic quality: thought vacillates
between the image of the cosseted falcon and its latent nature as bird of
prey. The mystery lies in the sense of grief that seems to accompany
the end. Has the girl who 'blooded' him in love's chase left him proud
or humiliated? Perhaps both, for innocence has been destroyed. The

1. An interesting recent interpretation of Kürenberc's song by Peter Wapnewski
(*Euphorion*, 53, 1959, 1–19) suggests that the falcon escapes, but does not find another
mistress, that the silken fetters and the plumage 'all red gold' mean only the ornaments
that the woman speaking had given the falcon. But such an interpretation does not (and
I think cannot) give a convincing account of the force of the poem's last line. Moreover,
it seems to me clearly implied in the second stanza that the silken fetters and complete
gilding of the plumage are things the woman had not seen before.

force of the lyric lies in its incantation. There is development, but only towards intensity, not as with Kürenberc towards complexity.

Kürenberc uses the falcon image once more in a quatrain that has affinities with Guillaume's songs of sexual boasting—yet it reflects not the wilful, high-spirited play-acting of the French poet but a gentle irony that extends to self-mockery:

> Women and falcons   are easily tamed:
> if you lure them the right way,   they come to meet their man.
> This is the method a fair knight used   to win a noble lady.
> When I think of it, I feel   a joyful confidence myself!

> Wîp unde vederspil   diu werdent lîhte zam:
> swer si ze rehte lucket,   sô suochent si den man.
> als warb ein schœne ritter   umb eine frouwen guot.
> als ich dar an gedenke,   sô stêt wol hôhe mîn muot.

Whatever extravagant protestations their predecessors in France and Germany had made in love-songs, Guillaume and Kürenberc have no intention of worshipping or serving a lady who does not allow love for love. Their ideal is a full-blooded mutual love that, in defiance of refined convention, recognises sexual desire in women as well as men. In one of his more serious songs Guillaume, after trying to tease his beloved out of her reticence—'it looks as though you want to be a nun' —and pleading with her, has a moment in which light cajolery gives way to a passionate affirmation:

> What good will *you* have if I shut
> myself in cloisters, and you've got
> no lover? Lady, we can have
> the whole world's joy if we both love!

The finest of Guillaume's songs is a celebration of mutual love, the challenge that is met despite all its agonies, uncertainties and dangers:

> In the sweetness of new spring
> the woods grow leafy, little birds,
> each in their own language, sing,
> rehearse new stanzas with new words,
> and it is good that man should find
> the joy that most enchants his mind.

I see no messenger or note
from her, my first source of delight;
my heart can neither sleep nor laugh,
I dare not make a further move,
till I know what the end will be—
is she what I would have her be?

Our love together goes the way
of the branch on the hawthorn-tree,
trembling in the night, a prey
to the hoar-frost and the showers,
till next morning, when the sun
enfolds the green leaves and the boughs.

One morning I remember still
we put an end to skirmishing,
and she gave me so great a gift:
her loving body, and her ring.
May God keep me alive until
my hands again move in her mantle!

For I shun that strange talk which might pull
my Helpmeet and myself apart;
I know that words have their own life,
and swift discourses spread about—
let others vaunt love as they will,
we have love's food, we have the knife!

Human love (love that is found and won, not mere love-longing, as
so often in the stylised nature-prelude of medieval love-songs) can be
a source of goodness and joy, in harmony with all that is sweet in
nature. Why then does it cause lovers so much pain? Social pressures
can keep lover and beloved apart and force them to meet furtively,
there are days when they cannot even send each other messages, there
is the fear of malicious gossip, in which the outer world seems to find
a strange, perverse pleasure. And these pressures, frustrations and
fears have an effect on the morale of the lovers themselves, make them
quarrel when they are together and uncertain of each other when
apart. He has not heard from her—does that mean her love is lessening?
Now he is afraid to make an outgoing gesture towards her—is she
really all that he had hoped and imagined? The conventional idyllic
image of nature in spring is not right for human love. Guillaume evokes
another, an image that takes cognizance of the darkness and dangers,
but also transcends them. A love that even momentarily triumphs over
its obstacles has its own desperate beauty, and whets and renews
desire more than an endless idyll could.

In the last stanza, with the tender cover-name (Prov. *senhal*) that the poet gives his beloved, and with his triumphant acceptance of love whatever talk may threaten, we feel that pessimism has been wholly overcome—the slanderers and gossipers are pathetic, impotent figures, whereas in the fulfilment of mutual love lies strength and sustenance.

Kürenberc's brief stanzas contain no map of love as comprehensive as this, but he too summons his beloved to wholehearted commitment to a mutual love that cuts across social niceties; then a flicker of humour hints that the lover may become as jealous as the husband:

> Loveliest lady,   now do as I do—
> joy and sorrow   I'll share with you;
> as long as I have life   I'll cherish you;
> but if you love a worthless man,   that I shan't allow!

Even a high romantic moment need not exclude the poet's gently laughing at himself. So too he can regard the lovers' fears of slander, and their stratagems to protect themselves against the outer world, with a smile:

> As the morning star   conceals its light,
> do the same, lovely lady,   when I come in sight:
> let your eyes rest   on another man,
> and not a soul will know   how things stand between us then!

Behind the playfulness is the assurance that love is unalterably returned: the poet knows that his beloved's eyes will sparkle when she sees him and will remain lustreless if she looks at another.

A marked difference of imagination between the French and the German poet reveals itself in some of the *personae* that they create. Guillaume exploits his vein of mordant humour and sexual fantasy in a lyrical fabliau. He uses a stock fabliau plot—of lascivious women who take as their lover a deaf-mute, so that he will never betray their secret: it is one of the many lighthearted story-patterns of amours and deceptions which exist at all times and places in oral tradition, and which occasionally are transformed into a subtle work of art, by a Petronius or a Boccaccio, a Chaucer or a La Fontaine. Guillaume's distinctive contribution to the genre is to tell such a tale in the first person: he himself is the hero-victim. The story is told nonchalantly; there is a deliberate, extreme contrast between manner and matter, between the cool, matter-of-fact pose and the preposterous sexual imagination lit up by a capricious, cruel humour. From the zany opening—

> I'll make a song, since I'm asleep,
> walking, and standing in the sun—

through the mocking challenge of the ladies' approach—

> You seem a right and proper man,
> as far as I can tell—

to the grotesque torture-scene (a fierce cat is made to inflict a hundred scratches on the 'mute's' naked back, to elicit whether he is feigning) and the outrageous climax of desire more-than-gratified, all narrated with a surrealist meticulousness, it is a flawless piece of mummery.

Kürenberc's dramatic genius is rather for intimate moments; what is remarkable is the conciseness with which he can evoke a complex state of feelings, and the complete imaginative insight that he has into a woman's role in love as well as a man's:

> To reject a dearly loved man   is a shameful thing,
> to retain one's lover   is a noble thing—
> this is what I love and praise.
> Ask him to be gracious to me,   as he was before.
> Remind him of what we spoke   when I saw him last.

By looking at the surviving songs of these two poets we can glimpse behind them traditions of love-lyric of enormous vivacity and scope: they are relying on a wide, sophisticated range of expectations in an audience for such lyrics, they take for granted that this audience will be familiar with the mercurial nuances of a subtle poetic language, they count on the recognition of love as a complicated thing both poetically and humanly. It is scarcely possible to surmise how much of the poetic art of Guillaume and Kürenberc was their own exclusive creation; what is certain is that neither was creating *ex nihilo*.

(2) *Troubadours and trouvères*

From several generations of poets in southern France after Guillaume's death (1127) a wealth of love-lyric survives that has often been presented in the past in a far too homogenised fashion. Phrases such as 'the code of courtly love' or 'the conventions of troubadour lyric' have badly blunted the perception of what is poetically alive and individual in this world of songs. It is this that I should like to characterise by some illustrations, though no brief selection of specimen passages can do justice to the variety of the material.

The famous, indeed legendary, troubadour of love-longing is Jaufre Rudel, who was composing perhaps two decades after Guillaume's death. The finest stanzas among his six surviving songs have an exquisite limpidity:

Amors de terra lonhdana,	Love from a far-off land,
Per vos totz lo cors mi dol;	for you all my being aches;
E non puesc trobar mezina	I can find no remedy for it
Si no·n au vostre reclam	if I do not hear your call
Ab atraich d'amor doussana	with the lure of soft love
Dinz vergier o sotz cortina	in an orchard or behind curtains
Ab dezirada companha.	with my longed-for beloved.

None the less, in the movement of such a stanza there is something enigmatic: only with the last line, when the *companha* is mentioned in person, does it become fully clear that *Amors* in the first line had been a personification of the love that she feels. The distance between the lovers is a theme that recurs in several of Jaufre's songs:

Luenh es lo castelhs e la tors	Far away is the castle and the tower
On elha jay e sos maritz . . .	where she lies, and her husband too . . .

Thus the poet is often with his beloved only in his thoughts or waking dreams, and Jaufre at times leaves deliberately blurred and dreamlike the transition between her imagined and her real presence (as here, in the fourth line):

Ma voluntatz s'en vai lo cors,	My will goes forth at a run,
La nueit et dia esclarzitz,	both by night and in radiant day,
Laintz per talant de son cors;[1]	down to her, as I long for her body;
Mas tart mi ve e tart mi ditz:	but it is late she comes, late that she tells me
'Amicx, fa s'elha, gilos brau	'Beloved, crude jealous people
An comensat tal batestau	have begun making such a clamour
Que sera greus a departir,	as will be hard to dispel
Tro qu'abdui en siam jauzen.'	so that we can have joy together.'

The lady is unmistakably on her lover's side, and at least occasionally, with her help and the help of friends, and also of God (whom the lovers nearly always imagine as favourably disposed, even towards adulterous love), a joyful meeting can be arranged in which love is consummated:

1. For this line I follow the text of M. de Riquer, *Los trovadores* I, 162.

Er ai ieu joy e suy jauzitz
E restauratz en ma valor,
E non iray jamai alhor
Ni non querrai autrui
          conquistz . . .

Now I have joy and a joyous welcome,
and all that is good in me is renewed,
and I shall never look elsewhere
nor ever seek another's
          conquests . . .

Mout mi tenon a gran honor
Tug silh cui ieu n'ey obeditz
Quar a mon joi suy revertitz:
E laus en lieys e Dieu e lor,
Qu'er an lur grat e lur prezen,
E, que qu'ieu m'en anes dizen,
Lai mi remanh e lay m'apays.

They hold me in great honour now,
all those whose advice I obeyed,
for I have returned to my joy:
for this I praise her and God and those,
who now have their reward fulfilled;
and, whatever I may say within,
there I remain, and pasture there.

Jaufre goes on to see this blissful sexual fulfilment as the vindication of that *fin' amors*, that noble, gracious love, which 'never betrayed anyone'.

The lover in these songs is a rather different figure from the Jaufre of the well-known legend, who, in the words of the thirteenth-century life, 'became enamoured of the Countess of Tripoli without having seen her, because of the good that he heard tell of her by pilgrims who came from Antioch'. The legend may have arisen out of a confusion: once Jaufre wrote a parodistic song, with a refrain of echoing laughter, a song imitating Guillaume's jest of being in love with a lady one has never seen. And Jaufre wrote one renowned serious song about a lady who lived far away, which contains *as fantasies* some of the thoughts out of which the 'biography' might have been embroidered: 'Oh if only I were a pilgrim in her land . . . then if it pleases her, I'll have lodgings with her. . . . For her sake I'd even let myself be called "scurvy knave" among the Saracens'. The embroidering did not cease with the *joglar*'s 'vida': even today many scholars believe that this song, *Lanquan li jorn son lonc en may*, is about love for a lady whom the poet has never seen, or even, who is not a human lady at all. But the text contains nothing of this: what Jaufre says is that he wants to see this far-off beloved '*truly*, in such a place that the bedroom and the garden forever seem a palace to me'. The expression is delicate, but the meaning I think is unmistakable—to see her truly is to see her naked, in a place where she and Jaufre can make love.

For this lady who lived far away, the biographer added, Jaufre composed 'many lyrics with good melodies and poor words'. The four melodies that survive are indeed as subtle and delicate as any in troubadour music. And is there not a grain of truth in the stricture on the words? At their best they are like a lucid reverie; and yet there is no great imaginative richness: the emotional range is narrow, and there is little sense of dramatic development within the songs, or of the crystal-lisation of thought and feeling in a memorable image.

The picture is very different when we turn to Jaufre's younger con-temporaries, Bernart de Ventadour and Raimbaut d'Orange. Bernart does have moments in which he expresses the hyperboles of anguish and of timid, submissive devotion to an unyielding lady that are popularly taken to epitomise troubadour love-poetry: he is in helpless torment because 'Love has captured me, and mercy is the only key that can open the dungeon into which he has cast me, and I can find no mercy there'. Seeing his lady he 'trembles with fear like a leaf before the wind; I have no more sense than a child, I am so overcome by love. . . . Gracious lady, I ask nothing of you but that you take me as your servant, for I shall serve you as my noble lord, whatever the reward may be'. Yet this is only the smallest part of the spectrum of love reflected in Bernart's songs. The lover's timidity itself can become almost a weapon of seduction, the first in a series of steps in which the lady's feelings are played on in diverse ways, until all her possible defences are cut off and she must give in. Such casuistry is brilliantly deployed in a song in which the poet claims he is afraid even to declare his love (though from the start we can guess that this is an invitation to a woman, rather than an interior monologue, and the poet himself admits it at the close): Bernart claims he is too frightened to speak,

> because I have never seen a body better shaped
> for making love so loath and slow to love.

What he adduces as a reason for his fear is in fact the beginning of his sexual enticement of the beloved. At once he disguises this by repeating familiar asseverations of love-worship:

> I love *midons* so much, hold her so dear,
> hold her in such great awe and fear,
> I never yet dared speak to her of me,
> I seek and ask nothing of her at all,
> and yet she knows my pain . . .

From these Bernart passes into erotic daydreams (which again are meant as a lure to the lady rather than as solitary reflection): if he could put a spell on all his enemies and turn them into children, so that they would not know how to slander those in love,

> then I would kiss her mouth in every way,
> that for a month the kiss-marks would remain!

> I would indeed find her alone,
> sleeping (or pretending to),
> and so steal a sweet kiss from her,
> since I'm unfit to ask for one.
> For God's sake, lady, how we waste our love!
> Time passes by, we lose the better part—
> we ought to speak by means of secret signs
> and, since we have no daring, use deceit.
>
> Indeed a lady deserves blame
> who puts her lover off too long,
> for to talk over-much of love
> is a great shame, and seems untrue—
> for one can love, and make pretence elsewhere,
> or lie when there is no one else about.
> Sweet lady, if you deign to give me love,
> I shall never have to lie to you.

The daydream is crossed by a flicker of humour which suggests that the lady may be feigning and in her heart already approves, and a moment later—the lover must steal a kiss from her in sleep because he is afraid, or unworthy, to ask for one in waking life—we arrive at a shrewd burlesque of the clichés of submissive love. At once this leads into a buoyant, sensual invitation—'Now let us sport us while we may'—in which the poet, now confident of her 'willing soul', speaks for the first time as if they were wholly agreed, allied against a prying outer world. Again the wit comes through—in the *double entendre* of the 'secret signs' and in the last, ironic allusion to the lover's timidity, with which the arguments had begun; now it is assumed that it was her timidity as much as his that had made love's fulfilment seem hopeless.

The lovers must now together use deceit (*gens*)—the last word of the stanza sparks off a new train of thought about honesty in love. Bernart holds the romantic cliché of the lady, who is so perfect that she never yields, up to the light of reality. Such an attitude in the lady, he claims, tends to reduce love to mere words; in the end it makes the lover's protestations hollow. What Bernart says, however true, is still a part of his seducer's casuistry: in effect he means 'You must not put me off any longer, or you will force me into living a lie. Is it not better to dissemble a true love before the outside world than to have dissemblance between ourselves? Can love in the last resort mean anything real to us if it is not shared and fulfilled?' All this, I believe, is implied in the wonderfully concise lines of the last stanza. Remarkable throughout are the subtle, effortless transitions, the agility of mind and feeling, the transformation, ever more apparent, of solitary reflection into a passionately and proudly argued plea.

In another song Bernart, like Guillaume, explicitly sets up as his ideal a candidly reciprocated love in which no convention is allowed to conceal the truth of feeling:

En agradar et en voler	The love of two true lovers lies
Es l'amors de dos fins amans;	in their mutual will and pleasure;
Nulla res no i pot pro tener,	nothing can be good in it
S'ilh voluntatz non es egaus;	if they are not equal in desire;
E cel es ben fols naturaus	he is an innate fool who blames
Qui de so que vol la repren,	love for what love demands, and makes
E·lh lauza so que no·lh es gen.	unworthy claims on love himself.

The essence lies in giving, not taking: 'that which loves nothing without grasping is not love—it has only the look and semblance of love'.

In a lyrical debate (*tenso*) with the troubadour Peire d'Auvergne, in which Peire automatically parades all the received notions of refined love, Bernart rejoins:

> Peire, if for two years or three
> the world were fashioned to my will,
> I tell you truly, ladies would
> never be wooed by us at all—
> then they'd endure such grievous pain
> that they would honour us so much,
> they'd woo us without being wooed.

It is a playful exaggeration for the sake of debate, but it underlines once more Bernart's concern to explore where mannerism ends and emotional truth begins.

This is perhaps most marked in a number of Bernart's songs that are concerned with disloyalty in love and with the unravelling of *odi et amo*. In one the note is a bitter acceptance by the poet of all that falls short of his ideal, an acceptance that leads to its own melancholy sense of peace: even if love rewards arrogant and deceitful men rather than gentle, open ones, even if the woman is making sport of him and tries to reproach him for her own inconstancy,

a sos ops me gart e·m estui,	may she keep and enfold me as her own,
e si non em amic amdui,	and even if we're no longer friends
d'autr' amor no m'es vejaire	it does not seem to me my heart
que ja mais mos cors s'esclaire.	will ever be lit by another love.

In another song, the lover's feelings at his humiliation burst into violence:

Una fausa deschauzida	A false, degraded woman,
träiritz de mal linhatge	traitress from an evil stock,
m'a träit (et es träida,	has betrayed me, and is betrayed—
e colh lo ram ab que·s	strikes herself with the switch she
fer);	cuts—
e can autre l'arazona,	and when a man addresses her,
d'eus lo seu tort l'ochaizona;	accuses him of her own fault,
et an ne mais li derrer	and vilest men get more from her
qu'eu, qui n'ai faih lonc	than I, who have waited for her
badatge.	long.

He would like to forget her—to wait without hope is mere calf-love, it 'reduces a man to a boy'— but he finds he cannot:

mas pero qui m'en razona,	Yet if a man speaks to me of her,
la paraula m'en es bona,	there is goodness in his words,
e m'en esjau volonter	willingly I rejoice in it
e·m n'alegre mo coratge . . .	and my heart grows light . . .
qu'e·lh perdo s'ela·m perdona . . .	I'll forgive her if she forgives me . . .

Again, in a song that begins not with the customary spring-prelude but in the cool manner of a legal discussion, a *jugement d'amour*, the deserted lover asks, shall he continue to love the disloyal lady, and be despised by the world for his horns? Or live on, devoid of love, unable ever to compose love-songs again? No, he would rather share her than lose her utterly, though he knows this is cowardice, inspired by a faint hope that she will reward him again on account of his tolerance. Then, before the envoy, come the moving lines that crystallise the relationship in an instant, in the enigmatic gesture that may equally conceal weeping or the first wavering of love:

manhtas vetz m'es pois membrat	Many times since have I called to mind
de so que·m fetz al comjat:	what she did at our leavetaking,
qu'e·lh vi cobrir sa faisso,	when I saw her cover her face
c'anc no·m poc dir oc ni no.	so that she could not tell me yes or no.

Bernart's sensibility and trueness of expression represent one of the summits in Provençal love-song, but remarkable developments were still possible in other directions. There is the intellectual brilliance of Bernart's contemporary Raimbaut d'Orange, always light, though occasionally serious too, in the play of hyperbole, conceit and paradox; in the last two decades of the twelfth century, there is the swift associative freedom of Peire Vidal, achieved on a tightrope stretched between anguish and delight; and again, the formal virtuosity of Arnaut Daniel. Already in the generation after Guillaume it had become common practice in composing a canzone to repeat the rhymes of the first strophe in each succeeding one (a feat that poets elsewhere in Europe scarcely ever tried to emulate); but no one had sustained strophic forms or rhymes like these:

Doussa car', a	Sweet face, with
totz aips volgutz,	every wished-for quality,
sofrir	suffer
m'er per vos mainz	I must, for your sake, many
orguoills,	signs of disdain,
car etz	for you are
decs	the goal
de totz mos fadencs,	of all my follies,
don ai mains brutz	through which I have many base
pars,	companions,
e gabars;	and mockery;
de vos no·m tortz	they do not turn me from you,
ni·m fai partir	nor am I drawn away
avers,	by riches,
c'anc non amei	for I have never loved
ren tan, ab meins d'ufaut;	anything so much, or with less vanity—
anz vos desir	rather I desire you
plus que Dieu cill de Doma!	more than God the men of Doma![1]

But it was not, or not primarily, for dexterity of this kind that Dante called Arnaut *miglior fabbro*: the canzone of Arnaut's that he commended most highly, as being 'illustrious' in its construction, *Sols sui qui sai*, is the least showy one—it is remarkable neither for its metrical pattern nor for unusual language, but for a sense of lucid order and control, a form that grows effortlessly out of the harmony of thought and means of expression.

Dante seems not to have known the songs of Arnaut's much-travelled contemporary Raimbaut de Vaqueiras, a troubadour whose poetic versatility and verve make him one of the truly outstanding lyric poets of Provence, in themes both of love and of war. As love-poet Raimbaut

---

1. Doma—according to Toja, the most recent editor, Domme (a small town in the Dordogne) rather than Puy de Dôme. The reference to the piety of its monks must be topical; the comparison of the lover's desire with the religious man's desire for God occurs elsewhere too in troubadour poetry.

composed numerous tours de force—they include a love-song in five
languages; a dialogue in which Raimbaut woos a girl in Provençal and
she refuses him in Genoese; a sparkling dance-song, unequalled in its
verbal and melodic conjuring; and a woman's love-lament of haunting
simplicity. But Raimbaut's finest qualities can perhaps best be glimpsed
by way of the sheer exuberance of poetic invention in his *Truan, mala
guerra*, the song of the 'siege of Biatritz'. Lady Biatritz so far surpasses
other woman that they in their envy wage war against her: from all
over Italy they come, and even Sardinia, armed for a tournament. They
build a city that they call Troy, with a rival ruler, and lay siege to the
citadel of Biatritz's perfections:

> The city Troy now vaunts
> its host will be arrayed,
> and as the tocsin sounds,
> the old commune's plot is laid:
> they in their arrogance
> command all ranks deployed,
> saying this—
> that lovely Biatritz
> has sovereign dominance
> of all that they once had;
> so disgrace
> now strikes them, comfortless.
> The trumpets sound, out cries the mayoress:
> 'Let us demand her looks and courtliness,
> her youth and grace'; all cry 'It shall be thus!'

With speed and excitement Raimbaut conjures up the physical
details of a siege. Biatritz, armed only in her excellence (*pretz*), over-
comes all her enemies in the joust, shatters their war-chariot and forces
them to flee back to their Troy. Abruptly the vision ends, as the poet
makes a double envoy for his beloved, praising her peerless, irresistible
body—she is his 'fair warrior' (*Bels Cavaliers*), no longer in the
fantasy-tournament but now in the sports of joyful love.

Northern France, so rich in narrative love-poetry, has no tradition
of love-lyric comparable in range and stature to the Provençal. If the
pair of love-songs by Chrétien de Troyes belong to his earlier work
and may be placed in the 1160s, they are among the first northern
testimonies that survive; they are technically of considerable accomplishment, but lifeless and colourless alongside the great romances of
that decade, the *Roman d'Enéas* and the *Roman de Troie*, Thomas's
Tristan and Chrétien's own *Erec*, *Cligés*, and *Lancelot*.

From near the close of the century a considerable number of northern French love-songs survive; but while the music is often full of inventiveness and grace (with trouvères such as Blondel de Nesle, Huon d'Oisi, and Gace Brulé), the words again and again are those of a bloodless *complainte d'amour*, elegantly turned and capable of an indefinite number of minor variations:

> Coment avrai ne secours ne aïe
> Vers fine amour, là où nuls n'a puissance?
> Amer me fait ce qui ne m'aime mie,
> Dont ja n'avrai fors ennui et pesance;
> Ne ne li os mon corage gehir
> Celi qui tant m'a fait de maus sentir,
> Que de tel mort sui jugiés à morir
> Dont ja ne quier veoir ma delivrance.

> How then shall I win succour or assistance
> in gracious love, where men are powerless?
> It makes me love, unloved, her from whose presence
> I shall have naught but harm and heaviness;
> nor do I dare reveal what my heart wills
> to her who makes me suffer such great ills
> that I have been condemned to die a death
> from which I have no wish to seek release.

This stanza, by Gace Brulé, may stand for countless others like it. Yet occasionally, though very rarely, in this genre, a trouvère would compose a song in which words as well as melody were individual and alive. When in the song *A vous, amant* (text and melody below, p. 241) the Chastelain de Couci, who met his death in the fourth Crusade in 1203, says farewell before departing to 'her who was my lady, my comrade, my beloved', he reflects on the claims to allegiance of God and of his love. He sees the Crusade itself as a divine mandate, which he begins to regard, with bitter irony, as the retaliation of a jealous God against the joys of human love:

> God does not wish to give gratuitously
> all the delights that I have had in life—
> rather, he makes me pay for them so dearly,
> I greatly fear the paying may be my death.
> Have pity, Love! If ever God acted basely,
> basely he now divides a virtuous love.

The irreverence is not wholly serious, though behind it lies a serious purpose: the poet wants to sharpen the confrontation between the two aspirations in which he believes in order to ask, are they really irreconcilable? It is by way of the witty, extravagant formulation that the question grows in depth. In the next stanza a crucial test is proposed: God demands the love of one's enemies; can the lover love even those envious slanderers who had tried to separate him from his beloved? Implicitly God is on their side, is like them even—he too sets obstacles in the way of the joys of human love. And yet the song concludes with a moving but serene stanza in which the Chastelain commends his beloved to God's keeping, as if none of these conflicts existed. How is this possible? Because he sees that loyalty and honour cannot in the last resort mean different things to God and man, that if a love is true by the highest human standards, then the lovers are also at one with God:

> Wherever I go, in God's name I beseech you
> to keep your promise, if I come back or not;
> and I pray that God may grant me as much honour
> as the truth that I have shown you in my love.

Crusade songs form, we might say, several sub-species in the medieval lyric: apart from songs to rouse support for a Crusade (which exist in Latin, Provençal, French, and German), there are the laments of lovers, both men and women, on whom a Crusade has forced separation. These are commonest in Old French; the most dramatically passionate is the anonymous woman's lament *Jherusalem, grant damage me fais* (discussed above, p. 107); but among the many farewells composed by men at this time, the Chastelain's seems unparalleled in the elliptical but penetrating quality of its reflections.

The handful of surviving songs by a contemporary of the Chastelain's, likewise a nobleman and a fellow-crusader, Conon de Béthune, have all the qualities implied by the untranslatable word *esprit*: they are many-sided lyrics, adroit and vivacious, often witty, with a fine sense of colloquial dialogue, mercurial rather than profound, as in the song in which the poet changes his mistress:

> The other day, after Saint Denis' feast,
> I was in Béthune, where I've been frequently,
> and I recalled men with an evil air
> who have told lies about me knowingly,
> saying I've sung of women foolishly.
> But they don't know the meaning of my song:
> I've sung one lady only—who has done
> so much to me that I've avenged the wrong.

Conon goes on to vigorous self-defence: if people blame him, it is only because right and wrong have become out of joint—

> If a thief's brought to justice rightfully,
> does this touch honest men? No, not at all!
> Not at all, in God's name, who knows what's right.

With the rejection of the beloved the tone changes once more: the surrender to the new love, that 'illumines and enflames my entire body', is expressed in the most exalted terms of love-worship. The transitions between the varied moments are swift and effortless.

Perhaps the most individual of all French love-lyrics of the period is the *Douce dame* of Jacques d'Autun, a trouvère of whom nothing else is known. It is another song of parting, but the circumstances are left enigmatic. It is possible that this trouvère was a contemporary of the Chastelain and of Conon de Béthune, though he may also be somewhat later: we cannot look beyond the thirteenth-century trouvère song-books in which the poem first occurs.

This is an unheroic parting—the poet begins by telling his lady that he has made every possible effort to avoid it, spending time and money, going everywhere for help. Then he looks back on their love together, and a flicker of mirth crosses the lament at the memory of their oneness:

> Mout fui herbergiez hautement
> La nuit que jui lez vo costel.
> Ainc sainz Julïens, qui puet tant,
> Ne fist a nul home mortel
> Si biau, si bon, si riche hostel.
> He las! chaitis, he las! coment
> Vivrai mais toz jorz languissant,
> S'ancore ne l'ai autretel,
> Car nuit ne jor ne pens a el?

I was given most noble lodgings at night when I lay by your side—not even Saint Julian, so efficient, ever gave a mortal man so fair, so good, so rich a hostelry. Alas, poor me, alas, how shall I live, for ever languishing, if I never have such again?—for night and day I think of this alone.

Then (in one manuscript only out of the five) comes the amazing stanza:

> Mout fist Amors a mon talant
> Qant de moi fist vostre mari.
> Mais joie m'eüst fait plus grant
> S'ele m'eüst fait vostre ami.

E

Or n'i atant fors que merci:
A vos et a Amors me rent,
Et se pitiez ne vos en prent,
Par tans em plorront mi ami
Car longues ne puis vivre ensi.

Love indeed fulfilled my desire when he made me your husband, yet he
would have given me even greater joy had he made me your lover. Now I
hope only for his mercy: I commend myself to Love and to you, and if pity
does not touch you, my friends will soon have cause to weep: I can no
longer live like this.

This poem seems to affirm, as Héloïse had affirmed to Abelard, that
a love which is given in absolute freedom and makes no claims as of
right is even more wonderful than the love that can exist within the
contract of marriage. And it is in a lover's language rather than a
husband's that the poet speaks in the lines that follow. At first this may
seem inappropriate: what might it mean for the beloved and Amors to
show pity, when she is already wholly his? So too in the next stanza,
what power have the 'felon mesdisant', who are conventionally feared
because they disclose an illicit love to the outer world, over married
love? In the new context of this song the appeal to the lady's pity and
the outcry against slanderers are completely transformed: they are her
kinsmen, who try to influence her wickedly, by imputing base motives
to his departure. He can only throw himself on her mercy, and rely on
her intelligence (*sage estes et conoissant*), that she does not doubt his
constant love. Her 'pity' will be to reassure him of her faith in him.
He must even, it seems, take their child with him on his voyage:

Dame, je n'ai confortement
Q'en vostre debonaireté
Et en un sol petit enfant
Q'en voz biaus costez engendré.
Graces en rent a Damedé,
Qant il de vos m'a laissié tant;
Norrir le ferai docement
Et mout bien l'edefïeré,
Por ce que vos l'avez porté.

Ma doce dame, a Deu comant
Vostre sens et vostre bonté
Et vostre gent cors avenant
Et voz iex plains de simpleté:
La compaignie ou j'ai esté
A qui nule autre ne se prent . . .

Lady, my only comfort lies in your generosity, and in the one little child that I begot in your beautiful body. I give thanks to God that He has left me so much of you; I shall have him tended gently and brought up very nobly, because it is you who gave him birth.

Sweet lady, I commend to God's care your sense and your goodness, your lovely graceful body and your eyes full of innocence, the intimacy which I have known, to which no other can compare . . .

Each word and each detail seems chosen with loving care. That out of the stylised patterns of trouvère love-song a moment of such authenticity should emerge is remarkable, even unique. But in the lucid, unobtrusive, gently melancholy language, in which even the simplest utterance can have grace, we can perceive at their finest some of the characteristic qualities of the medieval love-lyric in northern France.

(3) *Minnesang*

In the last quarter of the twelfth century Provençal and French strophic forms came to be imitated by German Minnesinger. Where Kürenberc had scarcely ventured beyond a traditional rhymed quatrain akin to that of the *Nibelungenlied*, a slightly younger generation of poets was considerably influenced in form, and to some extent in language, by the aristocratic lyrical traditions of troubadour and trouvère. It was not a question of 'importing' from the South a new, exalted and romantic, conception of love: this was an ancient, native and familiar element in northern as well as southern poetic tradition. We have already seen how Kürenberc satirises the lover who holds his lady in such high reverence that it pleases her not a bit; an early eleventh-century *Wechsel*, half Latin and half German, in which the lover twice beseeches 'coro miner minne' (put my love to test), seems to imply the same notion of love-service as was elaborated in Provence; behind this again, tenth-century Scaldic verse shows us some fascinating instances of a poetry of idealised love-worship. In twelfth-century Germany, such themes find expression not only in the lyrical poetry that shows southern influence, but in songs which in their starkness of form and language are free of such influence and probably prior to it: a fervent quatrain, in which the lover sees the return of his love as a celestial, miraculous condescension on the lady's part, a grace incommensurable with his own unworthiness:

Auwê lîp vor allem lîbe,	Oh dear one beyond all dearness,
wie kunde ich daz verdînen,	how could I deserve it,
umbe got und umbe dich,	through God and through yourself,
daz dû, vrouwe, woldest	that you, lady, were disposed to
minnen mich?	grant me love?

Or again, the lines in which the Burggraf of Rietenburg with utmost simplicity affirms the ennobling nature of love-service:

Sît si wil versuochen mich,   Since she would put me to the test,
daz nime ich allez für guot.   I accept all for the best.
sô wirde ich golde gelîch   I shall become like gold
daz man dâ brüevet in der gluot   that is tested in the blaze,
und versuochet ez baz: and, being tried the more,
bezzer wirt ez umbe daz,   is finer than before,
lûter, schoener unde clâr.   pure, clear, lovelier too—
swaz ich singe daz ist wâr: what I sing is true:
gluote si ez iemer mê,   should she burn it even more,
ez wurde bezzer vil dan ê.   it would be better still by far!

The southern influence, when it emerges, is most marked on the formal side; in details of expression it is also perceptible, but at a relatively superficial level. Essentially the 'classic' lyrical poets of Minnesang, whose work falls chiefly in the decades 1190–1220, made a profoundly distinctive contribution to the love-lyric.

If we turn to one of Heinrich von Morungen's songs, the effect is unlike anything we have met in love-lyric at an earlier date. Here is a poet who casts a spell, who from the first word to the last can compel his listener to surrender to a unique train of thought, to elicit a half-hidden meaning as from hieroglyphics:

Ich hôrt ûf der heide   On the heath I heard
lûte stimme und süezen klanc.   clear voices and sweet sound;
dâ von wart ich beide   through this I became
fröiden rîch und trûrens kranc. strong in joy, infirm in grief:
nâch der mîn gedanc   she towards whom my thoughts
      sêre ranc   pressed on
      unde swanc,   and swung,
die vant ich ze tanze dâ   at the dance I found her—she
      si sanc.   was singing.
âne leide   Without pain
      ich dô spranc.   I danced there too.

Ich vant si verborgen   I found her hiding,
eine und ir wengel naz,   alone, and her cheeks wet,
dô si an dem morgen   for on that morning
mînes tôdes sich vermaz.   she had surmised my death.
der vil lieben haz   Even my loved one's hate
      tuot mir baz   is more welcome
      danne daz,   than that,
dô ich vor ir kniete dâ si saz   when I knelt before her as she sat
und ir sorgen   and quite forgot
      gar vergaz.   her cares.

Ich vants an der zinnen, | I found her on the battlements,
eine, und ich was zir besant. | alone, and was called to her.
dâ moht ichs ir minnen | There I might have well won
wol mit fuoge hân gepfant. | the forfeit of her love.
dô wând ich diu lant | And I thought I had
    hân verbrant | burnt up the world
    sâ zehant, | there and then,
wan daz mich ir süezen minne | but no, the bonds of her sweet
    bant | love
an den sinnen | had left my senses
    hât erblant. | dazzled.

In these three moments Heinrich takes us into the experience of vision or reverie in all its illogical intensity. He is drawn into the vision at first as into a world of innocent serenity, free of the anguish of desire—only the strange phrase *trûrens kranc* briefly suggests the expense of spirit that had preceded. The verbs of motion, *ranc unde swanc*, suggest a parallel between the movements of his thought and those of the dance he now enters, but also a difference—where they convey strain and effort, the dance seems effortless, beyond desire and beyond pain.

The next scene is juxtaposed with visionary suddenness. Heinrich creates a moment in which the woman he loves, and who had shown him no warmth in return, hears a false rumour of his death, which breaks down all her defences. The thought seems to be—if he appeared just then, when her desire was unconcealed, that moment would have an intensity even more unbearable than her everyday mask of coldness.

In the last encounter the vision rises to a climax and breaks. The entry into it has again a quality of strangeness—is it she who summons him? The impersonal *ich was zir besant* leaves it—I think deliberately —uncertain. Then, as the poet becomes certain that the beloved wants him unreservedly, it is as if *ich diu lant/hân verbrant/sâ zehant*—the phrase suggests not only the measureless longing apocalyptically engulfing the world and himself, but a new, carefree sense of exultation. We are left with the enigma of the last two lines: are they looking back on a moment of hallucination or of ecstasy? Are they the last moment of the vision itself, or the awakening into reality? The poet does not tell us—he leaves us only with a sense of love, whether imagined or real, joyfully returned and overwhelming the lover with its sweetness.

The magic of this song is inseparable from the extraordinary formal effect—it is a strophic form unparalleled in medieval lyric, vernacular or Latin. The deep echoing rhymes that dominate each stanza (always rhyming on the dark vowel *a*) are hypnotic, they help to create the trance-like setting in which the poet moves. Technically it is one of the most demanding forms in the whole of medieval lyric (and quite impossible to approximate even partially in a literal translation), yet there is not the least suggestion of virtuoso display about it, because it seems effortless—not a syllable is there merely for the rhyme's sake, the choice of each word seems determined not by external form but by the total imaginative pattern.

As Heinrich's thirty-three surviving songs are all on love-themes, it has often been stated or implied that his poetic range was narrow. I believe, on the contrary, that this limitation is only apparent, and that these love-lyrics reflect a mind and sensibility of quite exceptional complexity and penetration. This can scarcely be shown without detailed consideration of many of the other songs, but some suggestion of it may at least be given by contemplating alongside *Ich hôrt ûf der heide* not only the alba discussed below (p. 180) but this brief song of despairing, unrequited love:

Si hât mich verwunt	She has wounded me
reht aldurch mîne sêle	in my innermost soul,
in den vil tôtlichen grunt,	within the mortal core,
dô ich ir tet kunt	when I told her
daz ich tobte unde quêle	that I was raving and anguished
umbe ir vil güetlichen munt.	in desire for her glorious lips.
den bat ich zeiner stunt	Once I bade my own lips
daz er mich ze dienste ir bevêle	to commend me to her service,
und daz er mir stêle	and to steal me
von ir ein senftez küssen,	a tender kiss of hers,
sô wêre ich iemer gesunt.	that I might for ever be well.
Wie wirde ich gehaz	How I begin to hate
ir vil rôsevarn munde,	her rose-red lips,
des ich noch niender vergaz!	which I never yet forgot!
noch sô müet mich daz	It troubles me still,
daz er mir zeiner stunde	that they once refused me
sô mit gewalte versaz.	with such vehemence.
des bin ich worden laz,	Thus I have grown so weak
alsô daz ich vil schiere gesunde	that I would far rather—alive—
in der helle grunde	burn in the abyss
brunne ê ich ir iemer	of hell than serve her still,
diende ine wisse umbe waz.	not knowing to what end.

There is something dramatically extravagant about the opening lines, and for a moment, in the incongruity between the violent verb *tobte* (raved) and its object, a kiss from the lady's lips, the boundary between extreme pathos and the ridiculous almost disappears. Then at once the violence of language is resolved into playfulness: the rest of the stanza is a witty conceit in which the lover's and the lady's lips are personified, and in which a protestation of love-service is frankly acknowledged as a trick to win love by stealth.

The second stanza begins once more with exaggerated intensity, and because of what has gone before it seems easy to assume that the tone is a playfully teasing one. But again the unexpected happens— the second tercet is subdued in tone, the poet speaks of his humiliation with a muted restraint that compels seriousness. The verb that now conveys his sorrow is not *toben* or *quêlen* but *müen*—he feels not frenzy, but great weariness. From this note of limpness the stanza rises to a crescendo of passionate outcry, and subsides again at once in bewildered despair.

Despite the many transitions there is, I believe, a profound coherence here, in which the light conceit of the personified lips plays a crucial role. It bridges a trifling and a serious motif—the refusal of a kiss, and a lover's sense of his own foolishness and humiliation. The lover begins with grandiose passionate hyperboles that take him to the brink of the ludicrous. It is because he realises his pathetic foolishness that he dissociates himself from it—gleefully he says, it was only my lips, not I myself. This act of clowning is his self-protection; but as the second stanza shows, he finds it cannot sustain him all the time: the poem ends as it began, with a wild, tragicomic exclamation. To suggest its unique timbre by way of an anachronism, the song contains, so to speak, a touch of Donne together with a touch of *commedia dell' arte*. With harsh perceptiveness and concision Heinrich has conveyed an experience of frustrated love in which pathos and wit, self-dramatisation and even hysteria are conjoined.

Only Walther von der Vogelweide, whose lavish gifts enabled him to excel and to create afresh in every direction of the medieval lyric, can perhaps be said to approach Heinrich's originality as a poet of love. This originality might be seen as stemming from a tension between the kind of love-poetry that his aristocratic audience wanted or expected to hear and what he, their entertainer, poor and patronised but with the best mind among them, wanted to say or felt he could get away with saying. At times Walther has his own way by sheer charm, at others by adopting a mercurial, teasing manner in which he keeps his audience on tenterhooks: how much is said in earnest, how much in fun? They can take it as they wish—as a stimulus to thought and greater sensibility, or simply as their court jester's *blagues*.

Twice Walther takes the fashionable notion of a lover humbly and reverently aspiring to an exalted beloved, and bends it to his pleasure. He writes an elaborately rhetorical 'lofty song' (*hôhen sanc*), an adoring, itemised description of his lady's beauty. She is a divine masterpiece, exalted above her devotee like a celestial being:

> If without sin I dare avow,
> I would rather gaze on her
> than heaven, or the heavenly plough . . .

Walther treats the old *topoi* with new lightness and verve, but his song is also contemporary, full of sly witticisms at the expense of his poetic rival, the gently melancholy, idealising, 'correct' love-poet Reinmar. Then in the last stanza, when his description comes to what Mercutio was to call 'the demesnes that there adjacent lie', Walther deliberately scandalises the conventional discreetness of *hôhen sanc*:

> If I should praise what lies between,
> I should confess there's more I've seen:
> I'd not have wished to cry 'Get dressed!'
> when I saw her nakedness.
> She did not see me, as she pierced me
> with a stroke that even now stabs me
> whenever I think of the dear ground
> where she bathed and, full of grace, stepped out.

The shock-tactic is not an end in itself; by way of it Walther reaches a new romanticism, more delicate and less artificial than the romantic ideal of his opening variations. Yet the wit is still present, flickering in the rhymes of Walther's last couplet (*stat/trat*), a parodistic echo of the rhyme that Reinmar had used to excess in a recent song.

In another song Walther counters his lady's disdain by the thought that her renown depends on him as poet: if he is silent, it will fade, if she gives him joy, he can give her immortality. The final expression of this thought is again a mischievous echo of Reinmar, who, like many a languishing lover, had once said 'stirbet si, sô bin ich tôt'—'if she should die, it is my death'; Walther deftly turns this into his own *exegi monumentum*:

> If she rescues me from this distress,
> her life shares my life's glory; if I should die, it is her death.

Then, with a wicked gleam of irony, he carries the outrage against the romantic ideal of love-service even further:

> If I should grow old in serving her,
> she won't get much younger in those years;
> perhaps by then I'll have such different hair
> that someone young is more what she desires.
> Then with God's help, my fine young man,
> avenge me—use young rods on her old skin!

At times Walther criticises the modish exaltation of the beloved lady in a far more serious way: he sees it as having an invidious social basis, in which worldly rank counts for more than qualities of being. This is the thought behind his witty and moving dialectic comparing the unassuming word *wîp* (woman) with the more fashionable *frouwe* (lady):

> 'Woman' will always be woman's highest name—
> it honours her more than 'lady', if I'm right.
> If any look on being woman as shame,
> let her first heed my song, and then decide.
> Among ladies some are unwomanly,
> among women this cannot be.
> Woman's name and woman's being,
> they are both so lovable—
> whatever else ladies may be,
> let them at least be womanly!
> A doubtful praise can mean disdain
> —like the word 'lady' now and then—
> but the name 'woman' gives each one a crown.

Some of the most enchanting of Walther's love-songs are those explicitly written to and about young women who were not in high society, songs out of a less-sophisticated emotional world, tender and playful, sometimes wistful but never bitter. (One of these, the re-nowned *Nemt, frowe, disen kranz*, is discussed below, p. 201.) But these qualities can also light up a song to a lady in the world of the court (*ze hove*), and then for a moment even Walther's dark memories of his own humiliations in that world, where he, a poet, had been offered gifts of secondhand clothing as if he were a mere travelling performer, are transformed into a stream warm and iridescent with gaiety:

Lady, it is a most precious sheath
you have slipped on: your clear beauty.
Never have I seen a better dress—
you are a woman who is dressed perfectly—
neatly stitched in it are wit and harmony.
I have never accepted clothes that were used,
yet I would give my life for this dress.
The Emperor would become your strolling-player
for a gift of such blessedness.
There, Emperor, play!—No, my liege, play elsewhere!

The poetry of Heinrich and Walther is in almost every way incomparable with French trouvère love-lyric. A comparison between the French and German is possible and fascinating, however, in love-songs concerned with partings during the Crusades. Where the Chastelain had used wit and irreverence as openings to an essentially serious, searching meditation on the ultimate meaning of love and loyalty, the Minnesinger Otto von Botenlauben, departing for the German Crusade in 1197, composes a *Wechsel* full of exhilaratingly profane hyperbole, which lover and beloved in turn ask God to condone, for the sake of their love:

'Were Christ's reward not quite so sweet,
I would not part from my dear love,
whom still my heart returns to greet:
she can be my heaven indeed,
wherever beside the Rhine she live!
Lord God, now show some sign of pity,
that both for her and me I may   yet win your mercy.'

'Since he affirms I am his heaven,
I've chosen him to be my God,
that he need never leave me, one step even.
Do not look at us angrily, Lord God!
He is no thorn that hurts my eye:
he was born here to give me joy—
my joy a play of light gone out,   if he should die!'

It is basically a simpler poem than the Chastelain's: here there are no misgivings, doubts, hesitations or fears, only a swift surge of confidence in the supremacy of love. The man and woman set up human love as an absolute, which the Chastelain would not have dared. Yet it is not an exclusive absolute: their mutual idolatry is far more than play, but it is by no means profanity, because from start to finish they submit it like a blueprint for the divine approval, convinced that (provided God plays his part in the design and keeps the lover alive) the two loves, if they are ultimately interdependent, can also harmonise. Some eight years earlier another gifted Minnesinger, Friedrich von Hausen, had been preoccupied with the very conflict that Graf Otto had so blithely eliminated. At first he lightly wards off the fear that his love may be unacceptable to God:

> I love her; whenever before God I dare,
> I think of her.
> He should forgive me for this too:
> if I had sinned in this with great offence,
> why did he make her of such excellence?

But graver thoughts intrude:

> I had a joy that touched me very nearly:
> it never let me
> turn my spirit towards wisdom . . .

And von Hausen's final resolution is sterner and more uncompromising than Graf Otto's or the Chastelain's. He has been a 'correct' lover, he says—he has never complained against love's sorrows, or against the women who caused him sorrow in love:

> But this is my complaint,
> that I forgot God for so long;
> I shall put him before all women from now on,
> and only after that greet them with my heart's love.

With the death of Walther von der Vogelweide (c. 1230), the most brilliant age of Minnesang was over. In the generations that followed, love-lyric developed in two main directions: one was away from love in the high style, towards the vivacious, mordant dance-songs of Neidhart (see below, p. 204), and towards balladry; the other showed an increasing elaboration of the high-flown modes towards pure virtuosity and mannerism. Lengthy strophic structures such as the *Leich*[1] became more popular; the lyrical strophe itself became larger

---

1. *Leich*: see above, p. 25, n. 1. I accept the arguments of Handschin and Spanke that the twelfth- and thirteenth-century Latin, French and German examples of this form descend from the archaic sequences, the remarkable range of lyrical forms which can be traced back both in Latin and vernacular poetry at least to the Carolingian period (see above, pp. 38–40). Despite the almost complete absence of recorded evidence for the later tenth and the eleventh century, the tradition was in all probability an unbroken one.

and more intricately and richly rhymed; lines were linked by echo and
word-play as well as rhyme; syntax tended to the involved and over-
burdened, expression easily became extravagantly mannered, prettified,
or obscure. Fancy flourished, imagination lagged behind. Landmarks
in this later tradition include the *Leiche* of Tannhäuser (whose legend
was soon to eclipse his songs)—at their best sensual and exhilarating—
the graceful intricacies of Konrad von Würzburg, arches within
arches, immaculate in their craftsmanship, and the straining lyrical
stanzas of Heinrich Frauenlob:

> God greet my heart's proprietor,
> the love-abounding guest of my high ecstasy,
> who at each moment
> with adventures new, delightful,
> helps me to joy unendingly:
> it is a woman, who has placed
> upon my senses such a more-than-mighty load
> with love-abounding
> dear love pressing to joy's utmost
> mark, wherein my faculties   10
> often dissolve,
> her victory
> complete in me:
> blessed be this innocent, tender,
> gentle mastery![1]

Here the rhymes are relatively sparse, but the syllabic-rhythmic
pattern (which I have reproduced in English) remains identical through
five stanzas. A single sentence becomes a maze, a faded thread of
thought drawn through its twists and turns—it is a bizarre but astonishing feat of dexterity. Such techniques came to be learnt systematically.
In Mainz, where he died in 1318, Frauenlob is said to have founded
the first German school for lyrical composition. It is the sign of a new
era—the era of late Gothic, and of the Meistersinger.

(4) *A Latin lyric*

Insofar as we can discount the accidents of preservation, we may say
that the finest achievements in medieval love-lyric in the twelfth
century are to be found first in Provence and then in Germany; in the
thirteenth century, above all in Italy (see below, p. 151). Till the end
of the thirteenth century we have only a few traces of a tradition in

1. The strophic form is that of a canzone, with two identical 'Stollen' (lines 1–5 are
given an exact metrical reproduction in lines 6–10), and an 'Abgesang' with a pattern
distinct from these (lines 11–15).

England. The twelfth century, again, sees the most abundant and finest
flowering of love-lyric in Latin, where the written records enable us,
however fragmentarily, to follow a tradition back at least as far as the
early tenth century. In its musical development the Latin secular lyric
was intimately linked with the music that grew up around the liturgy;
from the late eleventh century onwards this paraliturgical tradition
became increasingly adapted to love-lyrics and to other types of
secular song; it profoundly influenced the music of vernacular lyrics,
and conversely was frequently enriched by theirs. This is true in the
highest degree of France and Germany, where the Latin love-lyric was
cultivated most extensively; we have rather less evidence for Spain and
England, least of all for Italy. At the same time it is certain that the
Latin secular lyric became to a large extent international: the manuscript tradition of some of the most celebrated songs enables us to
follow them virtually over the whole of Europe.

What are the distinctive qualities and achievements in the Latin love-
lyric? Let us attempt to draw some general inferences from one outstanding and characteristic composition:

Annualis mea	My bride of May,
sospes sit et gaudeat!	joy and blessings on her!
arrideat,	May she smile
cui se hec chorea	as the dance around her
inplicat, quam replico	weaves in and out, to follow
et precino:	my melody—
pulchrior et aptior in mundo	in the world there's none so fair
non est ea!	and deft as she!
Fervens illa mea	She is my fire,
ignis est, sed suavitas	blazing, and yet gentleness
et bonitas	and sweet goodness
renitent ex ea.	radiate from her.
provocant me talia	I am provoked by these
ad gaudia,	to such great joys,
tristorque cum suspiriis sub	yet I grieve in the throes of
lite Venerea.	Venus, full of sighs.
Hospitalis mea,	My welcome guest,
candida et rubea,	shining white and red,
siderea—	starry-eyed—
Venus, amoris dea,	oh love-goddess, to you,
me tibi subicio,	Venus, I surrender,
auxilio	I have such need
egens tuo—iam caleo et	of your assistance now— I burn
pereo in ea!	and die for her!

Collaudate meam   All of you, praise
pudicam, delectabilem,   my innocent, delectable,
        amabilem!   so lovable
amo ferventer eam,   girl I want ardently,
per quam mestus vigeo,   she for whose sake I live
        et gaudeo,   in joy and grief,
illam pre cunctis diligo   et   adoring her as goddess   whom I
veneror ut deam.   love beyond all loves.

There is, first of all, an unusual blend of simplicity and sophistication: the exhilaration and sparkle of youth are conveyed by means of
an exceptionally skilful form, in which the patterns of rhythm and
rhyme dance gracefully together. The subject is ostensibly a May-game,
in which the dancers circle around the girl they have chosen as their
'bride of the year' (*annualis*). But does this May-game belong to a real
village world? There the allusions to Venus might well seem out of
place. Is it, then, a dance performed in a Petit Trianon of the poet's
imagination? There seems too much immediacy and spontaneity for
that. Again, the theme seems to be well known and straightforward,
an evocation of the lover's state of mingled joy and suffering—yet it is
treated with unusual subtlety. Who is the beloved? She is the consum-
ing love that the lover feels within him (a subjective state), and a source
of *suavitas* and *bonitas* outside him (an objective goal); in the third
stanza, by a deliberate ambiguity, she almost merges with the goddess
to whom he prays and submits himself, and if at the close he venerates
the girl *ut deam*, it is because of this imaginative fusion between her
beauty and the gleam of divinity that this beauty can reveal to him who
loves and longs for it. Such complexities are suggested, not stated, in a
lyric that gives a dominant impression of elegant lightness and speed;
there is a sense of intellectual dexterity about the whole, but at the
same time a candid quality, an essential simplicity that allows such a
form and such a range of thought to be linked with the uncomplicated
world of May-games without incongruity.

Here we approach the characteristics that in my view especially
distinguish the Medieval Latin love-lyric—allied to its considerable
refinement of form are two qualities that provisionally I shall call
its pervasive wit and its innocence. Wit here implies, as in Elizabethan
and seventeenth-century English poetry, a particular approach to
language and dialectic in verse, an approach that is perfectly compatible
with deep seriousness, as well as with feigned seriousness or mirth. If
we think of Romeo jesting with his friends, or pining for Rosaline, or
winning Juliet's love, or dying for Juliet's sake—the functions of the

language in these contexts differ widely, yet in them all the approach to language remains fundamentally the same: there is an integral quality of play in this approach that Shakespeare felt no need to eliminate even from the most sublime or tragic moments, a play that is intuitive or at least habitual. Naturally all the more gifted vernacular love-poets have moments of wit; in the Latin it is not so much a matter of more or less frequent moments as a condition intrinsic to the language itself—perhaps partly because, however well it had been learnt, it always remained in the last resort a learnt and not a native language, and therefore a language in which from the outset the intellect was exercised.

When I use the word 'innocence' of the Latin love-lyric, it is to suggest a literary rather than a moral quality.[1] It is a complete absence of those traces of self-doubt or self-criticism that reveal themselves from time to time in the finest vernacular love-lyrics from Guillaume and Kürenberc onwards, and give certain songs a special poetic resonance, certain poets a special dimension. It is not a question of emotional range—the Latin poets may doubt the success of their love, may feel despair even, but all this within a poetic context that is never itself questioned. As far as I know, there are none of those astonishing moments in which a poet can at times see through himself, watching his own movements of thought and feeling and behaviour with a kind of vulnerable detachment. Whether in their poetry they are suffering or successful lovers, joyously sensual or worshipping from afar, they are innocents in that essentially they do not question themselves, never momentarily step back to observe themselves critically in their own attitudes. This again may be partly due to the limitations of a learnt as against a native language. (The only exception that springs to mind is in the Latin prose of Petrarch's *Secretum*: Augustine, Abelard and many others had in their Latin writings revealed much of themselves and probed their own consciences; but only Petrarch, I think, tries to see through himself probing his own conscience.) The use of this learnt language, highly sophisticated in its poetic forms and its modes of expression, but with a basic candour of poetic attitude underlying it, perhaps helps to explain that pervasive wit which conditions the poets' approach to their themes. At all events in so far as the Latin love-lyric has qualities distinct from the vernacular it seems to me to depend on these interrelated elements.

1. The frequently held opinion that the Latin love-lyric is more frankly sensual than the vernacular is perhaps occasionally, but by no means generally true; the opinion that all the Latin songs were addressed to unmarried women is as unfounded and bizarre as the legend that all troubadour songs were addressed to married ones.

(5) English and Galician love-songs

Apart from the Latin tradition, there are two vernaculars in which love-lyric tends to have the same underlying innocence: Middle English and Galician. The specific qualities of poetic expression, however, are very different in these languages. When we first encounter love-lyric in Middle English (shortly after 1200), the form and diction are without elegance. They are plain and pithy and concise:

> I am all bereft of sense,
> of the world's bliss I am bare,
> because of a peerless lady,
> crown of all who tread in bower.
> Since she first belonged to him,
> locked in a castle wall of stone,
> I have not been whole or glad,
> or a prosperous man.
> There's many a man urges me
> to stay and to live happily,
> but it's downwards, to death, that I long;
> on me, I can say truthfully,
> woes are harshly hung.[1]

What is remarkable here is not the evocation of the lover's state of feeling (though this has a rueful, down-to-earth tone that carries its own conviction), but the suggestion of a vivid background of events, swiftly adumbrated in two lines—

> sethen furst the heo was his,
> iloken in castel wal of stan—

which lend concreteness and dramatic power to the complaint. Behind the forthrightness of the language we perceive the adroitness and tact of a narrator who knows how to work evocatively.

The song is rounded with a phrase, *herde thet wo hongeth*, that has an almost proverbial ring. So too in the first three lines of a brief song written down half a century later, the proverbial effect allied with the effect of alliteration enables a poet to achieve an intense, gnomic compression (the melody is given below, p. 244):

> Foweles in the frith,
> the fisses in the flod—
> and I mon waxe wod.
> Mulch sorw I walke with
> for beste of bon and blod.

1. A note on the textual problems of this lyric is given below, p. 280.

Birds [are] in the woodland, the fishes in the sea—and I must grow mad.
I walk with great sorrow for the best of bone and blood.

It begins with the contrast characteristic of the stylised, often highly
rhetorical, nature-prelude common in love-lyrics: the implication is
that the birds and fishes, being in their element, are happy and fulfilled.
The lover's languishing state is conveyed (far more effectively than
in many more elaborate complaints) by the two stark words *waxe wod*.
The close has a haunting quality: the lover does not describe his state
further, nor does he describe the woman who causes it; he reiterates
his sorrow with utter simplicity, and mentions his beloved only in a
phrase which was probably even then an alliterative cliché. Why then
does it have this strangely powerful effect? Is it not because the opening
words still reverberate in one's mind, and compel one to associate the
last line with them?—She too is bone and blood, a physical being—
what right has she to be different from the rest of the living world? If
she is the best in nature, can the blood in her veins be colder than that
of the birds and fishes? These may be only subjective explications of
the effect; what I feel certain of is that the poet intended the opening
and close of his stanza to react on each other and to release associations
of unhappy love, and that his intention was not merely to juxtapose
familiar phrases so as to fit a sweet tune but to achieve a conjunction
that would enrich poetic meaning.

From near the end of the century a song of more joyful love-
longing begins (cf. the melody below, p. 245):

Bryd one brere, brid, brid one brere,	1–3: Bird on briar
Kynd is come of Love love to crave.	1: Nature
Blithful biryd, on me thu rewe	2: lady/bird, 6: take pity
Or greyth, lef, greith thu me my grave.	2–3: quickly/prepare, dear one

Still the language has that seemingly unpremeditated quality, the
effect at first is almost of a birdlike chatter, bubbling over with excitement. But the word-play here reveals a keen sense of meaning and of
ambiguity. The second line once more brings to mind the nature-
prelude, but it is more 'metaphysical' than hitherto: it is a personified
Nature who comes in spring to beseech the love-god to release love in
the world—alternatively, Kynd, daughter of the supreme God, who is
Love, descends from on high to crave love (in the world); both
meanings may be implied. The allusion to the goddess 'of philosophers
and scholars', light as it is, is unmistakable. The third line puns on the
first, when *b[i]ryd* is repeated, now with the overt meaning of 'lady'

rather than 'bird'; the fourth line continues the verbal conjuring
(*greyth* can mean both 'quickly' and 'prepare'). All this points to an
essentially literary playfulness; but we cannot exclude from these lines
yet another meaning, latent as a possibility, of the bird as the confidant
of lovers, who can take pity on the lover by bringing him a joyful
message from his mistress—this time a convention characteristic of
popular song.

In the two remaining stanzas the lover confides his longing to the
bird. Here too it may be possible to detect in the language a conscious
echo of popular balladry. With

> She is huit of lime, loueli, trewe,   5: limb
> she is fayr, and flur of alle

we are not far from *As ye came from the holy land*—

> She is neither white nor brown,
> but as the heavens fair . . .

just as, in the opening stanza, we come close to Sir Walter Scott—

> 'Who makes the bridal bed,
>   Birdie, say truly?'
> 'The grey-headed sexton
>   That delves the grave duly.'

For all its many-sided artifice, the language of *Bryd one brere* is still
composed wholly of native elements. So too in many stanzas among
the love-lyrics in the Harley collection, some of which may go back to
before 1300:

> Levedy of alle londe,
> les me out of bonde;
>   broht icham in wo.
> Have resting on honde,
> ant sent thou me thi sonde
>   sone, er thou me slo;
>   my reste is with the ro.
> Thah men to me han onde,
> to love nuly noht wonde,
>   ne lete for non of tho.

Lady of all lands, free me from my bonds, I have been brought to woe.
Bring about peace for me, and send a message to me now, before you kill me;
I rest as little as the roe. Though men are hostile towards me, I shall not
swerve from loving, nor cease for any of their sakes.

At a time when such pleas and protestations, and motifs such as the message and the spiteful enemies of love, had become stale elsewhere in Europe through excessive and unimaginative use, they could still be treated in plain English freshly and directly. Again a quatrain of *c.* 1300, only recently discovered, uses witty hyperbole with an adroitness and vivacity worthy of Kürenberc. The lover, out in the cold night, makes his rueful serenade:

> So longe ic have, lavedi,   5: lady
> yhoved at thi gate,   1: lingered
> that mi fot is ifrore, faire lavedi,   3–5: foot is frozen
> for thi luve faste to the stake!

Here too, as in *Bryd one brere*, we must reckon with the possibility of word-play—the stake as gatepost, and as the place of execution for love's victim. The fourteenth century in England, however, sees the lyrical language transformed under French influence, all too often an effete and epigonic influence:

> Mercy me graunt off that I me compleyne,
>   to yow my lyfis soveraigne plesauns;
> and ese your servaunt of the importabyl peyne
>   that I suffre in your obeysauns . . .

Language of this kind, alas, comes to dominate the late medieval English love-lyric. At times, however, as in the finest of the Rawlinson lyrics (see below, p. 195), this newfangled language could still be set aside; or again an exceptionally subtle and alive personality such as Chaucer could shape it to his pleasure and thereby win nuances of meaning and emotion as individual as those of Guillaume or Kürenberc.

The poetic innocence of Galician love-lyric is a different matter again. Here we seem to be confronted, from the earliest lyrical records, with a deliberately restricted range of poetic language and conventions: in the *cantigas de amor* as in the *cantigas de amigo* (see above, pp. 101 ff.), it is largely a question of what artistic permutations were possible with a given poetic equipment—a severely limited vocabulary and stylised 'types' of emotion and situation, devices such as parallelism and refrain, conventional modes of opening, conventional forms of address, conventions about the length and number of the stanzas. Even in these formidable fetters a number of *trovadores* achieved poetry of true intensity and, more surprisingly, poetry that could be varied and

individual. They seldom attempted to free themselves of these fetters—
they clung to a lyrical mode that must have been deeply rooted in the
popular as well as the paraliturgical traditions of their land. As
King Denis, himself one of the most distinguished of the later
trovadores, explicitly recognised, there were other ways of doing
things—

> Provençal poets compose very well,
> and they allege they do so out of love—
> but those who make their songs at flower-time
> and not at other times, I am convinced
> they do not know such anguish in their hearts
> as I experience for my lady's sake.

In effect King Denis here criticises the spring-prelude which is so
characteristic of Provençal love-lyric (and extremely rare in Portuguese) from the standpoint of sincerity: he prefers a love-poetry that
confines itself to the naked emotions of love, emotions such as that
anguish of love-longing (*coita*) which dominates so many of the
Portuguese songs. The nature-prelude is extrinsic to such an emotion,
a song that adopts it loses in sincerity (or, in literary terms, loses in
concentrated force and unity). To make his point the King wittily
assumes naivety: he pretends to believe that all the love-songs that
begin with a spring-prelude must really have been composed in spring
—so all those lovers must be mere fair-weather friends!

The question of sincerity also occupied other *trovadores*: in a song
by Joan Airas the poet affirms that men who are not in love may well
be as accomplished in declaring it as true lovers are—yet they will
never be believed, for only truth really carries conviction. Again King
Denis, 'when him list to feign', composed a conventional panegyric
on his lady's virtues and claimed this to be *en maneyra de proençal*.
It would be rash, however, on the basis of such passages to follow
those older scholars who see Portuguese lyric as intrinsically more
sincere than Provençal: there is no adequate evidence for deciding this
at a biographical level; what is certain is that the emotional truth of
the Portuguese poets is first and foremost a *poetic* effect, governed by
far-reaching artistic conventions.

A song that admirably illustrates some of the specific excellence of
the *cantigas de amor*, as well as some of the limitations that this
excellence entails, is *Como morreu* by Paai Soarez de Taveiroos, one of
the earliest *trovadores* of whom we have evidence, at the court of
King Sancho († 1213):

Como morreu quen nunca ben	As he died who never had
ouve de ren que mais amou,	joy from the creature he loved best,
e quen viu quanto receou	and had only what he feared
d'ela, e foi morto por én,	at her hands, and for her died:
Ay mia senhor, assi moir'eu.	*Ah my lady, thus I die.*
Como morreu quen foi amar	As he died who tried to love
quen lhe nunca quis ben fazer,	one who never wished his good
e de quen lhe fez Deus veer	and through whom God made him see
de que foi morto con pesar,	that he was dying painfully:
Ay mia senhor, assi moir'eu.	*Ah my lady, thus I die.*
Com'ome que ensandeceu,	As he died who first went mad,
senhor, con gran pesar que viu,	lady, with all the pain he knew,
e non foi ledo nen dormiu	and not once saw joy or sleep
depois, mia senhor, e morreu,	again, my lady, and then died:
Ay mia senhor, assi moir'eu.	*Ah my lady, thus I die.*
Como morreu quen amou tal	As he died who loved a girl
dona que lhe nunca fez ben,	who was never kind to him,
e quen a viu levar a quen	and saw her married to a man
a non valia, non a val,	unworthy of her now as then:
Ay mia senhor, assi moir'eu.	*Ah my lady, thus I die.*

It is a single sigh of disappointed love, given an exquisite objective form. The melody, as with most *trovador* lyric, has been lost, but the words have their own limpid music. They are among the simplest, commonest words of love—*morreu, amou, morto, amar, pesar, dormiu* —yet in the gentle anaphorai they come to cast a spell. For three strophes one is lulled by them, drifting with their melancholy, it seems drifting nowhere in particular. With the two moments of direct address in the third strophe there is an increased urgency, but only with the climactic final strophe is the full design revealed: the delicate hint of a dramatic background is just enough to suggest a new perspective and depth for what has gone before, to link the subjective, dreamy sigh to an outer world that the audience knows, that, as the last line brings home, is with us in the present, in which a woman may indeed marry the wrong man and be bound to him for life. The relative concreteness of the last stanza brings a shock, yet this shock illuminates, and is itself assimilated within, the total pattern: the symmetry of the language and the refrain, here as before, ensures that the spell is not broken. It has been common in the past to consider such songs as simple and spontaneous *cris de cœur*, and to contrast them with the artificialities of Provence. I would say that here simplicity and spontaneity have been polished to attain a high degree of artistic expressiveness, refined almost to the point of preciosity. It is the hard-won simplicity and spontaneity of the finest Elizabethan lyrics. The characteristic excellence lies in a balance between passionate directness and graceful refinement; in the patterns of intensive repetition and variation the elemental and the cultivated are brought into harmony.

The *cantigas de amor* set forth many aspects of unhappy love—the lover who loves too desperately to be able to take revenge for his lady's coldness:

> If I were able to unlove
> her who has always been unloving,
> if I could hurt in any way
> her who has never tired of hurting . . .

or the lover whose mind is numbed with the ordeal of declaring his love, not knowing whether he will be laughed at:

> For the little that I spoke today
> with my lady, I give thanks to God,
> and that my eyes beheld their great delight.
> But I am full of fear for what I said:
> *I can't recall, for my heart trembled so,*
> *whether I told my love to her or no . . .*

Or again, one who reflects with bitter irony on his lady's hardness:

> If I meet my death today,
> I know well what my love will say:
> '*I am Guiomar Affonso!*'
>
> When she knows that I have died
> for her sake, she will say indeed
> '*I am Guiomar Affonso!*'
>
> When I am dead, she will stand
> and say, her chin cupped in her hand:
> '*I am Guiomar Affonso!*'

Despite the dramatic possibilities inherent in the use of the refrain, which can be seen especially from this last song, dramatic development within the lyrics is rare: it is a single mood or impulse that is evoked, in the best songs with a clean-cut elegance, often also with an intensity that borders on unashamed extravagance. The cumulative effect achieved by the repetitions, verbal parallels and refrains tended to magnify rather than qualify the basic mood or impulse, and was thus conducive to emotional overstatement. It is not surprising, then, that alongside the songs of anguished love have been preserved many that treat the same range of themes lightly or parodistically, with gentle humour or outright burlesque.

Thus for instance there is a delightful group of three songs by Pero Garcia of Burgos, a later thirteenth-century poet of whom more than fifty lyrics survive, in which he makes a playful jest of the *comme-il-faut* lover's secrecy—he must never disclose his lady's name—of his awe before the beloved and his fear of her wrath. He is so afraid of anyone's discovering who she is that he names three ladies instead of one:

> Joana, I said, and Sancha, and Maria,
> in my song with its great grief of love,
> and yet I did not say for whom I pined
> among the three, nor whom I long for most,
> nor who is making me bereft of sense,
> nor who is bringing me so near my death—
> Joana, or Sancha, or Maria . . .

In the next song the inevitable happens—the lady who was meant realises his love (and his indiscretion), and is furious; the last song shows us a picture of the pathetic lover, seeking a melancholy solitude, but persecuted by all the people who go on asking him 'Who was she?'

Though texts such as these occur relatively late, we need not I think assume that lighter variations on love-themes did not exist at earlier periods: the first *trovadores* whose names and dates we know already show us the art of love-song at a 'late' or highly developed stage, and it is extremely probable that in the popular lyrical traditions of the Iberian peninsula (the antiquity and vivacity of which are strikingly indicated by some of the *kharjas*—see above, pp. 86 ff.) serious and witty types of love-song had always existed side by side.

(6) *From the Sicilians to Dante*

The earliest Italian love-lyrics of which we have record were written by a group of learned poets who, coming from various regions of Italy, had gathered in Sicily at the court of Frederick II. They were noblemen and professional men, the Emperor's courtiers and civil servants. It is commonly affirmed that their songs represent an absolute beginning, and that love-poetry in Italian came into being simply as an imitation of the Provençal mode. It is true that no datably earlier

Italian love-lyrics survive, but some of the more archaic poems in
other genres, such as the *Ritmo cassinese*, the *Elegia giudeo-italiana*,
and the *Ritmo laurenziano*,[1] show beyond all doubt the existence of a
rich and vigorous poetic tradition, and of an amazing range of poetic
art, prior and unrelated to that of Frederick's court. It seems wholly
improbable that this older tradition should have included no love-
songs. It is true that the canzone, a favourite form among the Sicilian
group, was adapted from the 'canso' of the troubadours—though I
know no instance of an outright copy of form or melody.[2] It is true that
the 'founder' of the group, the notary Giacomo da Lentini, was familiar
with the lyrical conventions and the love-language of Provence—but
it is more important to stress that he was no mere epigone. His is a
new poetic voice, subtle and individual, the voice not of a tentative
experimenter but of a mature, self-assured artist:

Meravigliosamente	In a wondrous way
un amor mi distringe	a love is binding me
e mi tene ad ogn'ora.	and holds me constantly.
Com'om che pone mente	As a man concentrates
in altro exemplo pinge	on an idea and paints
la simile pintura,	a picture that is like it,
così, bella, facc'eo,	so, lovely one, I do,
che 'nfra lo core meo	who within my heart
porto la tua figura.	carry the form of you.

The painter has the 'idea' (in Plato's sense of the word), the exem-
plar or ideal form of what he wants to paint, in his mind, and his
painting is an attempt to copy that idea in a physical mode. The copy
can never quite attain the perfect form of the idea. So too the lover has
an ideal image of the beloved within him, which is the perfect expression
of his own love; but in the outer world he is shamefast (*vergognoso*)
and can express his love only imperfectly. He cannot wholly attain his
ideal beloved; but through painting her he can come near her in
imagination:

Avendo gran disio,	Filled with great love-longing
dipinsi una pintura,	I painted a picture
bella, voi simigliante,	resembling you, my fair one,
e quando voi non vio,	and when I do not see you

---

1. The first two are discussed above, pp. 57 ff. The *Ritmo laurenziano* (*Poeti*, I, p. 5)
is a vivacious begging-song addressed to a bishop, composed probably around 1200.
2. There is one unique instance of a Sicilian poet, Jacopo Mostacci, translating part
of a lyric by a troubadour, Rigaut de Barbezieux. The form, however, is different.

guardo 'n quella figura,	I look upon that image
e par ch'eo v'aggia avante:	and think you are before me,
come quello che crede	as a believer thinks to
salvarsi per sua fede,	win heaven by believing,
ancor non veggia inante.	although he does not see it.

The painter and the lover, like the religous devotee, must make an act of faith, must believe in the reality of an invisible form, an idea in their minds. Then Giacomo subtly extends his basic metaphor (of the idea and the attempts at its physical expression) once again: his praises of the beloved are 'for art' (*per arti*), they let her see 'through signs' (*per singa*) what he cannot say in her physical presence. The canzone itself becomes his painting, his *figura*, his attempt at the physical realisation of the ideal love in his heart:

Canzonetta novella,	My little newborn song,
va' canta nova cosa;	go singing what is new;
lèvati da maitino	as morning comes, arise
davanti a la più bella,	before the loveliest one,
fiore d'ogni amorosa,	flower of girls who love,
bionda più c'auro fino:	fairer than burnished gold:
'Lo vostro amor, ch'è caro,	Say 'Give your precious love
donatelo al Notaro	to the notary who
ch'è nato da Lentino.'	is Lentino's son.'

In the gentle melody of its thought, and in the meditation on love as both perfect idea and aspiring, imperfect expression in the outer world, this song indeed is 'nova cosa'.

It is to this notary, too, that we owe the first instances of the sonnet form in Europe. There had been nothing quite like this form beyond the Alps: Giacomo may well have created it, though we cannot rule out the possibility that he was continuing, or developing, a native tradition. The sonnet, as its later destiny not only in Italian but in European lyric shows, was more than one metrical schema among others: there was something intrinsic to the form that made it captivating to succeeding generations—the light but firm unity that could be achieved through the conjunction or contrast, or both, of the pair of quatrains and the pair of tercets. There is the simplicity of order, and yet flexibility: though the four units are essentially two pairs, each of the four can be related to the others by parallelism, continuity, antinomy, or balanced juxtaposition. To illustrate by one of Giacomo's sonnets, which in its ethereal, beatific conception of the beloved, and in its certainty that her transcendent perfection is acknowledged by all mankind, is characteristic of one of the predominant strands in early Italian love-lyric:

Lo viso mi fa andare alegramente,	The vision makes me go about in joy,
lo bello viso mi fa rivegli-	the lovely vision wakes my hope
are,	again,
lo viso mi conforta ispessamente,	the vision gives me solace many times,
l'adorno viso che mi fa	the gracious vision through which
penare.	I feel pain.
Lo chiaro viso de la piú	The radiant vision of the loveliest
avenente,	one,
l'adorno viso riso me fa	the vision that fills me with exul-
fare.	tant laughter,
Di quello viso parlane la	this is the vision of which mankind
gente,	speaks,
chè nullo viso a viso li pò	because no other vision can match
stare.	this vision.
Chi vide mai così begli occhi	Who ever saw such fair eyes in a
in viso,	vision,
nè sì amorosi fare li	or eyes that make their looks so
sembianti,	full of love,
nè bocca con cotanto dolce	or lips with such great sweetness
riso?	in their laughter?
Quand'eo li parlo moroli	Whenever I speak to her I die
davanti,	before her,
e paremi chi vada in paradiso,	and then I seem to go to paradise,
e tegnomi sovrano	and hold myself more blessed than
d'ogn'amanti.	any lover.

Here the two quatrains are the most intimately united. Not only are they syntactically parallel, they are in direct continuity, a continuity strengthened by the anaphoric *viso*, as well as by the emotional bridge from *alegramente* to *riso*, across the contrasting *penare*. The tercets, linked by their rhymes, are in other respects an antinomy, contrasting both in syntax and meaning. The first, in which the words *viso* and *riso* recur once more, is still closely linked with the quatrains to which it is juxtaposed. It sets off all that has gone before against the final tercet; the basic proportions in this sonnet, we might say, are 11:3 rather than the far commoner 8:6; yet those last three lines are a strong enough climax to balance the rest—the proportions are harmonious, the contrast resolves itself in unity.

Another love-poem which, like Giacomo's, belongs to the earliest surviving poetry from Sicily, the celebrated *Contrasto* of Cielo d'Alcamo, shows a very different range of language and attitudes. It is a lyrical dialogue in which the man and woman speak, or perhaps sing, alternate stanzas; though we have no direct evidence, I think it highly probable that the dialogue was accompanied by dramatic action and mime. While it has affinities with some of the dance-songs and *pastorelas*[1] discussed below in Chapter 6, it contains no allusion to dancing, and is unlike the *pastorelas* in several respects: in its length (32 stanzas), in the absence of a narrative setting, and above all in that there is no obvious difference of social status between the lover and his lass. Cielo, a sophisticated and brilliantly witty poet, has made them speak a language in which exalted and refined phrases jostle with vivacious colloquialisms, sly irony with broad invective, homely and proverbial wit with elaborate *double entendres*. It is an eclectic creation, drawing on lively traditions both of popular and courtly love-song, as well as on a tradition of burlesque, and fusing these in a new and exciting way. At one of the most remarkable moments the hyperboles of love-worship are transformed into a macabre fantasy. As the girl declares she would sooner drown herself than yield, the lover replies:

'If you fling yourself in the sea, gracious and fine lady,
I'll dive in and follow you, all the way through the ocean;
then finally, when you are drowned, on the beach I'll find you,
    only that this one deed be consummated,
    and you and I in vice at last united!'

'I'll cross myself—Father and Son—and in St Matthew's name!
I know you are no heretic, your father's not a Jew—
but I have never heard a man say such words as these.
    If a woman dies, she's lost all trace
    of her freshness and delightfulness.'

'Indeed I know it, dearest love, but I can't help myself . . .'

One of the crucial points in the argument—will she yield without his first promising to marry her?—is wittily resolved at the *dénouement*:

'Your soul torments you, yes I know, like a man who's burning—
but the thing just can't be done in any other fashion:
if you don't do as I tell you now, and swear upon the Gospel,
    I shall never let you have my body:
    you could sooner take me and behead me!'

1. The pastorela (Old French *pastourelle*) is discussed further infra, pp. 167, 200.

'You want the Gospel, dearest love? Here in my shirt I've got one:
I snatched it from the monastery when the priest wasn't looking.
On this book I swear to you I shall never fail you . . .'

But no selective quotation can do justice to the intellectual agility
and human richness of the whole. While it is exceptional in its range, it
must not be imagined as an isolated exception to an otherwise homogeneous mode of ethereal love-worship: a number of other poems—
the touching, exquisitely stylised women's laments by Rinaldo
d'Aquino, or the partings of lovers, full of warmth and tender sensuality, depicted by Giacomino Pugliese, show us how wide a spectrum of
love the Sicilian poets could reflect in their songs.

Towards the middle of the century the influence of the Sicilian group
came to be felt in Tuscany and in Bologna, where the poet-king
Enzo, son of Frederick II, was taken prisoner in 1249. For several
decades the most prolific and influential poet in these regions was
Guittone of Arezzo, at first as love-poet, then, after becoming a friar
in 1265, as moral, political and religious poet. The term 'versifier' is
perhaps more appropriate, as Guittone's range of dialectic and exclamation, for all its impassioned earnestness, remains inescapably prosaic in
content and unmusical in effect. In recent years his verse has been much
praised for its rhetorical and moral strength, yet these qualities cannot
in my view outweigh Guittone's signal lack of ear and of imagination.

Among Guittone's disciples, however, there were some born poets.
The finest of these, Guido Guinizelli (*c.* 1230–76), grew up in Bologna,
where as a young man he would have known the circle of poets around
King Enzo. But when Guido began to write, it was in the shadow of
Guittone—a sonnet addressed to the older man begins 'O caro padre
meo' (just as a generation later Dante, echoing these words, was to call
Guido himself 'mio padre'). While Guittone's example may have
given Guido a certain intellectual toughness and a concern with moral
values, Guido's poetic language had at its finest a soaring, golden
quality that outstripped everything in Italian lyric before it:

Vedut' ho la lucente stella diana,
ch'apare anzi che 'l giorno rend' albore,
c'ha preso forma di figura umana;
sovr' ogn' altra me par che dea splendore . . .

I have seen the lucent morning star
that comes before the day yields its first light
take on the semblance of a human form:
I think her radiance passes all that's bright . . .

It is this verve of diction, and the lucid concentration of Guido's language of love, that led a younger group of lyrical poets in Florence, the poets of the 'sweet new style' (*dolce stil novo*) to regard him as their master. This Florentine group included the younger Guido—Guido Cavalcanti, Lapo Gianni and Cino of Pistoia; its greatest poet was Dante. It was Dante who later, when writing the *Divina Commedia*, coined the phrase *dolce stil novo* to characterise the achievement of this group, and who tried to show polemically what set them apart from their predecessors, Giacomo the Notary, Guittone, and Bonagiunta of Lucca (one of the first northern poets to come under Sicilian influence). The words occur in Dante's dialogue with Bonagiunta in *Purgatorio* XXIV:

'But tell me, am I looking at the man who wrote the new song that begins "Donne ch'avete intelletto d'amore"?' I said to him, 'I am one who, when Love inspires me, take note, and, in the manner that he dictates within me, set it down.' 'My brother,' he said, 'now I see the knot that kept the Notary and Guittone and me from attaining to the sweet new style I hear. Indeed I see how closely your pens follow him who dictates—which certainly did not happen in our case . . .'.

What does Dante claim for his love-lyrics and those of his friends (and implicitly perhaps for all true poets, old and new)? Chiefly, I think, that their poetic language was wholly given to the service of their theme; it was functional, free from superfluous ornamentation and rhetorical display. He claims that they approached the theme of love with a new inwardness and awe, determined to communicate their notions of love with the utmost immediacy, not to waste words on anything that did not flow directly from them. They tried to make style organically one with content. *Dolce* conveys this dedicated aptness of the style: it is the strong and candid sweetness of Cimabue, not that cloying sweetness, heavy with artifice, which the pre-Raphaelites imagined. As an eleventh-century Italian rhetorician had written, 'We call it sweetness when we impel the reader's spirit in accordance with the theme that is being treated', and as Dante himself wrote in his essay on vernacular diction, it is a question of avoiding 'useless equivocation, which always seems to detract from meaning'.

Long before Dante's invention of the term, however, the poets of the *dolce stil novo* had, especially through Cavalcanti's powerful personal influence, felt themselves to have poetic aims in common. They were members of a new intellectual and urban élite, and wrote their lyrics for this society, for the cultivated young women in it, but even more perhaps for one another; they seem convinced that their poetry would be scarcely fathomable by the rest of mankind. This comes out particularly in the songs in which these poets try to define the essence of love, songs that at times presuppose a range of intellectual reference such as no earlier lyrical poet had counted on. Paradoxically, the two most difficult and demanding of these songs became the most celebrated and influential of all: Guido Guinizelli's *Al cor gentil rimpaira sempre amore*, and Guido Cavalcanti's *Donna me prega*.

Guinizelli's canzone is a passionate affirmation of the value of love. By a chain of images from physics and metaphysics, linked by subtle associations and verbal echoes, he argues that human love is an essential function of human excellence. This excellence or nobility (*gentilezza*) is open to all mankind, it has nothing to do with birth; fundamental to it is the capacity to love. In succeeding stanzas Guido tries to characterise a man's experience of how a woman brings his love to full realisation. It is like the 'influence' of a star—a higher power determining one's being from within; it is like receiving and responding to the warmth and radiance of the sun; it is an acquiescence in her being and her wishes, so effortless that it is experienced not as obedience but as harmonious oneness. This experience of moving in serene harmony with the beloved has something more than human about it—in this the lovers are like the angels of the spheres, whose harmonious movement expresses their oneness with God. It is this wonderful conception of love that enables Guido confidently to argue, at the end of his canzone, that human love cannot be incompatible with love of God:

Lady, suppose God says to me, when my soul is before him, 'Have you not been presumptuous? You have traversed heaven and come at last to me, yet you sought me in vain love, by way of a semblance: it is to me the praise is due, and to the queen of the blessed realm, through whom all deception ceases'—I shall be able to say to him, 'She had the aspect of an angel from your kingdom: it was no sin if I set my love in her!'

Cavalcanti's *Donna me prega* is a darker song: he too is in the last resort certain of the worth of human love, but for him it is a certainty *despite*, rather than a certainty *because*. In five long, lightly-moving stanzas, dazzling in the virtuosity of their echoing rhymes, Cavalcanti argues the nature and effects of love. He claims that his dialectic is a 'demonstration' in the field of natural philosophy, and indeed this song came to be treated as a *quaestio disputata* and was furnished with learned Latin commentaries. In the opening stanza the poet, in real or

imaginary response to a lady's request, sets up an eight-point programme of enquiry, and these points are then treated in due order, one
in each of the eight half-stanzas that follow. Where is love's place? In
the sensitive part of the soul, where memory is—but it is conditioned
by an energy of vehemence, an influence descending from the planet
Mars, where the fullness of the divine light has already been much
diminished in its descent. Who brings love about? The beloved, whose
form is seen and enters the lover's mind. And yet in the mind this form
can never be truly known—the lover, for all his absorption, cannot, as
long as he loves, know whether it corresponds to the reality of the
woman he saw. Love is inspired by 'a form that is seen' (*forma veduta*),
but once the lover is committed 'the form cannot be seen, and so even
less the love proceeding from it' (*forma non si vede: dunqu' elli meno,
che da lei procede*): love itself is invisible. The paradox begun in the
second stanza is completed in the fifth, with the last question: can love
be shown visibly? Between them, other questions are answered, describing the characteristics and effects of love, which underline the
fateful nature of the paradox. To what faculty of the soul does love
belong? To sensation: that is why it can unbalance judgment and make
will prevail over reason. What is love's power? It can cause a man to
die; it wars against that serene and harmonious mode of being which
alone deserves the name 'human life'. What is its essence? Unbridled-
ness and lack of measure, restlessness, lamentation, fear, instability; in
an aside, recalling his predecessor, Cavalcanti adds that it most affects
those whose hearts are noblest. What are the impulses love brings
about? Sighs, and moments of furious desperation and helplessness.

After so much pessimism Cavalcanti asks, what gain or contentment
(*piacimento*) can love give—what, in effect, makes it deserve to be
called love? The knowledge that one's love is returned, the loving
looks of a woman who, unafraid and with radiant openness, can
promise love's fulfilment. Then the darker mood, the sense of the un-
knowable in love, prevails once more. Love 'lacks colour'—it cannot
be physically perceived; it is 'cut off from being': it is not a substance
but an accident, a quality inhering in the sensitive part of the soul,
which is dark, which lacks the light of reason. And yet, Guido affirms,
flaunting a final paradox, it is precisely out of this darkness that something beautiful, love's reward, is born: he characterises love as

> For di colore, d'essere diviso,
> assiso—'n mezzo scuro, luce rade;
> for d'ogne fraude—dico, degno in fede,
> che solo di costui nasce mercede.

Without colour or being of its own,
set in a dark place, it shuts out the light;
beyond all fraud I say, deserving faith,
from this alone is born merciful grace.

The poem concludes with an envoy filled with sparkling artistic self-confidence:

Tu puoi sicuramente gir, canzone,
là 've ti piace, ch'io t'ho sì adornata
ch'assai laudata—sarà tua ragione
da le persone—c'hanno intendimento:
di star con l'altre tu non hai talento.

You can walk with assurance, my canzone,
wherever you please, for I have graced you so
that those who understand your argument
will welcome you with all the praise you need.
You have no wish to stay with any others.

Is *Donna me prega* the masterpiece that its author claimed, and as which it was often regarded not only by Guido's contemporaries but right up to the Renaissance, in the circle of Lorenzo dei Medici? It is a performance of astonishing intellectual and verbal dexterity; as for its analysis of love, I would suggest not that it is over-conceptualised, as some critics have claimed, but that Cavalcanti has here used his conceptual equipment ingeniously rather than profoundly—the effect in the last resort is of brittleness as well as excitement, of strained preciosity as well as brilliance. At the close, however, we glimpse the poet not only as virtuoso but as a human being, prickly yet also magnanimous, and in this can still feel something of the spell that he cast on his friends.

With the Florentine group as with the Sicilian, it is important to stress the full artistic range. These poets delighted not only in *dolcezza* but also in a wider, more flexible poetic language. Many of their songs and sonnets constitute a verse correspondence filled with topical wit and private allusion, in a language that is often informal, colloquial or satirical, with a vivacity and vigour of its own. Again, from Guinizelli onwards we find the sonnet being used not only for the high flights of love but for some delightful experiments in stylised comedy and burlesque:

Whoever has seen Lucia in her fur hat,
grey and white fur, and seen how well it suits her,
whoever he is, from here to the Abruzzi,
I know he'd take it in his heart to love her.

> That dappled hat gives her a foreign air,
> she seems a daughter of France or Germany—
> and not a serpent's head that's been chopped off
> quivers as I do for her, frequently . . .

With the Sienese Cecco Angiolieri, who was a slightly older friend of Dante's and wrote a witty riposte to one of Dante's most exalted sonnets for Beatrice, such experimentation is carried a stage further: Cecco creates his own sophisticated comic mask and comic world, a world whose language is that of Plautine and Terentian comedy brilliantly transformed into an Italian and contemporary mode:

> 'Becchina, love!'   'What do you want, false traitor?'
> 'That you forgive me.'   'No, you don't deserve it.'
> 'Mercy, for God's sake!'   'You're becoming humble.'
> 'And always will be.'   'What assurance have I?'
>
> 'My loyalty.'   'You've not much of that, have you?'
> 'Towards you I have.'   'Stop fooling—don't I know it!'
> 'How have I failed?'   'You know I've heard about it.'
> 'Tell me, my love.'   'Off with you, plague upon you!'
>
> 'Want me quite dead?'   'A thousand years will do me.'
> 'You are unkind.'   'I'm sure you'll teach me better.'
> 'And I shall die.'   'Oh God, what a deceiver!'
>
> 'May God forgive you.'   'What, you haven't gone yet?'
> 'If only I could!'   'Keeping you back now, am I?'
> 'You keep my heart.'   'I'll keep it—doing penance!'

To perceive the remarkable imaginative and linguistic scope of Italian lyric before Dante is not to diminish Dante's own creative contribution. From the start his lyrics had a narrative power scarcely paralleled in those of his friends: even in the brief compass of a sonnet Dante could convey his experiences of love as a coherent pattern of events, and show us these events as taking place in mind and senses simultaneously. Moreover, by placing many of the songs of his youth in the prose romance setting of the *Vita nuova* he made them part of a haunting personal mystery, gave them a dimension that sets them apart from the earlier lyrics of the Florentine circle. But the culmination of Dante's lyrical powers came later—the poetry he wrote between the *Vita nuova* and the *Commedia* includes at least four songs that in their different ways have permanently widened the boundaries of what lyric can be and can achieve. One of these canzoni (*Amor che nella mente mi ragiona*) is an exultant celebration of the 'Donna gentile'

F

of Dante's mind, Philosophy; two (*Tre donne intorno al cor mi son venute*, and *Amor, da che convien pur ch'io mi doglia*) are meditations and visions from the depth of his exile; and one (*Così nel mio parlar voglio esser aspro*) is a song addressed to a loved woman:

1. I want to be as harsh in what I speak
   as is this lovely stone in all her acts,
   she who at all times seeks
   for greater hardness and a cruder being
   and clothes her person in a jasper-stone
   so that because of it, or her withdrawal,
   no quiver can let fly
   an arrow that can penetrate her naked;
   she kills, and it is vain to arm oneself
   or move out of the range of deadly blows
   which, as if winged,
   land where they will, leave every weapon smashed—
   I have no means, no power, to shield myself from her!

2. I find no shield she does not cleave apart,
   no place that may conceal me from her sight,
   for, just as flower crowns leaf,
   she occupies the summit of my mind.
   She seems as much affected by my pain
   as ships are by a sea where no wave stirs,
   and the weight that makes me sink
   is such it could not find its match in verse.
   Oh you tormenting, pitiless file
   that wear away my life insensibly,
   why have you no restraint,
   devouring layer on layer of my heart,
   as I'm restrained from saying who gives you force?

3. For my heart trembles more whenever I think
   of her there where another man may gaze
   (for fear my thoughts
   may be transparent and betray themselves)
   than ever I tremble at Death, who already gnaws
   each of my senses with the fangs of Love—
   that is, whose bite so tears
   the mind itself that all its powers fail.
   He has dashed me to the ground, stands over me
   with the same sword with which he murdered Dido,
   Love, to whom I wail
   crying for mercy and beseeching humbly
   while he seems bent on banishing all mercy.

4. From time to time he lifts his hand and makes
   my feeble life despair—that perverse Love
   who keeps me stretched
   prostrate upon the ground, too weak to move:
   then in imagination screams arise,
   the blood that is dispersed throughout the veins,
   fleeing, invades
   the heart, which cries for it, and I'm left white.
   He strikes me under my left arm so hard
   the pain reverberates within the heart;
   then I say 'If he lifts
   his hand once more, Death will have shut me in
   even before the blow itself comes down.'

5. If I could see her heart thus rent asunder
   by Love, her cruel heart that quarters mine,
   I'd feel no grimness then
   in the death to which her beauty makes me run.
   She strikes as much in shadow as in sun,
   that violent, deadly murderess.
   Oh why does she not howl
   for me, as I for her, in the hot abyss?
   For I would soon cry out 'I'll comfort you';
   I'd do it willingly, and thus, into
   the golden hair
   that Love has waved and gilded to consume me
   I'd plunge my hand, and then please her at last.

6. Once I had taken hold of those fair tresses
   that have become a whip and lash for me,
   I'd catch them as day breaks and spend
   vespers and compline in their company.
   And I'd not show pity or courtesy,
   no, I would play in jest as a bear does;
   and if Love takes those locks to whip me,
   I'd avenge myself with more than a thousand blows.
   What's more, I'd gaze into her eyes
   that unleash sparks that make my dead heart blaze,
   with close, fixed gaze,
   to take revenge on her elusiveness;
   and then with making love I'd grant her peace.

7. My song, go to that woman straight
   who has struck my heart and robs me
   of what I hunger most for:
   go, plunge an arrow in her heart—
   sweet honour is won in carrying out revenge.

At the time that Dante wrote this canzone the *topoi* of the complaining lover—the arrows with which the love-god pierces him, the torments and wounds and slow death which Amor and the lady herself inflict on him, the lady's unyielding mercilessness—had been exploited so much and become so well worn that it might have seemed scarcely conceivable that something new could still be said by way of them. Though less common, there were also other accepted associations between love and pain—such as those of 'a lover's pinch that hurts, and is desired'. Dante here relies on both these types of love-language, the emotional and the physical: magnifying and intensifying them almost to cracking-point, he relates them and welds them together. Where the cruelty and unyielding rigour of the beloved had been at worst a cliché and at best a sensitive projection of a man's role in love, Dante probes into the cruel woman's part, or even for the first time truly creates it. She is no longer merely the postulate of a certain poetic genre, we are suddenly confronted with new questions, questions about her—what sort of person could this cruel fair one be? How does her mind work? What are her feelings? Is she cold or sensual? Is she testing her lover's sincerity, or does she enjoy seeing him suffer?

Dante begins by declaring the resolve which emerges fully at the poem's climax—to match the beloved's harshness with harshness of his own. Not only in his language and style, but in his whole fantasy of love as revenge. The humble lover whose merciless mistress can do with him what she will had often been satirised—it is in such a context, for instance, that the troubadour Raimbaut d'Orange had recommended harshness to the lover—but Dante carries Raimbaut's thought through on a very different plane. This is already hinted at, I believe, from the third line: the woman at all times demands and achieves (*impetra*) a greater hardness in herself. The word *impetra* may also suggest, she turns her hardness into stone within her. There is the further implication in the third and fourth lines that her hardness is a challenge to the submissive lover: she is longing to be met with hardness too. But she is armed against any dart of love—Dante expresses this commonest of thoughts with a turn of phrase that gives it a new, vehement sensuality, emphasised by the final words 'la colga ignuda': these are not simply arrows that, if they landed, might touch her heart (induce a change of feelings), but arrows which should penetrate her naked body.

So too her resistance is not pictured passively—it is an active, deadly warfare, aimed not simply at warding off the lover's advances but at reducing him to utter helplessness. The overtones of the language at the opening of the second stanza suggest it would be as impossible for him to escape from this attack as for the soul to escape from God (compare, for instance, the range of expressions in Psalm 138 [A.V. 139], 7 ff.). The sense of the beloved's awesome power passes into a moment of lyrical exultation accepting this power, then at once into bitter irony at the sovereign indifference with which the power is used, and then into an outcry against the waste of life it causes. At the end of the second and opening of the third stanza a new theme is sounded, with an intense hypersensitiveness that is Dante's own. Many love-poets protest their unswerving secrecy in never disclosing their lady's name, but Dante in the *Vita Nuova* had given unique expression to his mortal fear that his love for Beatrice might unwittingly become apparent in public, and to the fantastic lengths to which he went to guard against this. For him it was a matter of life and death—there, lest he offended against his high ideal of love, here, lest his desperate thoughts should be revealed. The word *morte* releases a new series of images of the lover being tortured by a slow death. The language is, as Dante promised at the outset, harsh (*aspro*): these are among the most extreme and painful images of love's torments in medieval lyric. Beginning in the second stanza with the file that wears away the lover's heart layer after layer (*a scorza a scorza*), they come to a climax in the fourth stanza, when the torturer (who is almost indistinguishably Love or Death, and ultimately a projection of the woman herself), beats and stabs an exhausted, prostrate body.

Are these images mere extravagances, taking a convention to a hyperbolic extreme? The answer is given in the last two stanzas, where Dante develops a complementary sexual fantasy, one which is not only emotional but physical and in which the woman becomes an emotional and physical being in her own right—previously her existence was defined only through what she, or the love of her, did to Dante. Her cruelty is too vehement to be a mere sign of cold indifference, it must be a perverse expression of a fiery sensuality. This is the basis of Dante's fantasy—if only the passionate ardour that takes the guise of passionate cruelty could be revealed for what it is, the lover could meet it with a fierceness that would match her own, and in which she would find a satisfaction such as no man's submissiveness could ever give her.

The sixth stanza is a counterpart to the fourth, a vision of the woman's (or Love's) cruelty 'avenged' by her lover.[1] But where before

---

1. I believe that all the terms of 'revenge', of treating the beloved as a slave and an enemy to be subjugated, are images of a specifically *erotic* fantasy. Both the close of the fifth stanza (*e piacere' le allora*) and the close of the sixth (*e poi le renderei con amor pace* —which I would interpret with Friedrich as the consummation of physical love, not with Contini as merely 'forgiving her and restoring her to my love') suggest to me that the 'revenge' scene that comes between these lines is essentially an erotic encounter, conceived as bringing violent sensual delight to both lovers. The peace is the quieting both of her cruel war against him and of the restless sexual dissatisfaction which caused his aggression.

the images had evoked the woman's total subjection of her lover's mind, now with the 'revenge' it is a question of the lover's domination not only of her mind but of her body and senses. Here the cruelty is inseparable from the rough fierceness of love-play. The revenge would lie in making love from earliest morning till latest night, violent love, in which the lover playfully and sensually, with countless blows, 'tames' his turbulent beloved, subjugates her with his determined gaze, and brings her peace in the consummation of love.

All the intolerable strain that social and literary convention put on a truly passionate man and woman could be overcome in an instant by a brave affirmation of what the conventions hide. Two centuries earlier Guillaume of Aquitaine had exclaimed, or pleaded—

> Lady, we can have
> the whole world's joy if we both love!

The same thought impels Dante's subtle envoy. The canzone which he is now sending *is* his 'revenge': it can become the arrow thrust in the woman's heart, the one thing that may shatter her defences and lay bare to her the secret feelings that she had been afraid to face, feelings that no merely submissive complaint could liberate. It could make real the whole fantasy to which Dante had been spurred by the thought 'If I could see *her* heart thus rent asunder/by Love . . .'. If it touches her to the quick, it will be both revenge and honourable victory, a triumph of love.

Dante has taken the language of the suffering courtly lover's complaint and intensified it till it reached a mythical dimension, and then has found its necessary counterpart and conclusion in an exciting sensual fantasy. The first moves to the brink of unreality, where it is suddenly lit up by the incandescent power of the second. Together these form an exploration of the torments of love which is perhaps the most prodigious achievement in the medieval love-lyric.

5

THE *ALBA*[1]

The love-lyrics we have considered until now have been concerned mostly with the state of being of men or women in love. There is another range of love-songs in the Middle Ages that have a more objective, narrative or dramatic, frame, songs that grow out of imagined events rather than an imagined state. The majority of these songs can be grouped in two principal genres—*alba* and *pastorela*, as they came to be called in Provence.

In both *alba* and *pastorela* we are shown the encounter of a pair of lovers. In the *alba* their meeting and their parting are expected; in the *pastorela* these belong to chance. The *alba* shows a secret meeting: the lovers meet by night (or occasionally at the point of dawn), they know that the coming of day will cut short their joys, and that the very quality and poignancy of their love is conditioned by this. Daylight brings back the claims of the real, waking world, which both lovers must acknowledge; it is the background against which secret love has beauty.

The *pastorela*, by contrast, shows a meeting in the open, in broad daylight. It is not prearranged. Where in the *alba* the lover has already gained the woman's love, in the *pastorela* she has still to be won: it has more the character of a seduction, or battle between the sexes (and this is most often accentuated by a social difference—the man is a sophisticate, the girl, as the name of the genre indicates, a country lass). The situation in the *alba* holds no surprises: from the start the beauty of

1. This chapter was completed before the appearance of Professor A. T. Hatto's valuable symposium *Eos* (The Hague, 1965). I have allowed the passages where my conclusions diverge from his (e.g. on the significance of *Phebi claro*) to stand unchanged: in the present context it would have been impossible to add a detailed scholarly discussion such as this important work deserves.

meeting and the anguish of parting are fully known. The *pastorela*, by contrast, often keeps us guessing till the close: who will win the skirmish, he or she? Will she refuse him, or yield to him at last?

Songs of both kinds have existed in many ages and places—as indeed both kinds of meeting have in real life. Certain elements in both genres seem to recur spontaneously, others to become stylised in a particular tradition. It is often almost impossible to demarcate these. Scholars in the past have suggested, for instance, that the *alba* in medieval Europe began as a woman's soliloquy, and that this developed later into a dialogue between two lovers. Finally, at some time in the twelfth century, it was said, a third character was added to the scene —the *gaita*, who keeps watch for the lovers against the lady's jealous husband, and warns them at dawn when they must part. Attempts have even been made at dating *albas* according to this principle—earlier if there is no mention of *gaita* or *gelos*, later if there is. Even from the very limited material that can be cited and discussed in this chapter, it will become evident that such a linear, evolutionary notion of the genre is without foundation. Ideally, to see the full extent of its inadequacy we should have to extend our discussion beyond medieval Europe—to show, for instance, that the jealous husband is mentioned in a Greek *alba* of the second century A.D., the watchman in a Chinese one of the fifth. So too in Arabic poetry of the seventh century it is the crier, the muezzin, who warns the sleeping lovers of the coming of dawn. Again, in China two *albas* in dialogue form survive from the sixth century B.C. —at least a thousand years before the first surviving Chinese dawn soliloquy. One of these ancient dawn-dialogues, beautifully translated by Arthur Waley, seems to me particularly illuminating in relation to the European *alba* tradition:

The Lady:	The cock has crowed; it is full daylight.
The Lover:	It was not the cock that crowed, it was the buzzing of those green flies.
The Lady:	The eastern sky glows; it is broad daylight.
The Lover:	That is not the glow of dawn, but the rising moon's light. The gnats fly drowsily; it would be sweet to share a dream with you.
The Lady:	Quick! Go home! Lest I have cause to hate you!

It turns on the conflict between the sweet deception and reality, with the inevitable victory—for the time—of the outer world of day. In this it foreshadows, in astonishing detail, one of the most moving *albas* in western literature, the farewell of Shakespeare's Romeo and Juliet. In Shakespeare it is the girl who first prolongs the love-fantasy: 'Wilt thou be gone? It is not yet near day.' In both *albas* there is the progression in urgency from the moment of the first dawn harbinger, the bird, when doubt is still conceivable ('It was the nightingale, and not the lark'), to the expanse of light, when doubt is on the brink of absurdity ('Yon light is not daylight, I know it, I'), to the final necessary acceptance of the 'truth' of light. In both it is the woman who is ultimately the first to dispel the illusion, to accept the day unflinchingly ('It is, it is; hie hence, be gone away! . . .').

The anonymous Chinese poet quite unmistakably portrays the same emotional and imaginative world as was known to the poets of the medieval European *alba*, and to Shakespeare as the inheritor of a medieval tradition. Paradoxically, the oldest surviving *albas* in a European language, the Hellenistic ones preserved in the Greek Anthology, are of a wholly different tone and spirit, graceful but artificial and cold:

> Loveless dawn, why do you rise so swiftly over my bedroom,
>   where till this moment I felt the warmth of dear Demo's skin?
> If only you'd reverse your swift course and be Hesperos,
>   you who shed the sweet light that is so bitter to me!
> Indeed once before you went backwards: for Jove and Alcmena—
>   it's not as if you didn't know how to turn roundabout!

This *alba* by Meleager (*c.* 140–*c.* 70 B.C.), for instance, consists primarily in the elegant unfolding of a conceit. The complaint is witty, not emotionally intense. Meleager alludes to the myth of Alcmena not because it gives him faith as lover, but because it gives an edge to his device of juggling with impossibilities. The outcry of Chaucer's Criseyde at the first dawn she faces with her lover Troilus, containing the same allusion, affords a sharp contrast:

> O nyght, allas! why nyltow over us hove,
> As longe as whan Almena lay by Jove?

Criseyde makes no pretence at hoping dawn will not come: this parting is too serious for her to pretend.

It is unlikely that the *albas* of medieval Europe owe their existence to the survival and adaptation of a Hellenistic literary motif. Rather, they seem to be a 'genuine progeny of common humanity': while vernacular European *albas* were not written down till relatively late, there are a number of indications that love-songs with a dawn theme were traditional and popular in Romance-speaking areas long before we have written records of them. A remarkable Latin dawn-song with a Provençal refrain survives in a late tenth-century manuscript (the melody is given below, p. 237):

> When Phoebus's bright beam has not yet risen,
> Aurora brings her slender light to earth;
> a watchman shouts to slumberers 'Arise!'
> > Dawn graces   the dank sea,
> > draws forth the sun,
> > then passes.   Oh watchman,
> > look how the dark   grows bright!
>
> Our lurking enemies are bursting forth
> to intercept the idle and the rash—
> the herald pleads and calls on them to rise.
> > Dawn graces   the dank sea ...
>
> From Arcturus the north wind is released,
> the stars of heaven hide their radiance,
> the Plough is drawn towards the eastern sky.
> > Dawn graces   the dank sea ...

Many aspects of this song are controversial, above all the refrain,[1] and my suggestions towards an interpretation can only be tentative. It seems clear to me at least that the song as it stands is not a lovers' *alba*. The enemies dashing out of ambush are not a host of jealous husbands; to imagine them as spying on a kind of *maison close* filled with 'idle and rash' lovers would be to reduce the song to farce. The guard and herald are soldiers, and it is a military ambush for which they are sounding the alarm. But are the enemies also human soldiers? Or possibly demons, whose attacks are described in military terms, and against whom the bravest and most vigilant souls warn the weaker *milites Christi*? Convincing parallels for either interpretation can be

---

1. It seems to me unnecessary to emend the MS. I construe the lines as:

> L'alba par'   umet mar,
> atra sol,
> poy pas'.—   A bigil,
> mira clar   tenebras!

Twice in the refrain the MS has *Lalba part*. . . . This would be 'Dawn appears . . .'. But the rhymes *mar, clar* suggest that *part* may be only a copyist's slip.

found: on the one hand in a watchmen's song composed at Modena in 892, when a Hungarian invasion was threatening—

> Oh you who guard these ramparts with your arms,
> do not sleep, I entreat you, but keep watch . . .

or again in the ancient Norse *Bjarkamál*, when the warriors of Hrólf kraki are roused to defend his hall—a lay recited before St Óláfr's last battle in Norway in 1030—

> Day has arisen,
> the cock's wings are beating,
> it is time for labourers
> to shoulder their task.
> Wake, wake,
> finest of friends . . .
> I do not wake you for wine
> or for women's love-whispering—
> no, I wake you
> for the savage game of war!

A 'psychological' interpretation of the military attack could find support in an older tradition of Christian dawn-songs, going back to Ambrose and Prudentius in the fourth century. For Prudentius, it is Christ who, at the first light of dawn, summons mankind to vigilance:

> Take away these beds, for they
> belong to sickness, sleep and sloth! . . .
> Keep watch, for I am near at hand!

Even if, as I believe, the immediate reference in the Latin–Provençal *alba* is to a physical battle, this spiritual perspective seems also to be present, enriching the words by its associations. The structure itself of the Latin lines would support this: spiritual connotations are at least latent in the dominant contrast between heaven and earth. The two opening lines evoke the sky's serenity; then the first note of peril on earth is sounded. In the second stanza the earthly dangers are conveyed with greater urgency. After this the last stanza seems almost inconsequential: the troubles of the soldiers are forgotten, dawn ends its serene progress, as if to say that, whatever turmoil there may be on earth, heaven continues its distant motions undisturbed.

Against the long Latin lines is set the swift, incisive Provençal

refrain (seven trisyllables in the original). Musically there is a marked
contrast: the long lines are sung each to the same melody, while each
phrase of the refrain has new notes. The refrain sounds vivid and
excited, the strophes, even when describing danger, are measured and
imperturbable. Was the refrain composed by the author of the Latin
lines? I think not. There is a small but telling discrepancy between
stanzas and refrain. In the stanzas the watcher addresses the sleepers, in
the refrain—unless this is radically emended—the watcher himself is
addressed. Who could be addressing the watcher? Not one of the
drowsy soldiers, surely? Dozens of later *albas* give a better answer—all
those *albas*, in fact, that consist of a dialogue between the watcher and
one of the two lovers, who see and speak of the dawn together while
the other lies asleep. It seems likeliest to me that the Provençal lines
come from just such an *alba*, and were adapted by the Latin poet to
his more exalted composition, for the sake of a pleasing musical
contrast and greater popular appeal. It is possible that a popular
tradition of erotic *albas* went back to the very beginnings of Romance
patois, and that the dawn-songs of Ambrose and Prudentius were
themselves a learned and sacred rejoinder to a vogue of profane *albas*
that have not survived in writing. But even if such hypotheses are too
audacious, the precious and difficult lines of our refrain point unmistakably to the existence of vernacular *albas* in the tenth century.
And there is no reason whatever why these should have been Europe's
first.

In the eleventh century we have proof of the existence of early
Romance *albas* from the Spanish side, once more among the Mozarabic
kharjas (see above, p. 86). Though these are notoriously difficult of
interpretation, their evidence cannot be brushed aside.[1] The girl, at
the moment of expecting her lover, rails at dawn (28):

Vay, ya sahhara,	Go away, sorceress,
Alba, qu'est con bel fogore!	Dawn, with your fiery beauty!
Cand vene, vedes amore!	When he comes, you see our love!

She confides in her mother (36):

Non dormiray, mamma,	Mother, I shall not sleep
a rayo de manyana—	in the morning's beam—
bon Abu 'l-Qasim	dear Abu 'l-Qasim
la faǧe de matrana!	is the face of my dawn!

1. Especially in the *kharjas* cited here, the verbal forms with apocope (*est*, *vene* in
28, *qued* in 25) are doubtful and have no decisive parallels elsewhere among the *kharjas*;
but no better alternatives have so far been proposed.

Or again, she consoles her lover with the thought that, when the night guard has had his fill of watching, they will still be able to snatch a time together (25):

Alba qued, meu fogore,	The dawn remains ours, my brightness,
alma de meu ledore—	soul of my joy—
bastando li-l raquibe	long enough for the spy
esta noḥte, [o] amore!	is this night, my beloved!

The role of dawn in these songs is unusual for an *alba*. It seems that here the lovers cannot lie together all night, only 'in the uncertain hour before the morning'. So the girl's attitude to dawn in the first of these *kharjas* is ambiguous: she needs dawn, the enchantress who brings the lover to her, but she fears and dislikes her too—this witch who stays, peeping at the lovers like a bawd, and reminding them by her very presence that the time for love is brief. If only she would bring the lover and then just disappear! In the second *kharja* the girl, lying awake in the first light of morning, awaits dawn eagerly: dawn is for her identified with the lover whose coming will make her radiant.

An eleventh-century Latin hand has written on a blank page of a theological manuscript at Sankt-Florian some words that are unmistakably the opening of a Latin lovers' *alba*:

Cantant omnes volucres,	All the birds are singing,
iam lucescit dies.	already day is dawning.
Amica cara, surge sine me	Rise, dear love, to go out
per portas exire!	through the doors without me!

Here it is the lady who has visited her (presumably clerical) lover, and who must creep out (of an oratory or cloister?) alone at dawn so as not to be seen. But one can also (by reading *sine* as an imperative, '*permit me* to go out through the doors') allow a different construction: that he is asking her to rise, not so much perhaps to give him leave to part (which she could do without stirring) as to help him out, closing the doors silently after him. A second stanza follows, too garbled to interpret with any certainty.

The simplest of the surviving Provençal *albas* is as brief as the Spanish and Latin ones (I see no reason to assume it is fragmentary, as many scholars do):

Quan lo rossinhols escria	When the nightingale, beside his mate,
ab sa par la nueg e·l dia,	heralds the night and the day,
yeu suy ab ma bell' amia	I lie with my fair beloved
jos la flor,	on the flowers,

tro la gaita de la tor	till the watchman on the tower
escria: 'Drutz, al levar!	cries 'Lovers, awaken!
qu'ieu vey l'alba e·l jorn	I see the dawn, the bright day
clar!'	breaking!'

All the other *albas* in Provençal are far more extensive, and more obviously products of a refined poetic art. Yet at least one aspect of the little nightingale *alba* also betrays a highly developed poetic technique: namely its syntax. The stanza is carved out of one piece; the thoughts are ordered and unified in a single, beautifully proportioned sentence, in which the principal clause is preceded by one temporal clause and followed by another, which itself serves as a frame for the imperative and explanatory clauses of the climax.

On the same page in the same (fourteenth-century) *chansonnier* as this song is one of the best known of all medieval *albas*, *En un vergier sotz fuella d'albespi*. Despite the great popularity of this song in modern times, its elements and structure have not yet, to my knowledge, been convincingly explained.

Deep in an orchard, under hawthorn leaves,
the lady holds her lover in her arms,
until the watcher cries, he sees the dawn.
Dear God, the daybreak! oh how soon it comes!

'If only God let night stay without end,
and my beloved never left my side,
and never again the guard saw day or dawn—
dear God, the daybreak! oh how soon it comes!

'Let us kiss, sweet beloved, you and I,
down in the meadows where the birds now sing—
defy my jealous husband and do all!
Dear God, the daybreak! oh how soon it comes!

'Let us create new love-sports, sweet beloved,
down in the meadows where the birds now sing—
until the watcher plays his pipe again.
Dear God, the daybreak! oh how soon it comes!

'In the sweet wind that came to me from there
I drank a ray of my beloved's breath,
my fair and joyous, gracious lover's breath—
dear God, the daybreak! oh how soon it comes!'

The lady is delightful, lovable,
admired by many for her beauty's sake,
and holds her heart most loyally in love.
Dear God, the daybreak! oh how soon it comes!

It looks as if there is nothing unusual about the opening stanza, which sets the scene. The lady's monologue, which fills the four following stanzas, begins with great intensity: it is not merely an asseveration but a prayer. Like so many lovers in medieval literature, she is convinced that God is on the side of human love. She prays for God's extraordinary favour, though the refrain, now part of her own lament, shows she is asking for the impossible, and knows it. Then she invites the lover in the tones of a *mal mariée* (*tot o fassam en despieg del gilos*), with deliberate sensual provocation in the fourth stanza (*fassam un joc novel*). I know of no other *alba* in which the lady seduces in this way. The language is not that of *albas*—it is echoing the Song of Songs (I translate from the Latin Vulgate):

> Come, my lover, let us go into the field . . .
> at dawn let us wake near the vines . . .
> There I will give you my breasts.
> Within my gates lies every fruit—
> new and old I have kept for you, my love.

Then comes the startling development of the fifth stanza, a mood of mystical meditation, and suddenly we realise that the lady is alone. It is a *memory* of that orchard which has stirred her with such physical force that it seemed she was drinking in her lover's presence with the wind. The image of the wind as messenger of the beloved, which occurs elsewhere too in troubadour poetry, derives not, as has recently been argued, from Arabic poets (though indeed they also use it), but once more from the Song of Songs:

> Awake, north wind, and come, south wind,
> breathe upon my garden . . .
> let my lover descend into his garden,
> and let him devour the flesh of its fruits.

It is from the Biblical love-song above all that this poet has learnt to pass imperceptibly from the meeting of the lovers to the memories and longings of the woman alone, from event to daydream, outer to inner world. This was already anticipated by a subtlety in the opening stanza: the use of the present tense. It is generalised and not time-bound; if the scene had been set in the past, it could only have described one (external) occasion.

The last stanza, the commendation of the lady, may seem an enigma or even an anticlimax. No other *alba* ends in this way. One might be tempted to ask, does this stanza belong organically with the rest, or could it be a later addition? I think the poet found it necessary to conclude in such a way. He has presented a woman glowing with life and passionate, but very different from the accepted 'portrait of a lady' in his society. That is why he ends by deliberately insisting on her courtly qualities, affirming that she is all that a *domna* should be. He is, one might say, forestalling objections: she is not impious in invoking God, not unrefined in spiting her husband, not unbecomingly lascivious in luring her lover; she is perfect, even by courtly standards. It is the achievement of this *alba* to have invaded the narrower world of *courtoisie* with the sensual and dreamlike qualities of the Song of Songs.

Guiraut de Borneil's *alba*, another of the most famous, likewise opens with an invocation to God. But here it is the watcher who sings.

> Glorious king, true light and radiance,
> most mighty God and Lord, be gracious now,
> hold my companion in your constant care—
> I have not seen him since the night came on,
> and soon it will be dawn!

After this resplendent opening, the watcher continues in less exalted tones, waking his friend, warning him of danger, cajoling him to rise; he claims to have been on his knees praying for the lover's safety all night. The exaggeration turns into humorous reproach: it was you who imposed all this on me, and

> now you're displeased both with my songs and me,
> and soon it will be dawn!

The reproach at last stings the lover to reply,[1] and his stanza has a buoyant quality worthy of the opening lines:

> Fair, gentle friend, I've found so dear a home
> I wish that dawn might never come again;
> the loveliest lady ever born of woman
> lies in my arms, and I care not a straw
> for jealous fool or dawn!

Other troubadour *albas*, unknown except to a few specialists, also have great poetic vivacity. In an anonymous *alba* the lover bursts into rage against the *gaita* for disturbing the night of love: 'May God the son of Mary curse you!... If I could lay hands on you, I'd kill you over and over.' In an *alba* by the troubadour Cadenet (early thirteenth century), the *gaita* steals the scene: in four stanzas, beginning 'Eu sui

---

1. I believe that this stanza (found in only two of the seven MSS of the song) is authentic.

tan corteza guaita' ('I am such a courteous watchman'), he characterises himself, with a blend of humour and compassion for lovers that anticipates Chaucer's Pandarus. He has such sympathy with true love that he takes delight in the longest nights, even though they are the coldest and harshest for keeping watch. He would never let a friend down, for any threat or risk. But if ever he had to watch for false lovers, he would try to conceal the dawn as best he could!

While the *albas* of Provence have a special place in European poetry, the written evidence suggests that many more were composed in Germany than elsewhere in Europe. The oldest manuscript to preserve a German *alba* is the celebrated Codex Buranus (*c.* 1220), which contains six lines where a woman sings:

Ich sich den morgensterne brehen—	I see the day-star breaking forth—
nû, helt, lâ dich nicht gerne sehen!	now, my brave one, be sure you are not seen!
Vil liebe, dêst mîn rât.	Dear love, take my advice.
Swer tougenlîchen minnet,	What virtue lies
wie tugentlîch daz stât,	in a secret love
dâ friunschaft hûte hât!	over which friendship keeps watch!

These lines (which in my view are probably complete in themselves, not fragmentary)[1] stand out among medieval *albas* by their serenity: at the moment of farewell this woman does not cry out or lament; after she has warned her lover (and even in this her tone is gentle rather than urgent), she reflects only on the beauty of the love she shares with him. This love is beautiful to her because it is completely *courtois*: secret, full of *virtù*, protected by mutual friendship. The last line seems to be a deliberate transformation of the 'watcher' theme: these lovers need no external friend as guard, it is their own friendship which defends, not the castle-tower, but the quality of their love.

This earliest-recorded German *alba* presupposes an older tradition. Such a tradition does not survive except perhaps in one song, recorded in the later, Manesse manuscript, a song more archaic in its tone, the often quoted *Sláfest du, friedel ʒiere*. While some scholars have claimed that this *alba* was 'faked' at a relatively late period, I am convinced by those who see it as 'the oldest German *Tagelied*':

> 'Are you asleep, dearest one?
> They will wake us all too soon.
> A little bird, so fair to see,
> has perched on a branch of the linden-tree.'

1. So also, I have since noted, A. T. Hatto, *Eos*, p. 446.

'I had fallen asleep so gently—
now, little girl, you call and warn me.
Without pain there can be no love.
Whatever you command I'll do, dearest love.'

The lady began to moan.
'You ride off and leave me alone.
When will you next come back to me?
Oh, you are taking with you all my joy.'

What is special about this song lies neither in its thoughts nor its language. The thoughts are simple, even commonplace, the metre is somewhat rough, a phrase like 'so fair to see' (*sô wol getân*) a glaring fill-in for the sake of a rhyme. Yet there is something direct, truthful and touching here which more than compensates. The key to the poem's quality lies, I think, in the word *kint* in the sixth line.[1] The girl who speaks in the first stanza is still almost a child, chattering with excited curiosity. She does not yet know for herself what a leave-taking means. The knight answers almost irritably at first, then with weary resignation: he knows this is how secret love has always been. But his reliance on her at this moment—'whatever you command I'll do'—makes her suddenly feel a grown-up woman. In the last stanza she is not *kint* but *frouwe*. Suddenly she realises what loneliness will be hers, and her words, which from an experienced lover would sound banal, are moving because it is she who says them, discovering through them the universal feelings of women in love. The sparse words convey nothing but the essential; each sentence is a gesture made with grave simplicity.

Of the three greatest poets who wrote around the year 1200, Heinrich von Morungen and Walther von der Vogelweide each composed an *alba*, and Wolfram von Eschenbach composed no fewer than five. These five mark a turning-point in the literary development of the genre. Unlike the earlier twelfth-century *albas*, Wolfram's are written in complex canzone forms. This does not, paradoxically, make them seem more artificial: the formal elaboration is accompanied by an elaboration of realistic detail. Four of the five songs have a narrative thread; in one only the woman speaks, the others are dialogues between watcher and woman, watcher and man, man and woman respectively. The speakers are individualised by their words more subtly and fully than ever before. Moreover, Wolfram depicts not only the emotions

1. While MHG *kint* can suggest 'young woman' or 'young man' as well as 'child', I am convinced that the extreme youth, as well as the inexperience, of the girl are poetically important in the context of this poem (see discussion below).

but the behaviour of the lovers. He shows that their fears and griefs at parting are themselves the strongest possible erotic incentives, the farewells become high moments of sexual passion. The fifth of Wolfram's *albas* is a palinode, a farewell to the form itself: the poet bids the watchman to be silent—the love in which he has his role is as nothing compared to that love where no one 'need fly away from his beloved because of morning.... An open, sweet wife can give such love'.

Among the four *albas* proper, one stands out especially by its startling opening: the lady speaks:

> 'His claws have riven openings through the clouds,
> he is rising with great power,
> I see him grow grey, day-like, about to break—
> the day, who means to take
> companionship away from the fine man
> whom I so fearfully let in;
> I'll guide him back now, if I can—
> it was his many virtues bade me do it.'

Such a personification of dawn is unparalleled in the *alba*. The image 'dawns' only gradually: at first, for two lines, it is nothing but a cruel, monstrous animal of menacing strength—only in the third line does it grow 'day-like', only in the fourth does it explicitly become day itself. Thus Wolfram evokes the moments from numb apprehension to conscious fear in the lady's thoughts. She begins to make a practical resolution, but it is cut short: in her fear she feels the need for self-justification. In the next stanza she tries to bribe the watcher—for the sake of loyalty (*triuwe*)!—to pretend it is not day. He answers courteously but firmly—he has a different notion of what *triuwe* means. Once again the lady is touchingly disingenuous: 'My lover and I', she says, 'are always frightened at your call.' She reproaches the guard for often coming sooner than he need. Then the last stanza opens with another menacing image of light; her terror suddenly turns into reawakened desire, which overwhelms both lovers—a sensuality born out of the danger itself:

> At the lightnings that the day shot through the glass,
> as the watchman sang to warn,
> she felt panic for the man who lay with her. She pressed
> her little breasts against his breast.
> The knight did not forget his brave desire
> (which the guard's song tried to avert):
> by kiss and other ways, closer and closer,
> leave-taking yielded to them love's reward.

Heinrich von Morungen's *alba* is, like Wolfram's, astonishing in its
range of human insight; in its conception it is very different. There is
nothing dramatic, no meeting or parting of lovers, only memories,
images, and hopeless hopes. Lover and beloved speak alternate
stanzas, as if to each other, but they are not together. Each is standing
in empty space, his thoughts so filled with the other that they overflow;
yet the lovers cannot hear each other.

Owê, sol aber mir iemer mê
geliuhten dur die naht
noch wîzer danne ein snê
ir lîp vil wol geslaht?
der trouc diu ougen mîn:
ich wânde, ez solde sîn
des liehten mânen schîn.
dô taget ez.

Alas, shall her body never again
stream its light through the night for me?
—body whiter than snow,
formed so perfectly,
it deceived my sight:
I thought that it must be
a ray of the moon's light;
then the day came.

'Owê, sol aber er immer mê
den morgen hie betagen?
als uns diu naht engê,
daz wir niht durfen klagen:
"owê, nu ist ez tac",
als er mit klage pflac
do'r jungest bî mir lac.
dô taget ez.'

'Alas, shall he never again
greet daybreak here with me?
If night could pass away,
so that we need not cry
"alas, now it is day",
as was his way
when last he lay at my side.
Then the day came.'

Owê, si kuste âne zal
in deme slâfe mich.
dô vielen hin ze tal
ir trêne nidersich.
iedoch gedrôste ich sî,
daz si ir weinen lî
und mich al ummevî.
dô taget ez.

Alas, they were numberless,
her kisses as I slept.
Then to the ground would fall
the tears she wept;
and yet I solaced her,
that she, without a tear,
embraced me utterly.
Then the day came.

'Owê, daz er sô dicke sich
bî mir ersehen hât!
als er endahte mich,
sô wolte er sunder wât
mich armen schouwen blôz.[1]
ez was ein wunder grôz
daz in des nie verdrôz.
dô taget ez.'

'Alas that so often, gazing,
he lost himself in me,
uncovering me to gaze on
me, poor in my nakedness,
without a sheet, without a dress.
It was a miracle that he
could never tire of this.
Then the day came.'

---

1. I retain the widely accepted emendation *mich armen*. The two MSS have respectively *mîn arme* ('my arms') and *mîn armen*. Despite a recent scholar's ingenious attempt
to defend the reading *mîn arme*, I find the meaning 'to gaze on my naked arms' wholly
incongruous in Heinrich's context.

In the first pair of stanzas, filled with images of light, the thoughts of lover and beloved are dreamlike wishes; in the second pair, filled with tender sensual detail, they are physical memories, painful and blissful at the same time. The first stanza plays on the theme of reality and illusion in the three kinds of light—moonlight, daylight, and the radiance of the beloved's body. Then the lady in her stanza accepts the reality of daylight—but by means of another illusion, by imagining a day of sheer light, 'the morning when the long night dissolves' (to quote from another of Heinrich's songs), a day from which night has been banished and hence no transitions or partings can intrude.

If these visions of uninterrupted radiance and endless love cannot come true, the second pair of stanzas shows that they have at least a partial reality in physical love. The kisses 'beyond number', the beloved's 'total embrace' of her lover, and his 'never tiring' of her body, all point towards this, whilst the refrain, as before, shows that such realities cannot last. The final stanza is a uniquely moving insight into a woman's sexual doubts: how can she know that her naked body is desirable? and for how long? But the poetic depth here stems also from the relation between the last stanza and the first: the miracle for her, that the lover should never cease to contemplate her body, awed by its beauty, is, in the lover's experience, the miraculous moment when he cannot believe that a human body could have such radiance. The physical reality of her last stanza and the poetic illusion of his first circumscribe the single wonder of mutual love.

Heinrich's *alba* is the summit of the genre. No thirteenth-century poet even approached such achievement in this form again. Later *albas* in Germany as well as in Provence tend to be more elaborate, full of metrical virtuosity; in Provence the *alba* was turned into the complaint (*planh*) of a lover sleepless with longing, who lies waiting for dawn to come, or again into a spiritual *alba* in which the poet's 'beloved' was the Virgin Mary. In Germany the more conventional types of *alba* continued to be frequently composed, even by the Meistersinger. Outstanding among the thirteenth-century songs, in my opinion, is one by a poet Von Wissenlo, of whom we know nothing more than that four *albas* survive under his name. After a quiet opening stanza, in which the watcher warns, the interchange between watcher and lady mounts swiftly to a moving climax. The lady gazes at her sleeping lover:

> 'Beautifully
> this man, who aspired always to a pure, prized woman's gift,
> has fallen asleep in my arms.'

> 'If you love your good name or his life,
> let his sleep not go on!'
> The lady, pure in love, started in fright;
> she said: 'Woe to you, day, alas
> that you would cut away from me a man
> such that no woman in Christian or pagan land ever won
> so dear a one!'

The poet evokes a woman who is a perfect lover: at the close of the first stanza she is one 'who has never forgotten steadfast virtue', and in each stanza the word *reine* is repeated and applied to her: it suggests not only her radiance and womanly perfection (as so often in love-lyric); I think that here the word *reine* also has its full religious force —'immaculate', 'sinless'—that for this poet *reinekeit* consists not in the avoidance of sexual love, but in loving sublimely well.

A handful of thirteenth-century *albas* survive in the other Romance languages—French, Italian, and Galician. Three of the four extant French 'aubades' are particularly well known from anthologies: *Gaite de la tor*, with its dialogue between watchman and lover, its refrains and its virtuoso rhyming; the gentle melancholy of *Quant voi l'aube du jour venir*; and (most unusual in this genre) the gaiety and self-conscious charm of *Entre moi et mon ami*, conjuring up a world of adolescent make-believe:

> Last Tuesday night, in a wood by Béthune,
> my love and I went to play
> all night by the light of the moon,
> until it was day,
> and the lark sang 'Beloved, away!'
> And he gently replied
> 'It is not yet light, my adorable one—
> so help me Love, the lark has lied!'
>
> Then he drew close, and I did not resist—
> he kissed me a good three times,
> more than once I also kissed!
> (what harm was in this?)
> We wished that night hundred times multiplied—
> just those words left aside:
> 'It is not yet light, my adorable one—
> so help me Love, the lark has lied!'

In Galician, only one *alba* is famous: Nuno Fernandez Torneol's *Levad', amigo*, with its surging lyrical opening—

> Arise, my love, asleep in the cold morning,
> all the birds in the world are telling of love.
>   I move in joy.—

passing by variations of wording and parallelism to a bitter close, the landscape laid waste when the lover has gone:

> You took from them the branches where they perched,
> and parched the fountains where they used to bathe.
>   I move in joy.

It is very beautiful—yet, dare I ask, are not the pathos, the symbolism, and the contrast of the refrain a little too neatly calculated? More moving, to my mind, is an *alba* that by comparison seems almost artless, one of three composed by a *jogral*, Juião Bolseiro, who visited King Alfonso's Castilian court. In essence it is a *cantiga de amigo*, containing no dialogue, only the thoughts of a girl alone at night:

> Without my love alone I stay,
> not even my eyes can sleep at night;
> with all my strength I beg for light—
> God does not yield in any way.
>   Yet were I with my lover now,
>   light would be with me now!
>
> Whenever I slept with my true love,
> night was as nought and could not last;
> now night endures, arrives, goes past—
> and no light comes, day cannot live.
>   Yet were I with my lover now,
>   light would be with me now!
>
> Whenever he seems to lie with me,
> the man who is my lord and light,
> comes dawn in which I've no delight,
> though now night falls increasingly.
>   Yet were I with my lover now,
>   light would be with me now!
>
> I pray a hundred *Paters*, more,
> that he who died on the true cross
> may quickly show me light for this—
> yet they are advent nights he gives!
>   Yet were I with my lover now,
>   light would be with me now!

Like Heinrich von Morungen, this poet plays with light and dark, though in a simpler way: each can mean fulfilment or abandonment in love. Thus the refrain itself can convey both love-longing—the desire for light—and the dread of light, the despair that even fulfilment can last only till dawn. The repeated counterpoint of light and dark gains in intensity and leads to the final prayer, in which the one word *avento* resolves the play of opposites: the nights of advent are the longest nights of the year, those in which the anguish of waiting is most acute; yet they are also a preparation for the feast of joy that follows them, which could light up the sorrowful night as if God had come again to earth.

I know of only one medieval *alba* from Italy, which has been preserved in a remarkable way. In the official registers of contracts and wills at Bologna some notaries in the decades just before and after 1300 had the splendid idea of filling in blank spaces between items (where forgeries might otherwise be added!) with poetry. Often they chose well-known lyrics of the *dolce stil novo*, but at other times they recorded popular songs of the Emilian region, which are not known from any other source. Among these is an *alba*,[1] inserted into the register of 1286 by a notary named Nicholaus Phylippi:

Pàrtite, amore, adeo,	Leave me, my love, farewell!
ché tropo çe se stato.	you have been here too long.
Lo maitino è sonato,	Morning has rung—
çorno me par che sia.	I know that day is here.
Pàrtite, amor, adeo,	Leave me, my love, farewell!
che non fossi trovato	so that you are not found
in sí fina cellata	in such a hiding-place
como nui semo stati.	as we have known.
Or me bassa, oclo meo—	Kiss me, light of my eyes—
tosto sia l'andata,	the parting must be soon—
tenendo la tornata	looking to the return
como d'inamorati;	as lovers do,
sí che per spesso usato	so that, often used up,
nostra çoglia renovi,	our joy's made new,
nostro stato non trovi	and our state of being never
la mala çelosia.	meets base jealousy.
Pàrtite, amore, adeo,	Leave me, my love, farewell!
e vane tostamente,	go quickly now!
ch'ona toa cossa t'aço	Everything you brought I've made
pareclata in presente.	ready for you.

1. I cannot conceive why in Professor Hatto's symposium (*Eos*, p. 391) this song is called a fragment.

Its kinship with the rest of the family of *albas* is evident. Yet there is also a distinctive note, which is not tragic, or pathetic, or vehement, or dreamlike, or sensual—a note of firm but tender solicitude, and at the end, a delightful, housewifely practicality.

6

DANCE-SONGS

One of the prime functions of lyric throughout the Middle Ages was to accompany dancing. From the beginnings of Christianity dance-songs often played a part not only in secular festivities but in religious worship, and were performed in many churches: we know this largely from numerous attacks on the practice by those churchmen who felt that the dance-songs were too reminiscent of pagan cults, or heretical in their content (they were specially favoured by Gnostic communities), or simply liable to encourage dancing and singing of a less sacred kind. The wide distribution and frequency of the condemnations shows how popular and ineradicable the practice was: for the times and places from which no denunciation survives we may assume that the religious dance-songs were favoured or at least condoned—not that they did not exist.

The most beautiful testimony to the nature and meaning of liturgical dance-song is a Latin wedding-hymn from Spain, *Tuba clarifica*, of the ninth century or perhaps earlier. It opens summoning the people of Christ to express their joy in music, 'with shining trumpet'—but the first theme of joy is not the wedding itself but the Redemption, the forgiving of Adam and Eve:

> Truly ring out the deifying might,
> intone the opening of heaven's gates,
> which the dire hatefulness of poison had shut:
>   now Christ is opening all!

The present tense at the close of this stanza links the theme of Adam and Eve—developed in the two that follow—with that of the wedding-hymn:

> All the while epithalamia are performed,
> with paradisal voice they seize back grace:
> the voice cries: Multiply, make dryness full,
>   adorn the bridal bed . . .[1]

Since Christ opened the gates of heaven, every wedding can be a fresh exemplification of the Redemption, a new opening of paradise, for a couple united not in sin but in grace, giving birth to new, redeemed human beings. Music, song and dance are reflections of this divine joy in an earthly mode, and at the same time reach heavenwards in thanksgiving:

> Music, exult with dance, with tambourines,
> and give your everlasting thanks to him
> who through the cross's glory has snatched out
>   the souls the serpent bit.

> Oh little bride, come now, take up your pipe,
> your lyre and flute, ring out your canticles—
> harmoniously, with David's melody,
>   play and sing the events.

The events (*gesta*) are simultaneously the actions of the wedding-ceremony and the greater event of the Redemption that is reflected in them. After a prayer to God to fecundate and bless the present wedding, the song concludes with another joyful summons to music and dance:

> Jubilate, lute, cymbals, together clash,
> echo now, zither, psaltery, join the dance
> for the high God aloft who rules all things
>   always in all ages!

The group of instruments has Biblical associations, especially of the victorious entry of the Maccabees into Jerusalem (I Macc. XIII, 51). Here too a victory is celebrated: in the Redemption, and in its unfolding in each marriage that is blessed, heaven is recaptured—*epithalamia . . . receptant gratiam*.

It is not easy to assess how large or frequent a part dance-songs played in the Christian liturgy in the following centuries. Explicit statements that the clergy danced to a particular liturgical melody, or

---

1. I punctuate and construe the first three lines of this stanza as in AH 27, 207 (though correcting to *arida* in l.3).

on a particular feast, do survive from the Merovingian period right through to the fourteenth century, but relatively rarely. On the other hand, many liturgical texts contain terms (such as *chorea, tripudium*) that allude to dancing; but a number of scholars claim (I do not know on what evidence) that these must be taken purely metaphorically. What is certain, at least, is that on the periphery of the liturgy dance-songs continued to flourish. On the eve of the greater feasts of the church year, the populace would gather in church to celebrate the 'vigil' with dance and song. Here these were an integral part of popular devotion. People danced even when an extended narrative piece such as the eleventh-century *Chanson de Sainte Foy* was sung to them—the author himself describes it as 'good to dance to' (*bella ·n tresca*). Again there are many clerical criticisms and injunctions about vigils, but chiefly to try to ensure that the dancing should be seemly and the words of the songs edifying. The nights were long, and love-songs, comic turns and provocative dances tended to creep into the programme. Only an occasional fanatic tried to ban vigils altogether as too dangerous.

The church and churchyard, however, as another persistent stream of clerical protest shows us, were also often used for popular festivities of a purely secular kind. The churchyard, central and spacious, proved ideal for carolling during spring and summer (and on one fateful, legendary occasion, during the Christmas night);[1] and the church itself could be a useful dance-hall for evening entertainments or when the weather was bad.

Do we know what the dance-songs of the medieval populace were like? Many scholars would say we can never know: we have some Latin dance-songs written down from the eleventh century onwards, but these belonged to a clerical milieu; we have vernacular dance-songs written down chiefly in the thirteenth century and later—but these belonged to a cultivated society, not to the people. The people in the Middle Ages left no written records—their songs and dances, it is argued, are lost irretrievably.

I cannot share this agnosticism. I believe, for instance, that the two best-known types of medieval dance-song, the carol and the rondeau, are essentially popular forms. By this I do not mean that they must have been composed in the first instance by uncultivated men and

1. On Christmas Eve in the year 1021 twelve young men are said to have planned the abduction of Ava, the daughter of the priest at the church of Kölbigk. They send two girls into the church to fetch her, and she joins them all in a wild round dance in the churchyard. Their singing drowns the music of the Christmas service within. Through a divine punishment the dancers were unable to break their circle of joined hands, and were forced to dance day and night without rest for a whole year.

women, but that their melodic and poetic simplicity made them intrinsically suitable for dancing and festivities irrespective of class (as against more complex forms, such as the *estampie*, which would have been essentially at home only in a sophisticated society). It is highly probable that carols and rondeaux flourished long before any were written down, and there is no evidence whatever that they were originally restricted to an exclusive milieu. So too with the other principal types of dance-songs recorded: the fact that we very seldom have a text that can with certainty be called a direct transcription of something that was sung and danced in the widest circles—for the writer, as writer, was almost inevitably oriented towards a more limited public —does not warrant the assumption that the wider public danced songs essentially different from those that survive, or that we can win no conception of their dance-songs by way of those that were written down.

With these considerations in mind, let us look at a few medieval dance-songs for their own sake.

The oldest and commonest of dance-figures is the ring, in which the dancers, moving together with hands linked, can feel the excitement of solidarity and even at times a sense of elemental power. A moving ring of dancers is implied by many medieval dance-songs, as by the merrily ironic German refrain preserved in the Carmina Burana:

> Swaz hie gât umbe,   Who are these circling here?
> daz sint alle megede,   Girls every single one:
> die wellent ân man   they want to spend all summer
> allen disen sumer gân!   dancing without a man!

It was up to the men to pluck up courage and enter the charmed circle next to the girl of their choice.

Even the simplest dances will have alternated the circular movement with marking time or dancing in one place. At the centre of the ring of dancers there could be instrumentalists—to cite a Latin song, again from the Carmina Burana:

> Dance round the fiddlers, singing   in harmony,
> your feet in time, combining   delightfully,
>   sharing   the music's joy,
> or clapping hands, applauding   the melody.

But often the song itself was the dancers' only accompaniment.

The majority of dance-songs have a refrain, to be sung by all the dancers, and strophes, to be sung by one or more soloists. The circular movement in the dance can coincide with the strophe, or with the refrain, or again with an instrumental or vocal *reprise* between them—depending on the rhythm, nature and content of the particular song. A refrain could easily be picked up by everyone, only the soloist had to know all the words of the song. A dance-song could thus combine a part more demanding in its music or its steps, for the soloist, with a recurring simpler part in which all the audience could enjoy participating. At times, as in the oldest surviving secular Latin dance-song (a fragment on the last page of the 'Cambridge Songs', copied *c.* 1050), the refrain is little more than a play of sounds. The soloist is a woman gaily and impudently inviting her lover (who may well at the close have joined her in the centre of the ring of dancers in a *pas-de-deux*):

> Come to me, my dearest love,—*with ah! and oh!*
> Visit me—what joys you'll have! *with ah! and oh! and ah! and oh!*
>
> I am dying with desire—*with ah! and oh!*
> How I long for Venus' fire!—*with ah! and oh! and ah! and oh!* ...
>
> If you come and bring your key,—*with ah! and oh!*
> How easy will your entry be! *with ah! and oh! and ah! and oh!* ...

In the sounds of the refrain the chorus could mischievously imitate cries of longing, or of anticipated joy, of mock surprise, knowing complicity or pretended shock.

The two most frequent lyrical forms in medieval dance-song, the rondeau and the carol, can be characterised by the ways that they use the refrain. Each of these forms has a number of more or less closely related variants; neither form, in my view, can be reduced to a single archetype. What is constant in the rondeau range is the use of a refrain *within* the stanza; one of the best known kinds uses the whole refrain at the beginning and end of the stanza, and only its first half in the middle. Rondeaux of this kind were especially favoured in thirteenth-century France, where the finest have a self-conscious and exquisite grace:

> *Est il paradis, amie,*
> *est il paradis qu'amer?*
> Nenil voir, ma douce amie—
> *est il paradis, amie?*
> cil qui dort es bras s'amie
> a bien paradis trové.
> *Est il paradis, amie,*
> *est il paradis qu'amer?*

> *Is there a paradise, beloved,*
> *is there a paradise but love?*
> No indeed, my sweet beloved—
> *is there a paradise, beloved?*—
> whoever sleeps in his love's arms
> has found paradise.
> *Is there a paradise, beloved,*
> *is there a paradise but love?*

The most constant element in the carol range of forms is the use of a *vuelta* ('turning-line')—that is, the practice of making the last line of each strophe rhyme with the refrain. Thereby the soloist indicated to his audience when the refrain was about to recur, when it was their turn to participate. Another extremely common characteristic is for the part of the strophe preceding the *vuelta* to consist of three formally identical segments bound together by rhyme. To illustrate both these features from a delightful Italian dance-song, copied in 1287 into the 'Memoriali bolognesi' (see above, p. 184):

E·lla mia dona çogliosa
    vidi cun le altre dançare.
	And I saw my joyful beloved
	    dancing with all the rest.
		(Refr.)

Vidila cum alegrança,
    la sovrana de le belle,
	Full of enchantment I saw her,
	    sovereign of beautiful women,
		(i)

ke de çoi' menava dança
    de maritate e polcelle,
	joyfully leading the dancing
	    of married women and girls—
		(ii)

là 'nde presi gran baldança,
    tutor dançando chon elle:
	at the sight of her I was emboldened,
	    soon I was dancing among them:
		(iii)

ben resenbla plui che stelle
    lo so vixo a reguardare.
	to be able to gaze at her face then
	    was like looking up at the stars.
		(Vuelta)

E·lla mia dona çogliosa
    vidi cun le altre dançare. . .
	And I saw my joyful beloved
	    dancing with all the rest. . .
		(Refr.)

Al ballo de l'avenente
    ne pignormo ella et eo;
	While she was gracefully dancing,
	    we joined our hands, she and I;
		(i)

dissili cortesemente:
    'Dona, vostr' è lo cor meo'.
	reverently I addressed her:
	    'Lady, my heart's in your keeping.'
		(ii)

Ella resspose inmantenente:
    'Tal servente ben vogli' eo,
	She replied without hesitation:
	    'Indeed I want such a love-servant,
		(iii)

in ço vivirà 'l cor meo'.
    Si resspose de bon are.
	now my own heart will be joyful'.
	    So generous was her reply.
		(Vuelta)

E·lla mia dona çogliosa
    vidi cun le altre dançare.
	And I saw my joyful beloved
	    dancing with all the rest.
		(Refr.)

These formal characteristics (the triple segments, followed by *vuelta* and refrain) are found not only in many Italian secular *ballate* but in nearly all the Italian religious *laude*; similar features can be found in the French *virelai* and the English carol, in the Galician *Cantigas de Santa María* (see above, p. 71), and in the colloquial Arabic *zajal*.[1] The history of their diffusion is tantalising: where were the carol forms

---

1. The slightly more complex structure of the *muwashshah*, which was composed in classical Arabic, and in which the *vuelta* reproduces the *complete* rhyme-scheme of the refrain, is briefly indicated above, p. 87.

spread by direct paths of transmission? Where were they developed
afresh independently, to meet the basic needs of people who wanted
to sing and dance together? Insofar as a genetic explanation is possible,
it would seem that Arabic strophic poetry arose under the influence of
Romance dance-songs, and that already in late antiquity the Romance-
speaking world must have known songs in forms akin to the carol
range.

The alternations between soloist and chorus could be developed in
far more elaborate ways. As the manuscripts very rarely indicate the
distribution of parts, this must be inferred as far as possible from the
words themselves. A classic instance is Joseph Bédier's reconstruction
of the most sophisticated of the many dance-songs about 'Bele Aelis',
which were the rage of Paris around 1200. In Baude de la Kakerie's
song *Main se leva la bien faite Aelis* the words alone seemed an incoherent mosaic of fragments; it was Bédier's brilliant analysis that
showed them to be a coherent scenario, with parts for Bele Aelis, her
lover, and a chorus, with moments of soliloquy and moments of
dialogue, the chorus now supplying a narrative thread, now addressing
one or other of the protagonists, now standing apart to comment on
their thoughts and feelings. Similarly, it seems to me that one of the
most problematic Latin dance-songs in the Carmina Burana becomes
lucid if we suppose parts for various soloists and chorus. In the first
strophe the chorus-leader summons the dancers, young men and
women, together, and introduces them to the refrain (here the *vuelta*
is identical in each strophe). The third strophe, like the two final ones,
is clearly to be sung by a man; the fourth and fifth strophes are I think
best interpreted as showing contrasting reactions to love, the one by
two men, the other by two women. The performance of the carol,
then, may be provisionally reconstructed like this:

1. Coryphée: The time of joy is here now—   come every girl!
              Now share in the revels—   come every lad!
                    Oh, oh, all flowering with love,
                  I am all on fire with new-wakened love—
                  it is new love, new love, love that makes me die!

2. A woman: Philomena sings now,   caressingly—
              how perfectly she traces   her melodies!
                    Oh, oh, all flowering with love,
   All: I am all on fire with new-wakened love—
                  it is new love, new love, love that makes me die!

3. A man: She is the flower of maidens,   my dearest one;
                 she is the rose of roses,   for whom I burn.
                     Oh, oh, all flowering with love,
      All: I am all on fire with new-wakened love—
                 it is new love, new love, love that makes me die!

4. A man: The promise that she made me   gives me my strength.
   Another: The denial she gave me   makes me despair.
   Both: Oh, oh, all flowering with love,
   All: I am all on fire with new-wakened love—
                 it is new love, new love, love that makes me die!

5. A woman: I feel I'm mocked by being   a maiden still!
   Another: To have lacked all cunning   is my downfall!
   Both: Oh, oh, all flowering with love,
   All: I am all on fire with new-wakened love—
                 it is new love, new love, love that makes me die!

6. A woman: Philomena, for a   brief while, let be—
                 well up from my heart now,   my melody!
                     Oh, oh, all flowering with love,
   All: I am all on fire with new-wakened love—
                 it is new love, new love, love that makes me die!

7. A man: In the time of winter   a man can wait,
                 but spring stirs his senses   to love's delight:
                     oh, oh, all flowering with love,
   All: I am all on fire with new-wakened love—
                 it is new love, new love, love that makes me die!

8. A man: Come, my little loved one,   with all your joy—
                 come, oh come, my fair one,   or else I die!
                     Oh, oh, all flowering with love,
   All: I am all on fire with new-wakened love—
                 it is new love, new love, love that makes me die![1]

1. The Latin text (which survives only in the Codex Buranus, fol. 70v) is in several places garbled. I suggest that the following emendations should be adopted for reasons of metre and rhyme:

      1. Tempus est iocundum,   o virgines!
        Modo congaude*ndum*,   vos iuvenes!

      2. Cantat Phylomena   sic dulciter,
        modulans *amena*   *quam pulchriter!*

      3. Flos est puellarum   quam diligo,
        et rosa rosarum   *qua caleo.*

      8. Veni, domicella,   cum gaudio—
        veni, veni, *bella*:   iam pereo!

Apart from these corrections I have tried to translate the manuscript text unchanged.

G

In villages as well as cities the young *clercs* loved to dance their Latin songs with girls who had not studied Latin—so sometimes, as in the Carmina Burana, they noted German stanzas that could be sung to the same tune as the Latin ones, sometimes they composed 'macaronic' songs in which Latin and vernacular words alternated. A bright girl, however, could easily have picked up not only Latin refrains but some Latin stanzas as well: after all, they were not so different from the language she heard sung in church each Sunday!

Some of the most beautiful dance-songs of the Middle Ages are popular not only in the sense that they could be performed and enjoyed irrespective of learning or class, but in that they perpetuate beliefs and fantasies of the people which are older than, and essentially independent of, clerical and aristocratic traditions. Thus with the celebrated dance-song for young girls by the Portuguese *jogral* Joan Zorro:

> Let us dance now, come, oh fair ones,
> under these flowering hazelnut trees—
> and whoever is fair as we are fair,
>   if she falls in love,
> under these flowering hazelnut trees
>   she'll dance with us!
>
> Let us dance now, come, oh prized ones,
> under these fruit-laden hazelnut trees—
> and whoever is prized as we are prized,
>   if she falls in love,
> under these fruit-laden hazelnut trees
>   she'll dance with us!

The song turns on the age-old association of hazelnuts with fertility and erotic fulfilment. It is under the hazelnut tree that love has the best chance of being returned, even by those who have shown no love elsewhere. In a wide range of proverbial expressions going into the hazelnut trees ('in die Haseln gehen', 'aller aux noisettes avec un garçon') is synonymous with love-making; already in the ancient world sterile women were beaten with hazel twigs to make them fertile, and hazelnuts were given to the bride and bridegroom on the wedding-night. Whether consciously or simply following a tradition whose meaning they barely surmise, the girls in their dance are invoking the tree's power. Their song is traditional[1]—yet by no means uncultivated: its special quality is bound up with a kind of imaginative counterpoint between the archaic fantasy and its delicate, artistic treatment.

1. The fact that another version of the song survives, with only minor variants, by the clerical *trovador* Airas Nunes, again brings this out.

So too the anonymous English song of the moor-maiden (written down, with some other snatches of lyric, on a scrap of parchment in the early fourteenth century) must be understood in the light of the popular beliefs to which it alludes.[1] This makes it rather less enigmatic than has often been thought, though no less enchanting:

> Maiden in the mor lay—
> in the mor lay—
> sevenyst fulle, sevenist fulle.
> Maiden in the mor lay—
> in the mor lay—
> sevenistes fulle ant a day.
>
> Welle was hire mete—
> wat was hire mete?
> The primerole ant the, the primerole ant the—
> Welle was hire mete—
> wat was hire mete?
> The primerole ant the violet.
>
> Welle was hire dryng—
> wat was hire dryng?
> The chelde water of the, the chelde water of the—
> Welle was hire dryng—
> wat was hire dryng?
> The chelde water of the welle-spring.
>
> Welle was hire bour—
> wat was hire bour?
> The rede rose an te, the rede rose an te—
> Welle was hire bour—
> wat was hire bour?
> The rede rose an te lilie flour.

What is a moor-maiden? She is a kind of water-sprite living in the moors; she appears in a number of German legends, especially from Franconia.[2] It is appropriate that the English song should be a dance-song, as one of the commonest legends associates the moor-maiden

---

1. Some scholars have mistakenly proposed a Christian interpretation for the song, unaware that it was precisely the un-Christian, 'lewd, secular' nature of the words which led Bishop Richard de Ledrede, who held the see of Ossory in Ireland from 1317–60, to compose a sacred Latin text to replace them. (Cf. R. L. Greene, *Speculum* XXVII, 1952, 504–6).

2. Cf. H. Bächtold–Stäubli, *Handwörterbuch des deutschen Aberglaubens*, VI, 565, s.v. *Moorjungfern* (with principal references; further references in E. Fentsch, 'Volkssage und Volksglaube in Unterfranken', *Bavaria*, IV [1866], i, 203 ff.).

with a dance. She tends to appear at village dances in the guise of a
beautiful human girl, and to fascinate young men there, but she must
always return into the moor at a fixed hour, or else she dies. Sometimes
it is only for one hour in the week that she is allowed to leave the moor
and mingle with human beings—this perhaps is also why in the song
she waits in the moor 'sevenistes fulle ant a day'. Like other water-
sprites, a moor-maiden may be linked with a particular well-spring;
in two German folksongs such a well-maiden gives the children who
come to the spring flowers 'to make them sleep' (whether sleep here
implies death is not certain from the context). In the English song,
however, the well and the flowers evoke the moor-maiden's more-than-
earthly serenity and well-being: she has none of the cares and needs that
mortals have. Is the lyric simply a meditation on this theme? I think it
far more probable that the theme was made vivid for the dancers by a
mime. Then at the start of the song a girl playing the moor-maiden
would have lain as if asleep; the dancers approach her, admiring her
beauty, and some of the young men try to wake her, at first in vain.
Then, perhaps, a bell strikes: suddenly 'sevenistes fulle ant a day' are up,
she comes of her own accord into the centre of the round, and is at
once the acknowledged queen of the dance. An admirer offers her
dainties to eat, which she refuses; he offers her primroses and violets,
and these she pretends to eat. Another admirer offers her wine—again
she makes a gesture of refusal; instead she goes to drink at her well. All
the dancers make her a bed of flowers; she reclines on it; the bell
sounds once more, and she falls back into sleep, again as out of reach
as at the beginning. It is along these lines, I think, that we can picture
the living reality that such a song may have been.

So too the words of the Provençal song of the April queen, *A
l'entrada del tens clar*,[1] not only reflect ancient popular beliefs but
vividly suggest the mimetic presentation of legendary beings. Here
the leader of the dance is more than a pretty girl who has escaped her
old husband and joined her lover in the delights of spring: it is she
herself who 'makes joy begin again', she takes the part of a universal
queen, a being like the Persephone of the ancient world or the Flower
Maiden of the Celtic one, who is the incarnation of spring and the
source of the rebirth of joyful love:

> El' a fait per tot mandar, eya,
> non sia jusqu'a la mar, eya,
> piucela ni bachelar, eya,
> que tuit non venguan dançar
> en la dansa joioza.

1. cf. the melody below, p. 241.

She has sent her command all through the world: from here to the ocean no girl and no young man shall fail to come and dance in the joyous dance.

Her jealous husband is cast in the role of the old king: the king of the underworld, the Flower Maiden's captor and gaoler, who represents all that is wintry and dead, who is afraid that if his bride leaves him even briefly to return to a younger, brighter world, he will never get her back:

> Lo reis i ven d'autra part, eya,
> per la dansa destorbar, eya,
> que el es en cremetar, eya,
> que om no li voill' emblar
> la regin' avrilloza.

The king comes on from the other side, so as to break up the dance, for he is all aghast lest someone wants to rob him of the April queen.

The words 'from the other side' read like a stage-direction incorporated in the song: on the one side of the playground is the ring of dancers surrounding their queen, on the other, a group of *jelos* shouting in protest and harassing the dancers. It is to them that the refrain of each strophe is addressed:

> A la vi', a la via, jelos!
> Laissaz nos, laissaz nos
> ballar entre nos, entre nos!
>
> Jealous ones, away, away!
> Let us be, let us be!
> Let us dance on our own, our own!

Warned by the clamours of the *jelos*, the king enters and tries to break into the circle of dancers and snatch out the queen. But when spring comes the king of the old year is powerless—the young queen ignores him, and takes a 'light young man' as her consort in the dance. Her dance is a physical expression of the divine and universal joy in love that she personifies: anyone can see by her dancing 'that she has no equal in the world'.

Often the possibilities of a mime at the centre of the dance must be conjectured from hints in the song itself; at times, however, we have an explicit testimony. As Bédier showed, Jacques Bretel's poem *Le tournois de Chauvency*, which describes the festivities held at Chauvency in 1285, gives full stage-directions for one of the dances

performed there, the dance play called the *Chapelet*. The Countess of
Luxemburg is persuaded to play the lead; four knights lift her up and
promenade her through the hall; then they return to sit among the
spectators, and she remains, a chaplet of flowers in her hands. The poet
describes the scene meticulously, and with a bubbling sense of comedy:

She, tall and straight, and in the joy of her heart longing to give others
joy, took a step forward, her face upturned, her eyes lowered, sweetly
singing the song

> There's none more full of joy than I.

Then she took two steps forward, and at the appropriate moment a man
appeared before her, a minstrel with a fiddle, as candid and gentle as a maid,
whose role was to ask her, by request and command, why she was dancing
all alone in this way, so gracefully, bearing herself so nobly, and playing
with her chaplet without companion, without friend. Then he said to her
very gently, but so that all could hear:

> 'You who are made for love,
> what does your body crave,
>   so sweet?'

> 'Sir, what is it to you?
> I think you are too bold.
> I've made my pretty chaplet
> down there in the wood.'

When she finishes her song she takes two steps forward, at the third
she whirls about. She lifts her chaplet high, spins it around in her hands,
looking at it from time to time, then she places it on her head. A little later
she takes it off again, and plays with it gracefully. And the man who was
standing before her sings her this song:

> 'Sweet lady, do you want a husband?'

> 'No, for if he's not too good,
>   then I'd have no joy.
> I'd rather have my chaplet
>   than wed unhappily!'

> 'Sweetest lady, I'll find you one,
>   made just as you desire.'

> 'Kind sir, then bring him to me here,
>   down to this forest glade.
> I'll be off now, but you'll find me
>   sitting in the grassy shade.'

Hands on her hips, she now turns back, makes herself pretty, preens
herself, with little running dancing steps. At times she lingers thoughtfully,
as if overcome by love. She tries on her chaplet in many ways.

Meanwhile, the minstrel singles out a knight from the audience, one Andreu d'Amance:

'Sir, if it please you, I should like to present you to an excellent lady: with your help I can acquit myself well.' And the knight, shamefaced, replies: 'I am not the right man, there are better men than I.' 'Kind sir, I'll not go elsewhere—I could indeed do worse.' He plucks the hem of his robe and drags him towards the lady, who is turning her chaplet in her hands and singing with exultant heart

> Oh God, he stays too long—
> when will he come?
> His delay will be my death![1]

When she has sung at her pleasure, the minstrel brings the knight before her, still pulling him a little by the sleeve, the brave, clever, noble, debonair and courteous knight. Then he sings with loud voice

> 'Lady, the knight-bachelor's here:
> in prowess I know none his peer.
> Take him, lady, I am giving
> him to you; indeed you'd fail
> to find one better than him living.'

She, who is so well nurtured, takes the knight's hand and leads him away, singing with great joy

> Thanks be to God, I've won what I desired![2]

In this dance-play the participants, some of whose names are recorded by the poet, were knights and a noble lady. Yet the mime takes place not in an aristocratic society but in Arcadia—not in a world of arranged marriages, social barriers and feudal laws, but in that enchanted forest or countryside where the only law is love. In Arcadia love is not complicated by social pressures or by guilt—here the lover finds the girl that he chances to meet wholly lovable or desirable, and the girl, whether she returns or refuses his love, follows in the last resort only the promptings of her heart. This dream-world of spontaneous feelings and physical pleasures was a compelling image throughout the Middle Ages: for learned writers it became the garden of Venus, or the garden of Natura, or other bowers of bliss; in the lyric it is, as the French dance-songs keep telling us, 'down there by the

1. In this *refrain* the closeness of the language to that of many of the *kharjas* (see above, pp. 86 ff.) is particularly striking.
2. *Le tournoi de Chauvency* (ed. M. Delbouille, 1932), vv. 4215 ff. The narrative is in octosyllabic couplets, the snatches of song, which I have set off, are in a variety of metres. In 4233 (the messenger's first line), I translate the reading of the Mons MS. (*Douce pour les amors*).

little fountain', 'down there beneath the olive-tree', 'down there in the green meadow'—wherever a young man or woman waits for, and finds, love.

This too is the world of the *pastorela*—a range of songs that were often danced, and I believe also often mimed, in which the heroine is a shepherdess. Usually they take the form of a lyrical dialogue: a man of some status in the outer world, a knight or *clerc*, enters the Arcadian landscape, sees a pretty shepherdess there, and tries to win her love. By the outer world's standards he is above her in rank or education, but Arcadia ignores such standards: in wit and personality the shepherdess is her wooer's equal, if not superior; sometimes she decides she will not have him; and if she does yield to him it is not for the sake of his finery or possessions, but for the sheer pleasure of making love.[1] Some scholars have tried to see these songs as a learned offshoot of Latin bucolic poetry, others as a purely aristocratic medieval *jeu d'esprit*. These are at best half-truths: certainly the Arcadia of the medieval imagination has in part a classical background, certainly aristocratic tastes helped to give some *pastorelas* their particular artistic shape; but the essential conception—a dialogue in which a man of high degree woos a country girl—cannot be restricted in this way. As its occurrence in the ballads, folksongs and even nursery rhymes of later centuries shows, the inherent wit and appeal of such a theme is not confined to intellectuals or to the 'best circles'. Nor was it ever: we may be sure that shepherdesses have dreamt of winning—or of refusing—dukes for as long as dukes have dreamt of shepherdesses.

If it was in Old French lyric that the *pastorela* had the greatest vogue—nearly two hundred examples have been collected—the most memorable poetically are in other languages—Provençal, Latin, Italian—where at times an exceptional poet set his own stamp on the form: Marcabru's *L'autrier jost' una sebissa*, in which the shepherdess, with grim humour and stabbing shrewdness, demolishes her wooer's Arcadian fantasy as a romantic falsehood; Walter of Châtillon's sparkling and elegant confection *Sole regente lora*, with its witty classical echoes; Guido Cavalcanti's *In un boschetto*, where the poet moves reverently, almost as if sleepwalking, through a landscape of open and blissful love:

> Down in a glade I found a shepherdess—
> lovelier than a star she seemed to me.

---

1. In a few of the cruder songs in the *pastorela* range, the lover takes the shepherdess by force—but even this tends to be presented in an 'Arcadian' way, as if no harm were done.

Her hair was golden, full of little waves,
her face roselike, and her eyes full of love:
holding her little staff she grazed her lambs;
she wore no shoes, her feet were drenched in dew;
she was singing as if she were in love,
as if she were laden with all delights.

Lovingly I greeted her at once
and asked her, had she any company;
and very sweetly she then answered me,
she was walking in the wood all, all alone.
She said: 'Know this—when a bird is singing,
then my heart aches with longing for a friend.'

When she had told me of her state of feeling,
and I could hear birds singing in the wood,
within myself I said 'Now is the moment
for winning joy from this dear shepherdess.'
I asked her only for the grace to kiss
and to embrace her—if it be her will.

She took me by the hand, to show her love,
and told me she had given me her heart.
She guided me to a fresh little grove,
where I saw flowers of every colour bloom;
and I felt so much joy and sweetness there,
I seemed to see the god of love descending.[1]

This is perhaps the highest expression of the Arcadian ideal in medieval lyric, culminating at the close in an almost mystical celebration of earthly joy. The only Arcadian vision of comparable intensity that I know occurs in a song written some three generations earlier by Walther von der Vogelweide, a song that begins and ends with a dance. But where Guido, while his song lasts, shuts out all other worlds, Walther both conjoins and compares Arcadia with reality:

'Nemt, frowe, disen kranz':	'Lady, accept this garland'—
alsô sprach ich zeiner wol getânen maget:	these were the words I spoke to a pretty girl:
'sô zieret ir den tanz,	'then you will grace the dance
mit den schoenen bluomen, als irs ûffe traget.	with the lovely flowers crowning you.
het ich vil edele gesteine,	If I had priceless stones,
daz müest ûf ir houbet,	they would be for your hair—
obe ir mirs geloubet.	indeed you must believe me,
sêt mîne triuwe, daz ichz meine.'	by my faith, I mean it truly!'

1. Guido's 'pasturella' is in *ballata* form: the opening lines are a refrain, reintroduced at the close of each strophe by a *vuelta* (see above, p. 191). While some of Guido's *ballate* are literary rather than dance-songs, this one may well have been intended for dancing.

Si nam daz ich ir bôt,
einem kinde vil gelîch daz êre
    hât.
ir wangen wurden rôt,
sam diu rôse, dâ si bî der liljen
    stât.
do erschampten sich ir liehten
    ougen:
doch neic si mir schône.
daz wart mir ze lône:
wirt mirs iht mêr, daz trage ich
    tougen.

She took my offering
as a gently nurtured child would
    take it.
Her cheeks became as red
as the rose that stands besides the
    lilies.
Her shining eyes were lowered then
    in shame,
yet she curtsied graciously.
That was my reward—
if any more becomes mine, I'll hold
    it secret.

'Ir sît sô wol getân,
daz ich iu mîn schapel gerne geben
    wil,
so ichz aller beste hân.
wîzer unde rôter bluomen weiz ich
    vil:
die stênt sô verre in jener
    heide,
dâ si schône entspringent,
unde die vogele singent,
dâ suln wir si brechen beide.'

'You are so fair,
that I want to give you my chaplet
    now,
the very best I have.
I know of many flowers, white and
    red,
so far away, on the heath over
    there,
where they spring up beautiful,
and where the birds are singing—
let us pluck them together there.'

Mich dûhte daz mir nie
lieber wurde, danne mir ze muote
    was.
die bluomen vielen ie
von dem boume bî uns nider an daz
    gras.
seht, dô muost ich von fröiden
    lachen.
do ich sô wünneclîche
was in troume rîche,
dô taget ez und muos ich
    wachen.

I thought that never yet
had I known such bliss as I knew
    then.
From the tree the flowers
rained on us endlessly as we lay
    in the grass.
Yes, I was filled with laughter in
    sheer joy.
Just then, when I was so gloriously
rich in my dreaming,
then day broke, and I was forced
    to wake.

Mir ist von ir geschehen,
daz ich disen sumer allen meiden
    muoz
vast under dougen sehen:
lîhte wirt mir einiu: so ist mir
    sorgen buoz.

She has stirred me so
that this summer, with every girl I
    meet,
I must gaze deep in her eyes:
perhaps one will be mine: then all
    my cares are gone.

waz obe si gêt an disem tanze?	What if she were dancing here?
frowe, dur iur güete	Ladies, be so kind,
rucket ûf die hüete.	set your hats back a little.
owê gesæhe ichs under	Oh if only, under a garland, I
kranze!	could see that face!

It is at a real dance that Walther hopes to find a girl with so unique
a gift for love and joy that she could make real the poet's Arcadia. At
first we are shown dramatically how such an incurable romantic would
look to a girl who, however attractive in looks and behaviour, is not
unique: she hears him babbling exaggerated nonsense, and is acutely
embarrassed; yet she senses that his offering of his garland (and
implicitly of his heart), however absurd, is kindly meant, that it would
be wounding and ill-mannered to refuse, so she accepts and is not unfriendly, though still reserved, in her gesture of thanks.

With the last line of the second stanza comes a transition of extraordinary brilliance and swiftness: even as the poet starts to make a wry
aside—she was not the unique one, after all—his daydream begins,
which reveals the secret hope within him that he is resolved not to
reveal, not to cheapen, in waking life. Dramatically the effect is of a
man so possessed by his fantasy that imperceptibly his phrase 'If any
more becomes mine . . .' passes into 'Suppose there is more, suppose
it were like this . . .'. And the next moment he is already daydreaming,
he has given this particular girl the ideal girl's answer. He sees her as a
girl utterly generous and fearless in responding to his invitation to
love: she gives him her chaplet, which is her pledge of love; her true
chaplet has still be to made together with him, her capacity to love
still to find its fulfilment. Then all becomes effortless—no longer each
lover plucking his or her flowers, to make something of their hopes,
but flowers falling endlessly and freely on the united lovers.

The Arcadian dream that had grown so imperceptibly out of reality
breaks and leaves the dreamer desolately lonely, but not disillusioned.
He continues resolved 'to hope till hope creates/of its own wreck the
thing it contemplates'—this he sees as his essential task as poet of love.
At any moment in a dance the ideal might become more than a poet's
fantasy, at any moment he might blissfully recognise, in a girl's eyes,
the response that answers to his ideal. The response, I think, means
inseparably to his poetry and to his love—both are figured in the
garland: he is in search of the girl in whom all his love-songs will find
their destination. In the first line of the song Walther offers a girl his
garland to take to the dance; in the last line, where the word 'kranz' is
repeated, it seems as if all the women dancing are wearing a garland on

their hats. Are they all wearing *his* garland? Has he projected the entire dance? The words 'lîhte wirt mir einiu', so close to the words with which the daydream began, suggest 'perhaps the one will become real for me'—for Walther as poet or as Arcadian lover the true response for which he longs would mean the human substantiation of his ideal.

Another truly original German poet, a younger contemporary of Walther's, Neidhart von Reuenthal, wrote numerous songs both for and about dancing. Forcefully, often savagely, he evokes the world of village dances that he knew: it is a peasant world akin to that of Breughel paintings, not pretty but teeming with life, vigorous and far from squeamish in its appetites, where coarseness, brawls and jealousy can flare up as easily as gaiety; a world, too, that has its glints of fantasy:

> An old woman, who fought with death
> all through the day and through the night,
> > sprang up again
> > like a ram
> and knocked all the young ones down.

—this is one of Neidhart's wide range of images of the power of winter menacing the first stirrings of spring.

In the midst of this peasant world appears Neidhart himself—a persona created with a cutting self-mockery. He is the impoverished, *déclassé* knight moving among the peasantry, distrusted, hated and attacked by them, while he, envying their relative prosperity, pillories their loutishness and their attempts at aping the dress and the presumptions of their betters. He has a roving eye, and at times succeeds in turning the head of a pretty peasant lass—or of her mother—but the rustics tend to band together and crowd him out.

While it is impossible to judge how much of this is pure fiction and virtuosity in a chosen mode, it is clear that Neidhart knew the peasant world as well as the chivalric at firsthand, and that he had an audience in both: for his satirical peasant-baiting among the gentry, for his joyful dance-songs also, or even primarily, at the village dances themselves. It is this wider audience that made him legendary, so that in the late Middle Ages he became a clown-hero of carnival plays and farce. Long before that, however, Neidhart's achievement as poet had given the world of sophisticated lyric a new thematic and expressive range. I shall illustrate from a song, *Sinc, ein guldîn huon*, where the melody also survives (given below, p. 243), and has a verve and freshness that match the poetic language:

'Sing, my golden chick—I'll give you corn!'
All at once
I was glad:
to win her favour I feel joy in singing.
So a fool's kept cheerful by a promise
through the year . . .

Clear away the footstools and the chairs,
have the trestles
carried out,
for today we'll dance till tired of dancing!
Fling the rooms open, so as to make them cool,
that the breeze
gently blows
on the bodices of dancing girls.
Then, when the soloists have ceased to sing,
you will all be asked to join
in another
little courtly dance to the music of the fiddle.

Listen, I hear the dancing has begun.
Take your places
now, young men!
There's a great bustling herd of village women;
one could see a polka[1] going strong;
as the two
fiddlers stopped,
some cheeky boys thought they would have their fun
and in a flash started a drinking-song.
Through the windows the noise dinned,
Adelhalm,
as always, dancing between two girls . . .

The song is a whirl of moments flying past. The first image is of a
girl, whom Neidhart loves in vain, ordering him with amused, mocking
provocation to sing at a village dance. He is half-prepared to see this as
a sign of encouragement from her, and so he takes on far more than
she had asked: in the next image he is excitedly organising the whole
dance, and hoping to include in the programme at least a couple of
brief court dances (*hovetänzel*), in which he will shine and perhaps
impress her. But he has no chance: in the next image the loudest village
louts take over and the dance becomes an uproar. Neidhart suddenly
focuses all his attention on one vain and boorish man, Adelhalm, who
—as we now learn in three stanzas of bitter caricature—is his rival. The

1. The precise nature of the dance mentioned here (*ridewanzen*) is not known.

song concludes with a striking juxtaposition: Adelhalm crudely
mauling the girl (which she seems not to mind!), and Neidhart making
her a quixotic courtly flourish, offering her his poor little estate (whose
very name, as he often recalls in playing on it, means 'vale of grief') as if
it were a kingdom:

> This summer I saw him munching at her face
> as if it were bread:
> I went quite red
> with shame, as they sat next to each other.
> If she'd be mine, she whom I gladly serve,
> I shall give her a choice estate—
> Reuenthal—
> all as her own: it is my lofty Siena!

Confronted with images such as these, one is suddenly aware that
by comparison many if not most medieval dance-songs contain some
artificial sweetening. Here is an unidealised world, in which feeling is
still acute, in which sweat and savageness are as intensely perceived as
mirth.

7

LYRICS OF REALISM

Among the many medieval lyrics that cannot easily be grouped with any of the genres so far discussed, we may distinguish an important range that I shall tentatively call 'lyrics of realism'. The phrase is inadequate, and liable perhaps to misunderstanding, but I can think of no better. Here I should like to distinguish especially two kinds of lyric: lyrics that show the poet's response to specific historical circumstances, to people and events in the real world, and lyrics in which the poet disregards the expectations of his audience (in the way of genre and conventions) and writes primarily for himself. In the recognition of such lyrics we must clearly be on our guard—to portray realistically may also be to feign, to break through genres and conventions may be a virtuoso exercise in a special kind of genre or convention. (Was the Archpoet really a compulsive gambler and seducer? Did Rutebeuf really find his poor wife an intolerable burden? Did Cecco Angiolieri really wish his father dead?) What is important for a literary discussion, however, is not the conjectures about the historical truth that may or may not lie behind the verse, but to recognise and attempt to define a distinctive poetic language and personality where these occur.

The range of material relevant to a discussion of medieval lyrics of realism is both fascinating and immense. To do it justice will eventually involve a number of interdependent major projects of literary scholarship that have scarcely yet been broached: for instance, to trace the development of the realistic and topical *sirventes* as a genre among the troubadours from Marcabru onwards, as well as its influence in the rest of Europe; to relate the lively and prolific Latin tradition of realistic and moral-satirical poetry—the world of Hugh Primas and the

Archpoet, of Walter of Châtillon and Philip the Chancellor—to the kindred developments in the vernaculars, in the world of Walther von der Vogelweide or Peire Cardenal, Rustico Filippi or Rutebeuf; above all, to explòre and evaluate the astonishing wealth of topical, satirical and personal lyric from thirteenth-century Portugal, which has only now been made accessible in a critical edition by Professor Rodrigues Lapa.[1] Often, too, it is the lyrics of realism that present the most formidable linguistic difficulties, in the interpretation of colloquial idioms, terms of slang and invective, and topical allusions. Here I can do no more than make some brief probings, to communicate a few of the moments that I have found poetically and humanly most arresting.

The first major poet in medieval Europe whose lyrics are predominantly realistic in the two senses I have outlined is the troubadour Marcabru. To read his songs as a whole (forty-four are ascribed to him) is to find much that is wearying and obsessive: his repeated invectives against the corrupt society in which he lived, against its debasement of love and honour, his fiery denunciations of falsity of every kind on earth, however deeply Marcabru may have felt them, often cease to have any compelling poetic quality. But to read the finest of these songs (perhaps a dozen in all) is another matter: then Marcabru appears as an artist of prodigious force and range: a poet who in one song can see the crusade of 1147 exultantly, as renewing the face of the earth, and in another tragically, as breaking the heart—and the belief in God's goodness—of a girl who has lost her lover through it; who in his only two love-songs evokes a strange picture of enslavement to a good-natured but wanton woman, of whom he says the fiercest things in the lightest manner; above all a poet in whose attacks on his own world bitterness, coarseness, spite and cruelty can at times be transmuted and clarified in the intensity of a prophet's vision. In one such song, 'Pus mos coratges s'es clarzitz', Marcabru begins with words similar to those that open many a troubadour's love-song: his 'heart has become bright through the joy that makes me joyous': he has been endowed with that special joy which is no mere mood or impulse but a quality of being, which makes a person capable of receiving the grace of Love. As he waits to be chosen by *fin' Amors*, gracious Love, he resolves to purify his songs. For Love can reject as well as choose—he rejects and makes demented any who sully his name. With this thought Marcabru has already begun to move away from the *topoi* of love-lyric; it leads into his passionate denunciation, in which he tells who are the human beings who sully *fin' Amors*:

1. *Cantigas d'escarnho e de mal diƷer*, Editorial Galaxia, Coimbra 1965.

Such are false judges, such are robbers,
adulterous husbands, perjurors,
false-painted men and slanderers,
demagogues, cloister-pillagers,
and those fervid courtesans
who yield to other women's husbands—
all these will have hellish reward!

Homicides and treacherous men,
necromancers, simoniacs,
debauchees and usurers,
who live by an ignoble trade,
and men who practise sortilege
and stinking fortune-telling women
will all meet in the burning fire.

Drunken men and blackmailers,
false clergy and false abbots too,
false anchoresses, anchorites,
will suffer there, says Marcabru:
the false all have their place reserved—
gracious Love has promised it—
their grief there will be desperate!

Suddenly the fierce accumulation of blame ceases, the prophet stands
there cowed and ashamed. What right has he to judge and denounce,
to construct his private hell? Is he not himself as guilty as anyone?

Ah, gracious Love, fountain of good,
illuminating the whole world,
I ask forgiveness for these cries—
shield me from having to linger there!
I hold myself your prisoner
to have your comfort everywhere,
hoping that you will be my guide.

I quell my own heart by this song,
reproach myself more than the rest,
for one who assigns blame elsewhere
must truly know how to protect
himself from being stained by crimes
that he lays at another's door—
then he can warn and be secure.

The 'prophetic' stanzas could easily have been mere ranting; it is
Marcabru's moving awareness that the prophet's mantle does not fit
him which redeems them.

At the centre of the song there is something enigmatic. What does Marcabru mean by *fin' Amors?* It is a symbol, not an allegory. No single concept can be substituted for it without diminishing the poem —not God, or love of God, or love of neighbour, or faithful sexual love: it is all these and more. One might indicate it best by saying, *fin' Amors* is all that is true, truly loved or truly loving, in whatever mode, earthly or heavenly, it finds expression; all that is genuinely felt, devoid of treachery or dissembling, calculation or greed or fear. The wonderful comprehensiveness of Marcabru's symbol can be seen from the range of sins that he sees as offences against 'gracious Love' —the key is the recurring word 'fals': falsity in justice, in sex, in business, in religion, in any of man's dealings with his fellow-men or with God, all of which can be ruled by 'gracious Love', which at its highest is a divine love manifesting itself in human beings. To reduce Marcabru's symbol to a purely Christian religious notion, however, would again be to oversimplify it: for instance, here as in other songs he measures human love by a standard of emotional truth, which is its own law, rather than by the extrinsic standard of Christian morality. *Fin' Amors* can be embodied in a love-affair as well as in conjugal love —each can have its intrinsic standard of truth. True love is falsified and debased not only by courtesans and debauchees, but also by *lauzengiers*, those slanderers who spread tales about lovers' secrets. Even if Marcabru's songs show us a fierce and often unpleasant, by no means conventionally 'good' moralist, they also reveal glimpses of a passionate, independent and touching human being.

A generation later another outstanding troubadour, Bertran de Born, composed songs in which realistic elements played a leading role, songs for his own time. In temperament, outlook and technique Marcabru and Bertran are as unlike as could be, yet they have in common an intensity which can lend their songs an incandescent, visionary quality. Bertran transforms the politics of his day into an imaginative vision: his songs mirror, magnify, and distort, elements in his own life and in the wars and intrigues of princes. That his own life was turbulent and insecure, that his estate was ravaged by enemies, and that he was often involved in fighting for himself and others is certain. Poetically, Bertran projected this turbulent life onto so grand a scale that to Dante a century later he appeared as a demonic, strife-stirring figure, as the man who set Henry Curtmantle against his father Henry II and his brother Richard, a man who, even though Dante recognised the originality and power of his poetry, was assigned a unique and terrible place in the *Inferno*. But the historical Bertran was too insignificant a figure to be the Machiavel of his age, whatever his dreams and fantasies. If he loved fighting, it was not a dedication to evil, but rather a temporary escape from poverty. Yet the poetic *persona* of his songs is indeed of heroic temper: there he becomes a Roland, limitless in his zest for fighting, for whom the glamour of battle emerges even amid the awareness of its harshness and sordidness:

> If both the kings are chivalrous and brave,
> soon we shall see fields littered with remains
> of helmets and of shields, of swords and bows—
> and of men cleft asunder head to waist;
> and we shall see chargers race riderless,
> and many a lance bedded in ribs or breast,
> and joy and weeping, pain and cheerfulness.
> Loss will be great, but gain be greater still!
>
> Trumpets, tabors, pennons and bannerets
> and gonfalons and horses white and black—
> soon we shall see life is worth living for:
> usurers will be robbed of all they have,
> and on the roads no muleteer will pass
> in peace that day, nor burgher without fear,
> nor merchant calmly make his way from France.
> He will be rich then who robs joyfully!
>
> If the king comes, I'll put my trust in God:
> I'll be alive, or I'll be hewn apart!
> And if I live, it will be my great joy—
> and if I die, my great deliverance.

The occasion of this song is the hostility between Alfonso II and Richard Cœur-de-Lion: Bertran, who had been one of the faction opposing Richard before Curtmantle's death in 1183, later became one of Richard's most loyal adherents. In a sense one may say that such a song, like many of Bertran's, is propaganda, or that it 'represented public opinion' (Hoepffner's phrase). Yet the essence of such a song seems to me to be neither propagandist nor topical, but mythical. It is a myth consciously embroidered by the poet, an attempt to fire men's imaginations by a vision they could not have made articulate themselves—to give the impoverished lower knighthood, a class that had nothing to lose and could gain nothing but by fighting for it, to give Bertran's own class, in short, a cause, a sense that their future was not bleak and hopeless. Bertran plays on the best and worst elements in that audience (and perhaps in himself)—the love of glory and the thirst for plundered gain. He tries to fire them with his own hatred for

the securer, easier bourgeois world that could never be his or theirs: is
not danger itself thrilling? Is it not better to risk all than to 'sit in the
stye of contentment'? Such was Bertran's myth, barbarous, harsh and
splendid. It is salutary to recall that this is the same man who in 1187
repeatedly encouraged others to go on the crusade but would not risk
going himself, and who a few years later became a Cistercian monk.

Only one song survives from Bertran's great lord Richard Cœur-de-
Lion, which offers a fascinating contrast: it has neither Bertran's
flamboyant artistry nor his element of myth, but despite or perhaps
because of that, it reveals a person more intimately and directly. The
occasion is Richard's captivity: he is the prisoner of Leopold of
Austria, and the price of his ransom cannot be found. The poetry is so
unobtrusive that at first we might think, this man is not specially
talented; his tone is quiet, slow and rueful, but then we notice the glint
in his eye, a flicker of pride and a flicker of sardonic humour, and we
realise that this poetic voice is very much his own, and that a most un-
common personality has penetrated our imagination:

> Ja nus hons pris ne dira sa reson
> Adroitement, s'ensi com dolans non;
> Mès par confort puet il fere chançon.
> Moult ai d'amis, mès povre sont li don;
> Honte en avront, se por ma reançon
> Sui ces deus yvers pris.
>
> Ce sevent bien mi homme et mi baron,
> Englois, Normant, Poitevin et Gascon,
> Que je n'avoie si povre conpaignon
> Cui je laissasse por avoir en prixon.
> Je nel di pas por nule retraçon,
> Mès encor sui ge pris.

No man who is in prison can speak his thoughts aptly without speaking
as a man in grief; and yet for comfort's sake he can make a song. I have
many friends, but the gifts are poor—they will be shamed if for lack of
ransom I am a prisoner these two winters.
Indeed they know, my men and my barons—English, Norman, Poitevin
and Gascon—that I never had so poor a comrade that I would leave him in
prison out of greed. I do not say this as a reproach—yet I am still a prisoner.

The opening, which at first seems banal, turns out to be a subtle
captatio benevolentiae: Richard is singing 'par confort'—not, or not
primarily, to comfort himself, but to say uncomfortable things in a
comfortable form. The ironic touch here reflects back on the first two
lines: to hear of Richard from prison at all will make many of his

friends uncomfortable, will prick their consciences—and yet, the lines
say, even if one cannot pretend that one's life is other than it is, one can
at least say what one has to say pleasantly. Richard at first shows his
circumspection by the touches of impersonal statement ('the gifts are
poor', not 'my friends are mean'), and of hypothesis ('*if* I remain a
prisoner . . .'), which still leave it open for his friends to vindicate
themselves. The second strophe moves swiftly from the self-assured
sense of his own generosity to an uncertainty about others that finds an
outlet in ironic melancholy. Then the reproaches and appeals become
more direct and more bitter; there is a moment of arrogance ('The
plains are empty of fair deeds of arms/as long as I am prisoner'),
though even here the tone is despondent: this is addressed to knights
who, while they were with him, were beautiful and chivalrous, and
now are merely 'rich and thriving'. The most unpredictable moment
in the song is the envoy: a solemn invocation that seems devout and
touching turns, as it were in an afterthought, into a grimace of wicked
humour, as Richard, having thought of his favourite sister, suddenly
calls to mind the sister whom he cannot stand:

> Contesse suer, vostre pris souverain
> Vos saut et gart cil a cui je me clain
> Et par cui je sui pris.
> Je ne di pas de celi de Chartrain,
> La mere Looys.

Countess and sister, may your peerless nature be protected and guarded
by Him on whom I call and by whose will I am prisoner. (I'm not talking
of my sister in Chartres, the mother of Louis!)

In the same year as Richard composed his song in prison, a mercurial
Latin poet, the cosmopolitan humanist and diplomat Peter of Blois,
gave public, political expression to that same imprisonment. His song
will have been sent in 1192 to prelates at many of the courts of Europe,
to excite clergy and laity alike on Richard's behalf against Leopold of
Austria. Peter, who could write love-songs scintillating in their play
of words and rhymes, whose songs retracting and repenting the
frivolities of his youth were as elegant and witty as the frivolities themselves, who adopted as his one truly serious *persona* the image of the
prodigal son, here uses all his rhetorical craft to captivate his listeners
and win their support. The polemic is reckless, but the language
fastidiously chosen. The song is in a flawless rhymed sequence form.
It opens at a pitch that might seem difficult to sustain:

Quis aquam tuo capiti,	Who will give water to your eyes,
quis dabit tibi lacrimas,	who will give you tears enough
ut laudes regis incliti	to tell the praises of the noble king
fraudesque ducis exprimas? . . .	and the treachery of the duke? . . .

But each stanza caps the preceding one, magnifying Leopold's crime: he is a Herod, a Cerberus, he crucifies Christ afresh, he is a Judas and worse than Judas:

Iudas Christum distraxerat,	Judas made a bargain of Christ,
dux regem vendit Anglie,	the duke sells England's king,
sed crimen hoc exaggerat	but in his money-worship
idolatra pecunie,	surpasses Judas' crime—
nam impie	blasphemously
pacem cum rege finxerat	he'd feigned peace with the king
dum ei rex improperat	when Richard taunted him
quod fugerat,	for taking flight,
relicta crucis acie	deserting the army of the cross,
cedens in partem Sirie.	fleeing into Syria.

Throughout Richard is presented as Christ's champion, as the one man who could lead Christendom in reconquering Jerusalem. Therefore Leopold, by arresting the Crusader, has betrayed Christ; worse than Judas, he has betrayed not Christ alone but Ecclesia. In the final strophe contemporary events are seen in an Augustinian visionary pattern: the duke has 'sold the people of the Promised Land'. Peter here sees the inhabitants of the Latin kingdom of Jerusalem symbolically: they are an epitome of *Jerusalem caelestis*, of all who have made their peace with God. There *could* be such a city of God on earth, its king another David, but instead Leopold's plot 'confirms the tyrant of Babylon on David's throne':

> sed tua machinatio
> firmat in David solio
> tirannum Babilonis!

If the Latin kingdom loses its foothold in the Holy Land and Saladin recovers the region, it will mean the victory of Babylon over Jerusalem among mankind. It is hard to know whether to admire more the flamboyance or the sheer low cunning with which Peter has blown up the Austrian's demand for English money to eschatological proportions.

A century later, in Italy, another poet wrote a song about captivity, in which the personality of the prisoner is revealed in a different and more spectacular way than in Richard's song, but again with the immediacy of an unmistakable voice: it is the Franciscan poet Jacopone da Todi who, imprisoned by Pope Boniface VIII in 1298 (because he had been one of the leading 'spiritual' Franciscans, a group within the order that the Pope opposed with violence), shows us in what I think to be his greatest poem the inner drama of a prisoner's life. He shows us the peripety by which from bitter satirical complaint he arrives at serenity; and this peripety is reflected in an astonishing way in the poetic style, which spans from the goliardic to the mystical, and even transmutes the one into the other.

In the first part of the song a rigmarole of half-bitter, half-humorous complaint predominates. It has something of the 'underdog' tone of Hugh Primas' autobiographical complaint, *Dives eram et dilectus*—a tone that is now fierce and coarse, now sly in attack, now self-mocking. Jacopone's metre, too, recalls the Latin poet's, though his schema is a regular one of the carol/*lauda* type (see above, p. 191). Yet there is none of Primas' rigidity and one-track-mindedness: we see this already from the refrain, where after each stanza the troubling question recurs—

Que farai, fra Iacovone?	What will you do, friar Jacopone?
Èi venuto al paragone.	Now you must face your test.

Humanly, all possibilities remain open. There is a remarkable range of observation—from the grim physical details, to the psychological warfare, to reflections that turn realistic horrors into fantasies:

La prescione che m'è data,	The prison that's been given me,
una casa sotterata.	a house below the ground.
Arèscece una privata:	A privy drains off into it—
non fa fragar de moscone.	its scent is not of musk.
Null'omo me pò parlare;	No one's allowed to speak to me,
chi me serve lo pò fare,	only the attendant can,
ma èglie upporto confessare	but they force him to confess
de la mia parlazïone.	everything I've said to him.
Porto iette de sparviere,	I wear the gyves of a sparrowhawk,
soneglianno nel mio gire:	they tinkle as I walk—
nova danza ce pò odire	he can hear a new dance-music
chi sta appresso a mia stazzone!	who stops near where I live!

Soon a deeper irony appears: cannot the discomforts of which Jacopone complains be seen as the very things that bring him closer to his spiritual ascetic ideal? A basket of food is lowered into his dungeon on a pulley-rope—

Lo ceston sì sta fornito:	The hamper is filled up like this:
fette de lo dì transito,	slices of bread from yesterday,
cepolla per appetito;	an onion as apéritif—
nobel tasca de paltone.	noble pouch for a mendicant!

But here the self-mockery is taken a stage further—with a diet chiefly of bread, and no chance of exercise, the 'ascetic' *malgré lui* gets fatter and not thinner:

Tanto pane ennante affetto,	First I cut up so much bread
che ne stèttera un porchetto:	that a pig would have enough:
ecco vita d'om destretto,	yes, that's an ascetic's life—
novo santo Ilarïone.	I'm a second Saint Hilarion!

Then in a daring metaphor prayers become the coins with which he pays God for his prison fare (here for the first time the possibility of a mystical acceptance of the hardships is seriously hinted at):

Paternostri otto a denaro	Paternosters eight a penny
a pagar Dio tavernaro,	to pay God, my taverner—
ch'io non aio altro tesaro	for I have no other riches
a pagar lo mio scottone.	with which to pay my bill.

There follow reflections, wholly serious and bitter in a quite different way from anything before, on how little of such coin the friars now have, how deeply Francis's bride Poverty has been betrayed. Then Jacopone returns to his own predicament: perhaps the greedy friars find even his upkeep too great an expense? At this moment, the turning-point of the poem, invective passes into a triumphant acceptance of humiliation: no contempt or hate that can be shown him can match his own *odio*—the self-hate or self-contempt that is his own violent expression of accepting all humiliation for Christ's sake, or rather not of accepting it but of actively seeking it, like a knight seeking out an opponent in jousting, so as to win a lady's love:

Faite, faite che volete,	Do, do whatever you will,
frate, ché de sotto gite,	friars—you are the losers still:
ca le spese ce perdete:	you will lose the whole expense—
prezzo nullo de pescione;	not a pigeon's worth of gain!
c'aio un granne capetale:	For I have lots of capital:
che me so' uso de male	I've grown used to being hurt,
e la pena non prevale	and suffering does not prevail
contra lo mio campïone.	against my champion.

The gain that the friars of the opposing, Papal faction hope is that imprisonment will force Jacopone to accept their ideas and abandon his own ideal (St Francis's ideal) of what the Franciscan order should be. Jacopone proclaims that he will not yield—but he sees this as a fight not against others but against the elements of self-assertiveness that may still be smouldering within him:

Lo mio campïone è armato,	My champion is wearing arms,
de lo mio odio scudato:	shielded by my self-contempt:
non pò esser vulnerato	he's not exposed to any wound
mentr' ha a collo lo scudone.	with that shield around his neck.
O mirabel odio mio,	Oh my wondrous self-contempt,
d'onne pena hai signorio,	sovereign over any pain,
non recìpi nullo eniurio,	you have received no injury,
vergogna t'è essaltazione.	shame for you is exaltation.
Nullo se trova nemico,	Nowhere is an enemy,
onnechivèl' è per amico,	anyone at all is friend,
eo solo me so' l'inico	I only am my enemy
contra mia salvazïone.	opposing my salvation.
Questa pena che m'è data,	This pain that has been given me,
trent'anni che l'aggio amata:	I have loved her thirty years—
or è ionta la iornata	now at last has come the day
d'esta consolazïone.	I win her consolation.

As the psychomachia closes, saltier goliardic phrases begin to re-appear, and in the envoy, dispatching his song to the Roman curia and to the world, Jacopone echoes a stanza from near the opening: what was then a complaint uttered with savage satire—his incarceration is Rome's 'prebend' for him—is now heard in a new harmony, in which the stab of irony is inseparable from a sublime acceptance:

E di' co' iaccio sotterrato,	Tell how I lie underground,
en perpetua encarcerato:	in perpetual imprisonment:
en corte i Roma ho guadagnato	in the court of Rome I've won
sì bon beneficïone.	so good a benefice.

Imprisonment is a relatively rare theme in medieval lyric, and Jacopone's confrontation of it is unique. A far commoner theme, on the other hand, is poverty—begging-songs can almost be regarded as a genre in their own right. Here the most brilliant performances are those of the Latin Archpoet: in his poetry, with its subtle stream of irreverence, its always faintly mocking learning and eloquence, and through all its unfaltering sense of the grandeur of the poet's vocation, the figure of the begging poet achieves mythical stature. But to me the most real song of poverty is a German one: paradoxically the most real, for this poet speaks allegorically and is acutely conscious of his role as performer; he too, though in a very different way from Jacopone, accepts his destiny serenely. It is a song that survives in the Manesse manuscript, under the name 'Süsskind, the Jew of Trimberg':

> Where-to-Find and Not-to-Find
> often do me injury;
> Sir Direneed of Lackaland
> seeks out my company.
> Because of this my children often weep:
> it's a bad pasture for their little beaks . . .

Against the strained ingenuity of the opening, with its deliberate distancing effect, the pair of lines about the poet's children stand out with a startling colloquial immediacy, made sharper by the rare but homely expression *snabelweide* (almost untranslatable—approximately 'beak-pasturing-place'). The allegory is resumed for a few more lines, and the poet slips in the briefest, apparently most casual appeal to his aristocratic audience—the only direct indication he gives that the poem is a begging-song at all. Then he continues:

> Still with my art I undertake
> the journey only a fool would make,
> as nobles do not give me anything.
> For this I shall now shun their court,
> and I shall grow a long grey beard:
> from now on I shall take the road
> in the way an old Jew does.
> My coat will have to be long,
> I'll wear a wide-brimmed hat,
> my walk will have to be a humble walk,
> and I shall seldom sing them another courtly song,
> since noble lords bar me from what is theirs.

There is a choice of roles: the one, that of the travelling court poet financially at the mercy of his patrons, is an insult, and Süsskind flings this insult in his audience's face. The other role is a caricature: for someone whose life has been spent in the courts the popular image of the 'old Jew' could not help being another piece of play-acting. Yet he is resolved to change his part: in the caricature, he claims with a sombre wit, he will find his identity better than as court entertainer. There will be an element of external pretence—getting the details of his new costume right—but no longer the corroding inner pretence, the pretence of feeling at ease in a world that has not accepted one, the pretence of elegant mirth when one's children are crying with hunger.

In the great range of lyrics of realism in medieval Portugal, the majority are less grave in theme and tone than the songs so far discussed. In the songs that comment on political events, on the wars, intrigues and scandals of the time, even a serious disaster, such as the desertion of King Alfonso by his Galician chivalry at the battle of Granada, tends to give rise to laughter at the cowardice of the knights rather than to lamentation, and the laughter, though mocking, is good-natured more often than savage. Another favourite theme, the poverty and decline of the lower knightly class, the *infancões*, in the thirteenth century, is treated with a wealth of witty anecdote by way of illustration. Other songs again are broadsides launched against particular people: against an over-presumptuous *jogral* or a *trovador* who has gone down in the world, a miser or a pederast, and especially against some of the professional women singers, whose outspokenness and sexual freedom offered good pretexts for the delight of making songs about them. The most famous of these *soldadeiras*, Maria Balteira, was a favourite target for such poetic jests—no fewer than sixteen of the surviving songs allude to her gaily sensual life and art.

Among the most outstanding of the *trovadores* who composed topical and satirical lyrics are Pero da Ponte, whose work falls largely into the second quarter of the thirteenth century, and shows links with the Aragonese court of Jaime I, as well as with the Castilian one of Fernando III and his brilliant son Alfonso; the somewhat younger Pero Garcia of Burgos, who likewise frequented Alfonso's court; and the poet-king Alfonso himself, whose most remarkable poetic achievements are to be found among his topical songs rather than in his huge popular devotional collection (see above, p. 70), or in the somewhat conventional handful of love-songs that survive under his name.

Pero da Ponte's most memorable songs are those directed against women. The humour can be cruel, as when he writes of a courtesan in Toledo, nick-named 'Peixota' (the Fish):

> I've always heard it said that in Toledo
> there's a very poor supply of fish;
> but, to be honest, I just can't believe it . . .
> there lay a Fish, abandoned, under the bed,
> and not a single man would pick it up. . . .

At other times, even in malice, Pero's wit can be light. There was a lady whose education of her daughters seemed to prepare them less for marriage than for a career as *grandes cocottes*:

> Do you want your daughter to be taught
> a skill with which she will do well?
> Send her to Maria Dominga—
> she's an admirable teacher!
> What is her method? I shall tell:
> the lass will learn, in less than a month's time,
> learn the wise art—of wiggling her behind!

It is Pero too who composed the most sparkling of the songs about Maria Balteira, when the adventurous *jograressa* (for whatever motive) undertook a pilgrimage to the Holy Land. With great verve he spins his own fantasy about her return to Portugal, loading every rift with innuendo, sparing neither religious practices nor sexual:

> Maria Pérez, our crusaderess,
> returning from the land beyond the sea,
> came back so laden with indulgences
> that with the weight she could not even rise;
> but some are stolen, everywhere she goes,
> till no indulgences were left at last.
>
> Indulgences are very precious things,
> one must look after them most carefully;
> Maria's treasure-chest was not too safe
> a place for that—indeed it could not be,
> for since the time the padlock was first broken,
> her treasure-chest has always been wide open . . .

The best known of the younger poet Pero Garcia's *cantigas d'escarnho* is one in which he teases his colleague Roí Queimado for making songs in which he professed to die of love:

> In his songs Roí made himself to die—
> but then he rose again on the third day!

Here I think that the point, amusing as it is, is drawn out excessively: it is too slight a joke to support two dozen lines of verse. A far more brilliantly sustained piece, to my mind, is Pero Garcia's attack on avarice. There are a number of such attacks in Galician lyric, and many more in Medieval Latin, there especially against the Roman curia. They are rarely first-rate as poetry—only where, like Pero

Garcia, the poet is concise, avoids generalities, and is fired in what he has to say by a vital personal impulse:

> Lord God, how I was welcomed courteously
> when I reached Lagares the other day,
> while great showers of rain were pouring down:
> but God is gracious—for I met the judge
> Martin Fernándiz, and he said to me:
> 'You can buy bread, wine, meat in the next town,
> in San Paaio'—which was on my way.
>
> I tell you, I'd have been quite desperate
> had I not met the judge. What could I do?
> I was without a penny that day, too—
> but through God's graciousness I met the judge
> Martin Fernándiz: he came out to me
> and pointed out a nearby hostelry
> in which I bought my food—however much.
>
> Had I not found the judge, how well I know
> I'd never have met with such a host that day—
> for it was growing dark, I'd lost my way;
> but the judge I met helped me out: although
> it was a while till I knew who he was,
> he knew me at once, came forth, and humbly paid
> his best respects—and pointed out my road.

Nothing disturbs the unruffled surface of this song. At the same time it is beautifully varied: in each stanza the poet adds another touch about his plight, as if quite incidentally, but each time, until the crowning irony of 'he knew me at once', it reveals the judge still more despicably, without the poet's ever having to say so. The control is perfect, not once does Pero feel the need to raise his voice. The tone is as bland as any in the Galician lyric repertoire, yet every detail needed to complete the case against the judge is lightly and allusively sketched in. It is this that enables Pero to humiliate his miserly victim with superb elegance and panache.

Equally remarkable, and stylistically at another extreme, is Pero Garcia's diatribe against a wanton woman, Maria Negra. Humorously coarse language had always had its place in satirical verse, in Galician lyric as elsewhere; what is exceptional here is that the coarseness is not there for humour or raillery, or even for invective, but rather to create a grotesque vision, strong enough to exist in its own right, outrageous enough to compel acceptance, while it lasts, of its hyperbolic fantasy of hate:

Maria Negra, luckless woman, why
buy so many tails, why try so hard?—
since in her hand they just lie down and die,
unable to endure her, the ill-starred.
As for the great long weapon that she bought,
yesterday evening she ravaged it,
and now she holds another slimy-wet . . .

She lacks all fortune in her escapades,
to lose so many tails within a year—
they die on her, although she buys them dear:
for it's a dank house where she puts them down,
a stable where she leaves them, so that then
they die on her, and the crazed hag again
roars for more tails, stretched prone upon the ground.

King Alfonso's songs include a wide range of satire within the themes and conventions of his time, but his finest song is more serious and more individual than any of his outright satires. It is a meditation stimulated by his experiences: with gentle self-mockery he admits that he has never enjoyed battles or chivalric sports, that he has always been afraid of them; he calls to mind all the disloyalty he has suffered at the hands of his courtiers, his friends and his family, against whom he is quite defenceless. Life on land is epitomised for Alfonso by a nest of scorpions, a landscape of poisonous dryness and terror. In his dream existence the sea is a refuge from this land, it holds out the promise of a fresh life, unambitious, contemptible to the chivalric world and lacking that world's romanticism of love and arms, but with its own, more serene romance. Alfonso's reverie is too subtle, too fully an imaginative creation, for any part of it to be directly related to particular persons or events in his life. There are no allegorical correspondences. It is a symbolist poem, that establishes its own laws of association and is not bounded by requirements of fact: it is a portrait of a man's imagination running free.

There is a gentle rhythm in the repetition of themes and images that seems to reflect the very motion of being lulled in a ship on a softly stirring sea—the variations and recurrences in the language suggest the dreamy, hypnotic quality of the whole. It is an excellingly original and relevant use of the old traditions of anaphora and parallelism that played so large a role in Galician lyric. In satirical songs these are often a disadvantage: the point that can be made with concise wit in a single stanza is diluted by variations into the customary three stanzas or four; even in some of the examples I have given from Pero da Ponte and Pero Garcia it seemed as effective, if not more so, to cite individual

stanzas as to cite complete songs. Alfonso's song, however, must be
quoted in full: for him the traditional modes of variation are not
superfluous—it is by adapting them that he creates the unique fabric of
his poem. The unusually complex rhyme-scheme and syntax likewise
contribute to this fabric in an essential way: for each of the two pairs of
stanzas the rhymes form a perfect mirror-image—all the rhymes find
each other again, as unerringly as in his reverie the poet finds his true
self again. And whereas in satirical songs poets tend to be fond of
staccato effects, here in each stanza the syntax produces an astonishing
legato: in each the movement of thought remains syntactically unbroken for the full thirteen lines, mirroring the serene continuity of the
vision itself:

Non me posso pagar tanto	I cannot find such great delight
do canto	in the song
das aves nen de seu son,	of birds, or in their twittering,
nen d'amor nen d'ambiçon[1]	in love or in ambition
nen d'armas—ca ei espanto	or in arms—for I fear
por quanto	that these indeed
mui perigoosas son,	are fraught with danger—
—come dun bon galeon,	as in a good galleon
que mi alongue muit' aginha	that can take me speedily
deste demo da campinha,	from this demonic landscape
u os alacrães son;	where the scorpions dwell;
ca dentro no coraçon	for within my heart
senti deles a espinha!	I have felt their sting!
E juro par Deus lo santo	And by the holy God I swear
que manto	I would wear
non tragerei nen granhon,	neither cloak nor beard,
nen terrei d'amor razon	nor would I involve myself in love
nen d'armas, por que quebranto	or arms, for injury
e chanto	and lamentation
ven delas toda sazon;	come from these at every season—
mais tragerei un dormon	no, I'd pilot a merchant-ship
e irei pela marinha	and sail across the ocean,
vendend' azeit' e farinha;	selling vinegar and flour,
e fugirei do poçon	and I would fly from the poison
do alacran, ca eu non	of the scorpion, for I know
lhi sei outra meezinha.	no other medicine against it.

1. The two MSS. read *damiçõ*; Professor Rodrigues Lapa rejects the emendation to
d'ambiçon on the grounds that this word is 'rarely or never found', and suggests 'de
mixon' (of harvest). Yet this seems to me poetically less appropriate: the context demands
a word congruent with the aspirations of the chivalric world.

Nen de lançar a tavlado	I can take no pleasure here
pagado	in tilting,
non sõo, se Deus m'ampar,	nor, God save the mark,
aqui, nen de bafordar;	in mock-tournaments;
e andar de noute armado,	as for going armed by night
sen grado	or patrolling,
o faço, e a roldar;	I do it without any joy—
ca mais me pago do mar	for I find more enchantment in the sea
que de seer cavaleiro;	than in being a knight:
ca eu foi já marinheiro	long ago I was a mariner,
e quero-m' ôi-mais guardar	and henceforth I long to guard
do alacran, e tornar	myself against the scorpion, and return
ao que me foi primeiro.	to what I was in the beginning.
E direi-vos un recado:	I must try to explain to you:
pecado	the demon
nunca me pod' enganar	will never be able to trick me
que me faça já falar	now into speaking the language
en armas, ca non m'é dado	of arms, for this is not my role—
(doado	(useless
m'é de as eu razõar,	for me to reason thus,
pois-las non ei a provar);	I have not even arms to try)—
ante quer' andar sinlheiro	rather, I long to go alone
e ir come mercadeiro	and in a merchant's guise
algũa terra buscar	to find some land
u me non possan culpar	where they cannot strike at me:
alacran negro nem veiro.	the black scorpion, and the mottled.

It is perhaps appropriate to conclude this chapter by returning briefly to a poet half a century older than Alfonso, Walther von der Vogelweide, not only because he wrote some of the most unforgettable songs that are 'realistic' in the two senses I have outlined, but because in his own German tradition he himself to a large extent created the very possibility of realism in lyric. His point of departure was *Spruchdichtung*—a kind of didactic or gnomic verse that has very ancient roots in Germanic poetry, at its best pithy, crackling with shrewdness and wit, at its worst tediously sententious. Before Walther it was seldom particularised or given a topical bearing. Walther's artistry transformed the whole conception of *Spruchdichtung*: for him it became more specific, an often informal, always mercurial, pungent and personal mode of comment. Even in his most didactic pieces Walther conveys the particular movement of his own brain, not simply an impersonal chain of *sententiae*. Walther can make the *Spruch* reveal as much of himself as he chooses, can make it do whatever he requires.

When the scheming Pope Innocent III, pitting Otto of Brunswick, whom he had crowned Emperor, against the young anti-papal Frederick II, tried to raise money in Germany for a new crusade, ordering poor-boxes to be placed for this purpose in all the German churches, Walther makes of the *Spruch* a savage political weapon:

> Aha, in what a Christian spirit the Pope laughs
> when he tells his foreign henchmen 'Yes, I've done them down!'
> —He is saying things he should not even have thought—
> he says 'I've made two Alemans share a single crown,
> so that they wrack the Empire and destroy it:
> we'll in the meantime fill our coffers by it!
> I've herded them to my poor-box,[1] all that's theirs is mine,
> their German silver's wandering to a foreign base—
> come, all you priests, eat chickens and drink wine,
> and let the German lay-folk fast and waste!'

The deadly effectiveness is achieved by the simplest device: making the Pope speak in his own person. That he should condemn himself out of his own mouth is an incomparably more telling attack than any protest against him could have been.

At the other extreme of Walther's *Spruchdichtung* are poems that have nothing to do with ethics or politics, but contain some acute moments of self-revelation. One, on the day when Frederick II at last freed him from homelessness and gave him 'status', has already been cited earlier (p. 23). Another, in which remarkable human complexities emerge, is his elegy, or soliloquy, on the death of the poet Reinmar:

> It's true, Reinmar, I grieve for you,
> far more deeply than you would do
> if you were alive and I had died.
> I will admit quite truthfully,
> I'd not weep much for you personally—
> I weep for your noble art that is now destroyed.
> You could increase the joy of all the world
> when you cared to aim at something good.
> I grieve for your eloquent lips, and for your graceful song,
> that they have seen destruction in my time.
> Why couldn't you wait even a little time?
> I'd have kept you company—my singing won't last long.
> May your soul fare well, and our thanks go to your tongue.

1. The box (*stoc*) was in the form of a long, hollow stick—thus the implied contrast with the staff of the 'good shepherd' is unmistakable.

H

Walther had come to the court at Vienna as a young poet around 1190, when Reinmar, some ten years older, was the established and fashionable poet there. He had at first learnt much from Reinmar in poetic language and technique, and had found much to admire in the older man's introspective, melancholy, idealising love-songs. But inevitably he came to feel their limitations—their monotony and unreality, their confined and often anaemic diction—and showed his feelings by ironic and parodistic allusions to Reinmar's love-songs in his own (see above, p. 136), and before long Walther acquired the confidence to write songs that went deliberately against the conventions to which Viennese court society clung. Walther was forced to leave the court in 1198 and, despite a return visit later, was never fully accepted there again. We can surmise that Reinmar was not blameless in this. In Walther's meditation he speaks with a frankness that brushes aside all the routine modes of praise which normally prevailed in the medieval elegiac genre. We see him trying to distinguish his feelings about Reinmar as man and as artist. At first it seems easy to make a distinction, but gradually Walther finds it more difficult: did not the fact that Reinmar was too limited and inflexible, too little prepared to welcome the new ideas of a younger man, reflect itself also in his art? If he 'cared to aim at something good', if he had something to say that was truly his and truly worth saying, his was a 'noble art'—but, by implication, there were times when Reinmar did not do this, when he relied on his eloquence and gracefulness but was not prepared to think or feel afresh. Yet as these thoughts cross Walther's mind, he recognises that a poet's eloquence and grace are, after all, rare and beautiful qualities, and with the words 'Why couldn't you wait . . .' he seems to feel a not unfriendly impulse towards Reinmar the man as well: whatever his faults and limitations, he was a worthy rival; the world is a little sadder now for Walther since he has no one of this stature as sparring-partner.

Towards the end of his life Walther subjected his own poetry and ideals to a more searching critique than he had ever attempted for Reinmar's. What would his own aspirations look like in the eye of eternity? He has a strong impulse to gaze towards the eternal, to say a gentle but firm farewell to 'Frô Welt' and her always ambiguous gifts of joy. Above all, he feels that his earlier stream of poetry has run dry: he can still turn out a love-song, but only to oblige an audience—his heart is no longer in it. It is this thought that occupies him in the opening stanza of his incomparable introspective meditation that begins 'Ir reinen wîp, ir werden man'. The second stanza ('Lât mich an eime stabe gân') defends the notion that human nobility is an inner quality which has nothing to do with status in the world, and which truly fine human beings will always recognise regardless of a man's condition. Calmly, without a trace of assertiveness, Walther affirms it will be recognised in him: ever since childhood he has worked unflinchingly striving towards true excellence. The link with his opening thoughts is left implicit, but is unmistakable: for Walther this striving was his 'forty years' of labour as poet 'of love and how to lead one's life' ('von minnen und als iemen sol')—this is as valid a way towards true nobility as any other. The second stanza closes

ezn wart nie lobelîcher leben,	There was never life more praiseworthy
swer sô dem ende rehte tuot.	than doing justice to the goal.

But what if a poet in his old age is no longer certain of the 'ende' towards which he has lived? What if he is overwhelmed by a sense of world-weariness in the light of which his earlier aspirations to joy and beauty seem futile? What if he is tempted to think that this world-weariness is the true *contemptus mundi* and longing for the eternal, the soul's victory over the body's pleasures, the affirmation of a changeless heavenly love against a fickle earthly one? Walther shows us these thoughts as they invade his consciousness:

3. Welt, ich hân dînen lôn ersehen:	World, I can see through your reward:
swaz dû mir gîst, daz nimest dû mir.	what you give me, you take from me.
wir scheiden alle blôz von dir.	We are all naked, leaving you.
scham dich, sol mir alsô geschehen.	Have shame, if I am to be naked too,
ich hân lîp unde sêle (des war gar ze vil)	I who have wagered body and soul (it was indeed
gewâget tûsentstunt dur dich:	too much) a thousand times for you:
nû bin ich alt und hâst mit mir dîn gampelspil:	now I am old, and you play tricks on me—
und zürn ich daz, sô lachest dû.	if I grow angry you just laugh.
nû lache uns eine wîle noch:	Laugh at us a while longer, then:
dîn jâmertac wil schiere komen,	your day of weeping will soon come,
und nimet dir swatz uns hâst benomen,	rob you of what you robbed from us,
und brennet dich dar umbe iedoch.	and burn you for it nonetheless!
4. Mîn sêle müeze wol gevarn!	Let my soul make its journey well!
ich hân zer welte manegen lîp gemachet frô, man unde wîp:	In the world I have brought joy to many people, men and women—
künd ich dar under mich bewarn!	could I have kept my being whole!

H*

lobe   ich des lîbes minne,
    deis der sêle leit:
si giht, ez sî ein lüge, ich
    tobe.
der   wâren minne giht si
    ganzer stætekeit,
wie guot si sî, wies iemer wer.
'lîp, lâ die minne diu dich
    lât,
und habe die stæten minne wert:
mich dunket, der dû hâst
    gegert,
diu sî niht visch unz an den grât.'
	If I praise the body's love, the
	    soul feels hurt:
	she says that I am raving, it's
	    a lie.
	For true love she claims utter
	    constancy,
	how good it is, how everlasting too:
	'Body, desert the love that deserts
	    you,
	and cherish changeless love alone—
	I think the love for which you have
	    longed
	is not fish right down to its bone.'

Is the soul right, or is hers too easy a solution? If she remains unanswered, does it mean that Walther's attempt to seek the good by way of human love and human excellence, the ideal of his life's work, was mistaken? Walther answers the soul's claim by contemplating that ideal once more:

5. Ich hât ein schoenez bilde
    erkorn:
owê daz ich ez ie gesach
ald ie sô vil zuoz ime gesprach!
ez hât schoen unde rede verlorn.
dâ   wonte ein wunder inne:
    daz fuor ine weiz war:
dâ von gesweic daz bilde iesâ.
sîn   liljerôsevarwe wart so
    karkelvar,
daz ez verlôs smac unde schîn.
mîn bilde, ob ich bekerbet bin
in dir, sô lâ mich ûz alsô
daz wir ein ander vinden
    frô:
wan ich muoz aber wider in.
	It was a fair image I
	    perceived—
	alas that I ever gazed on it
	or spoke to it so many times!
	It has lost its beauty and speech.
	In it dwelt a miracle: it went I
	    know not where,
	and thus the image became mute;
	so prison-coloured grew its lily
	    and rose,
	it lost its fragrance and its glow.
	My image, if I am imprisoned
	within you, let me out again
	so that we find each other
	    joyfully—
	for once more I must enter in.

The 'fair image' Walther contemplates is, I suggest, an image of his ideal, of all the beauty and love towards which his poetry and life had been striving. In his moments of bitterness, exhaustion and disillusion this image tarnished and faded, the miraculous element, inspiration, that was bound up with it, disappeared—the old poet found he could only versify to order, it was no longer his ideal speaking within him. He cries out in regret that he should ever have chosen this way as his destiny: for his audience he must still, however lustreless he feels, live up to his image—the image has become his prison. But in the four last lines Walther arrives at an insight that goes beyond this. He asks for freedom from his image—not in order to reject it, but such a freedom as will enable him to find it again and re-enter it spontaneously and gladly. Now he knows that the image, even if he has wearied of it and neglected it, is *his* image, the 'ende' which his life must do justice to. If the soul tempts him to deny his image, to impose one that is not his own, she is wrong. The ultimate worth, the salvation, of a poet of human love and honour is as a poet of human love and honour. He must be free—to find and, at the last, fully re-enter, 'that which he always was'; not as if returning to a prison, but to a destiny that he has chosen and spent a lifetime trying to achieve.

This interpretation makes two important assumptions: that Walther in these stanzas is developing a profound and coherent pattern of ideas —that here we have not, as some distinguished earlier scholars have claimed, either a loose concatenation of independent stanzas, or more than one separate poem. Secondly, that the order which I have adopted for the last two stanzas, which is their order in all four manuscripts in which the poem occurs, is the right and inevitable one.[1] The majority of scholars today, despite the overwhelming manuscript evidence, reverse the fourth and fifth stanzas, and make the fourth the conclusion of the poem. This would make the poem more of a palinode, a renunciation of all that Walther had spent a lifetime trying to express in poetry; the soul would then have the last word. But it would leave the fifth stanza without a (to me) satisfactory meaning or function in the whole.[2] If we are not to start with the assumption that the poem is incoherent, I submit that the fifth stanza cannot belong anywhere but at the close: it is only as an answer to the soul's claims, as the final resolution of the conflict, that the poet's apologia makes sense. It is

---

1. Two MSS (BC) have the stanzas in the order that I have adopted (1 2 3 4 5). The third MS (A) has 4 5 1 2 3, the fourth (w^x) has 1 2 4 5 3. Despite these variations, the relation of 4 and 5 to each other never changes. Among the most notable earlier interpretations, that of Carl von Kraus (*Festschrift des Wiener Akad. Germanistenvereins*, 1925, pp. 105 ff.) proposed an order 1 2 3 5 4, while more recently Günther Jungbluth (*Deutsche Viertel jahrsschrift* 32, 1958, pp. 372 ff.) adopted and defended the order of the 'A' text.

2. It is sometimes argued that the fifth stanza, if placed before the fourth, could be read as the opening of a soul-and-body debate, that Walther's 'image' refers to his own body. It seems to me that expressions such as 'schoen' and 'liljerôsevarwe' make this unlikely: in so serious a context it would be quite inappropriate for Walther to refer to himself as an Adonis. Moreover, there is no mention of 'soul' in this stanza—here it is always 'ich', not 'mîn sêle'. If the 'bilde' is not Walther's body, then the frequent suggestion that 'ich muoz aber wider in' refers to the resurrection of the body on the Day of Judgment must likewise be ruled out.

not a victory for soul or body, but for Walther the human being, when, in the face of the doubts that have tormented him, he sees that it is not on the desertion of his lifelong ideals as man and poet, but on the joyful ultimate identification with them, that his worth in eternity depends. From the standpoint of orthodox belief in Walther's time, this may well seem a profoundly individual and unconventional utterance—as individual as the way of thought by which Walther arrived at it. At the same time we can see how great a consciousness of poetic vocation, how deep a sense of a unique role in human society, was possible in a writer of medieval lyric.

POSTSCRIPT 1977

The book completed a decade ago was planned as a literary introduction to aspects of medieval lyric, with a focus mainly on the interpretation and critical reading of particular texts. Ten years later, while more conscious of the limitations of such a selective and personal approach, I still venture to hope it has not lost all value. Perhaps a full-scale systematic history of medieval lyric will one day be written, or a manual produced in which the coverage is (at least up to the publication day) exhaustive. Yet even if such formidable instruments of research were to come into being, it might still be worth setting out some reasons for the belief that there is a range of lyric poetry in the Middle Ages, as richly varied and distinctive as in any period of Europe's history, which need not and should not remain the preserve of philologists and antiquarians—a poetry in which most barriers of language and of timebound conventions are readily surmountable, and poets can speak to us with individual voices even across a millennium.

The only substantial innovation in the present edition is a more detailed bibliographic supplement (pp. 262–76), devoted to work that has appeared in the last ten or twelve years. The chief aim in the original bibliography was to give a wide-ranging guide to the *primary* sources of medieval lyric. To achieve this in manageable compass, the choice of secondary literature had to be severely curtailed: it was confined to some standard works of reference, and to a few of the essays and studies I had found most stimulating in the course of writing the book. In the new supplement I have tried to balance editions with more general and more detailed studies, historical and critical, with studies of the music, versification, themes and imagery as well as of the wider background of medieval lyric. There is no question of compre-

hensiveness; for some languages I have been able to see more of the
recent work than for others, and my selection cannot please everyone.
But I trust that, whatever important omissions there may be, the works
listed will themselves contain sufficient references to guide readers
further in both older and newer scholarship.

In the course of the book many minor changes have been introduced,
in order to improve details in the texts, translations and critical
comments. The most significant change occurs in the translation and
discussion of Wilde Alexander's song about childhood (pp. 78–81),
because a recent scholar has emended a crucial corrupt word in the text
—I believe decisively—and this must modify the interpretation of the
whole. Another of the more controversial interpretations I proposed,
however (pp. 195–6)—arguing that the English *Maiden in the mor lay*
is a dance-song, and must be read as a profane, not sacred, lyric—has
meanwhile received a fortunate and unexpected confirmation in a text
discovered by Siegfried Wenzel (*Speculum* 49, 1974, 69–74): an
English preacher, writing around 1360, cites this lyric as a *karole* (i.e.
dance-song), and makes quite clear that for him the song is about a
moor-maiden, whose delights are those of a pagan Golden Age, and
not about the Virgin Mary, the Magdalen, or any other figure of
Christian hue. It would be difficult to argue that this almost contemporary witness was mistaken, or alone in his mistake. It is still
possible, of course, that for other medieval listeners the song of the
moor-maiden evoked sacred associations, just as it has done for so
many modern scholars—but as yet we do not know if this was so.

For another early English lyric (translated and discussed on p. 144),
I have added a new textual note (p. 280): the handwriting in the unique
manuscript is so faded and illegible that neither the standard edition
(by Carleton Brown, 1932) nor some recent and most valuable corrections to it (by Theo Stemmler, 1974) have in my view fully resolved
the obscurities of the text.

While this brief technical note and a new bibliographic section
could be added, there remains much else that—now, as ten years ago—
I should have liked to add but couldn't. The Middle Ages have left us,
for instance, a number of brilliant longer poems that are in some
essential aspects lyrical, and that I was eager to include. Yet reluctantly,
for practical reasons, I had to concur with the *OED*: that 'lyric' is
'Now used as the name for short poems (whether or not intended to
be sung) . . .'. To have presented longer poems as well, with appropriate interpretation and criticism, would have resulted in a book of
wholly different proportions and scope. This means that some major
poets, such as the Archpoet or Rutebeuf, flit through these pages as

hurriedly as Hamlet or Claudius through *Rosencrantz and Guildenstern are Dead*—as if they were 'attendant lords' and not protagonists. Or again it means that Ramón Lull's finest poem, the *Desconhort*, is evoked by a few allusions only and not cited or analysed. To these poets I hope to return on another occasion. An equally important omission was the discussion of that lyrical poetry which lies, in both a literary and a geographical sense, on the borders of what is here discussed: the Celtic and Norse traditions, the Byzantine, Slavonic, and Hispano-Arabic. But to treat or even sketch these lies outside my competence.

In the last decade much has been won for the study of medieval lyric that could not be signalled in the body of the book. To mention some things that seem to me of particular interest: there is, first of all, an exciting new range of recordings of medieval lyrics, both Latin and vernacular, by groups such as the *Studio der frühen Musik*. Even where transcriptions and techniques of performance may remain debatable, or where texts of lyrics have been treated inexpertly, it is possible to experience something of the living reality of many more medieval songs today than ever before. A fine bibliography of medieval music by Andrew Hughes (1974), and the collected *Scripta Musicologica* of Hygini Anglés (3 vols., 1975), are landmarks for the study of the music of the lyrics.

Among new anthologies of lyrical poetry, Martín de Riquer's three-volume *Los trovadores* (1975) brings together a large corpus of accurate texts and translations, and a wealth of historical insights that will long remain unsurpassed; Frederick Goldin has made a most attractive selection of troubadours and trouvères, and of medieval German and Italian lyrics, in two volumes with facing English translations (1973). Some important new editions of individual poets have also appeared— of troubadours such as William of Aquitaine (N. Pasero, 1973), Raimon de Miraval (L. T. Topsfield, 1971), and Guillem de Berguedà (M. de Riquer, 2 vols., 1971), of Minnesinger such as Neidhart (S. Beyschlag, 1975), Galician poets such as Martin Moya (L. Stegagno Picchio, 1968), and Italians such as Dante da Maiano (R. Bettarini, 1969) and Jacopone da Todi (F. Mancini, 1974). The text volumes of the *Carmina Burana*, in the edition begun by Hilka and Schumann, have been completed by Bernhard Bischoff (1970). For the comparative study of the forms of medieval lyric, István Frank's invaluable *Répertoire métrique* of troubadour poetry has now been complemented by similar instruments of research for Galician-Portuguese lyric (G. Tavani, 1967) and for Old French (U. Mölk and F. Wolfzettel, 1972). Repertories of the themes in early Sicilian and Tuscan lyric have been published (W. Pagani, 1968; E. Savona, 1973), and a repertory of imagery in Old French and Provençal poetry has been begun (W. Ziltener, 1972).

For those who seek recent discussion of medieval lyric, many directions could be indicated. Roman Jakobson, in two essays, on a song by Martin Codax and a sonnet by Dante (now printed together in his *Questions de poétique*, 1973), has attempted an elaborate analysis of sound-patterns in medieval lyrics, in the tradition of Dante's own enquiry in *De vulgari eloquentia*. New contributions to the difficult problem of assessing the popular elements in medieval lyric have been made in essays by the late Theodor Frings and Elisabeth Lea (see below, pp. 268–9), and by Margit Frenk Alatorre in her book *Las jarchas mozárabes y los comienzos de la lírica romanica* (1975). The understanding of medieval lyrical genres and their 'Typologie' has been furthered in essays by Hugo Kuhn (*Text und Theorie*, 1969) and several of his pupils. Some of the most notable recent contributions to the interpretation of medieval lyrics that I have come across have been in books by the late Guido Favati (1975) for Italian lyrics, by Douglas Gray (1972) for English, and Stephen Reckert (1976) for Portuguese. Walther Killy (*Elemente der Lyrik*, 1972) has brought stimulating insight to the central problems of interpreting lyrical poetry, discussing examples ancient and modern from several literatures.

Nonetheless, as regards the interpretation of medieval lyrics, much remains to be done. Most of the major poets and collections still need editions with stylistic, and not purely philological, commentary; many of the finest lyrics have never yet received detailed critical discussion. There is also a need for more precise study of the diverse social contexts of medieval lyric—here Anna Maria Clausen's recent monograph, *Le origini della poesia lirica in Provenza e in Italia* (1976), though limited in its use of texts, indicates some promising paths of enquiry. It is becoming more widely recognised that the historical understanding of medieval lyric is inseparable from sensitive interpretation of the texts, and from the perception of what, in an exploratory book, I once called 'poetic individuality in the Middle Ages'. The most perceptive scholars of recent years no longer treat the content of troubadour and trouvère poetry as if it were a homogeneous mass, or wish to legislate about such concepts as 'the chivalric system of virtues' or 'the code of courtly love'. On the whole these and similar *a priori* constructs, which became current seventy or eighty years ago, have fitted the actual texts poorly. The sociological implications of the lyrics will be elicited gradually, by meticulous reading, from the lyrics themselves. And even then we would expect them to remain subtle and shifting, not fixed and hard of outline. For some decades at least, I suspect, the most illuminating studies of medieval lyric will remain chary of literary and historical generalisation; rather, their device may well be Warburg's: 'God is in detail.'

Cambridge
June 1977   P.D.

MELODIES

The melodies of twelve of the lyrics discussed in the course of the book are given below in modern notation. I have drawn on the work of scholars with diverse techniques of transcription: there is still no unanimity on principles and method, the various styles of notation at different times and places in the Middle Ages present their own problems, and questions especially of the length of notes and the variations of rhythm still offer musicologists crucial points for debate. My aim has been to choose as varied and attractive a range of melodies as possible, but the choice has been determined partly by relevance to my literary discussion and partly by the availability of transcriptions. The style of transcription and of editing has in each case been taken over from the scholar who is named; sources are cited in full in the references on pp. 277–80..

The limitations of space for presenting melodies here, and my own lack of professional knowledge on the musical side, must not lead the reader to underrate the importance of the music in medieval lyric: the melodies are an essential complement to the texts; ideally, where the music survives, it would always be printed together with the words before the discussion of any lyric begins.

1 Gottschalk, *Ut quid iubes, pusiole* (? Reichenau, *c.* 850; the dating *c.* 825, suggested by several scholars, seems too early in terms of Gottschalk's stylistic development; if the song was composed in his artistic maturity, the poet's presence on the island Reichenau may be only in memory. Melody transcr. E. de Coussemaker; discussed above, pp. 34–6)

2 *Phebi claro nondum orto iubare* (Provence, s. X²; transcr. G.
Vecchi; discussed above, pp. 170–2)

3 *Mei amic e mei fiel* (Limoges, s. XI²; transcr. F. Gennrich; discussed above, pp. 50–1)

Co - lum - ba as - pex - it per can-cel - los fe - nes - - tre,

u - bi an-te fa-ci-em e - - ius su-dan-do su-da-vit bal - - sa - mum _

de lu - ci - do _ Ma - xi - - mi-no.

1(a)

Ca-lor so - lis _ ex-ar-sit _ et in te - ne - bras res - plen-du - it,

un - de gem - ma sur-rex - it in e - di-fi-ca-ti-o - ne tem - - pli

pu-ris-si - mi cor-dis _ be-ni - - vo - - li.

1(b)

Is - te _ tur - ris - ex-cel-sa de lig-no Li - ba - ni et ci - presso _ facta _

ia-cinc - to et sardi - o or-na - ta _ est, urbs _ pre - cel - lens _

ar-tes a - li - o - rum _ ar-ti - - fi - - cum.

2(a)

4 Hildegard of Bingen, *Columba aspexit* (Rhineland, *c.* 1150;
transcr. I. Bent; discussed above, pp. 75–8)   *continued on pp. 239–40.*

Ip-se___ ve-lox cer-vus cu-cur-rit ad___ fon- tem ___ pu-ris-si-me___

a-que___ flu-en - tis de for-tis-si-mo la- pi - de qui___ dul- ci- a

a-ro-ma- ta ___ ir-ri - - ga-vit.

2(b)

O pig - men - ta-ri- i qui es-tis in sua-vis- si- ma vi-ri-di-ta-te___

hor- to-rum regis, as-cen-den- tes in al- tum quan - do ___ sanc-tum sa-cri-fi-ci-um___

in a- ri- e-ti - bus per-fe-cis - - tis,___

3(a)

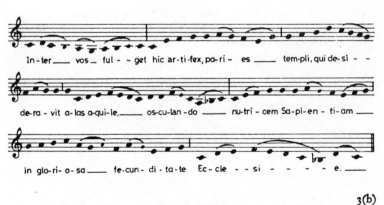

In-ter___ vos___ ful - - get hic ar-ti-fex, pa-ri - es ___ tem-pli, qui de- si - -

de-ra - vit a-las a-qui-le,___ os-cu-lan -do ___ nu-tri - cem Sa-pi-en - ti-am___

in glo-ri- o-sa___ fe-cun - di -ta-te Ec- cle - - si - - - - e. ___

3(b)

4 *continued* Hildegard of Bingen, *Columba aspexit*

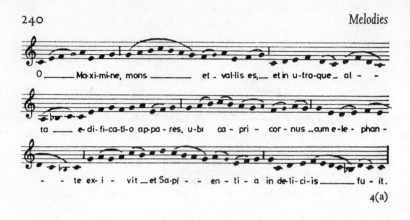

O ____ Ma-xi-mi-ne, mons ____ et - val-lis es,___ et in u-tro-que __ al - - ta ____ e-di-fi-ca-ti-o ap-pa - res, u-bı ca - pri - cor - nus ___ cum e-le - phan- - - te ex- i - vit __ et Sa-pi - - en - ti - a in de-li-ci-is ____ fu - it.

4(a)

Tu ____ es for-tis ___ et ___ su - - a - vis ___ in ce-ri-mo-ni- is et ___ in ____ choruscati-o-ne al - ta - ris as-cen-dens ____ ut fu - - mus ___ a - ro - - ma - tum ad co - - - lump- nam ___ lau - - - - dis,___

4(b)

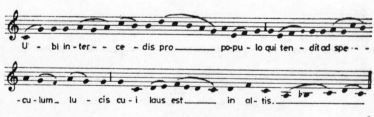

U - bi in -ter - - ce - dis pro ____ po-pu - lo qui ten - dit ad spe - - -cu - lum __ lu - cis cu - i laus est ____ in al- tis. ____

5

4 concluded   Hildegard of Bingen, *Columba aspexit*

5 *A l'entrada del tens clar* (Provence, ?s. XII[2]; transcr. F. Gennrich; discussed above, pp. 196–7)

6 Chastelain de Couci, *A vous, amant, plus k'a nulle autre gent* (Northern France, *c.* 1200; transcr. P. Aubry, text from MS. K; discussed above, pp. 127–8)

7 Philip the Chancellor, from *Dic, Christi veritas* (Paris, s. XII/XIII; transcr. H. Husmann; discussed above, p. 56)

continued on p. 243.

I

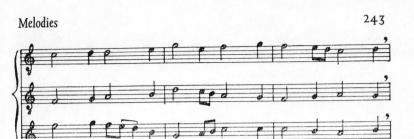

cum Ne- ro - ne aut in an- tro cum The- o - ne

7 *continued* Philip the Chancellor, from *Dic, Christi veritas*

1. «Sinc, ein gul - din huon; ich gibe dir wei – ze.» Schie - re
2. Rû - met ûz die schä- mel und die stüe - le! Heiz die

1. dô   Wart ich   vrô: Nâch ir   hul – den   ich vil   ger - ne
2.schragen Vür - der   tragen!   Hiu - te   sul wir   tan-zens   wer - den

1. sin – ge.   Al - sô   vreut den   tum - ben   guot   ge - hei –
2. müe - der.   Wer - fet ûf die   stu - ben   so   ist ez   küe –

1.-ze   Durch das   jâr.   Wür - de ez   wâr,   Sô   ge - stuont   nie
2.-le, Daz der   wint   An die   kint   Sanf - te   wæ – je

1. man - nes   muot   sô   rin – ge   Al - sô   mir der   mî - ne
2.durch diu   ü - ber - müe – der.   Sô die   vo - re - tan - zer

1. dan - ne   wæ – re.   Mac sî   durch ir   sæ - le - keit
2. dan - ne   swî – gen.   Sô sult ir   al - le   sin   ge - beten

1. Mî - niu   leit   Wen - den?   ja ist mîn   kum - ber   kla - ge - bæ – re.
2. Daz wir   treten   Aber ein   ho - ve - tän - zel   nâch der   gî – gen.

8 Neidhart, *Sinc, ein guldîn huon; ich gibe dir weize* (Austria,
s. XIII[1]: transcr. F. Gennrich; discussed above, pp. 204–6)

1. Ay Deus, se sab' o - ra meu a - mi - go com' eu
2. Ay Deus, se sab' o - ra meu a - ma - do com' eu
3. Com' eu se-nnei - ra es-tou en Vi - go e nu-
4. Com' eu se-nnei - ra en Vi - go ma - nno e nu-
5. E nu-llas gar - das non ei co - mi - go. Er - gas
6. E nu-llas gar - das mi-go non tra - yo. Er - gas

1. se-nnei - ra es-tou en Vi - go! E vou na - mo - ra-da!
2. en [Vi - go] se - nney - ra ma - nno!
3. llas gar - das non ei co - mi - go!
4. llas gar - das mi - go non tra - yo!
5. meus o - llos que cho - ran mi - go!
6. meus o - llos que cho - ran am - bos!

9 Martin Codax, *Ay Deus, se sab' ora meu amigo* (Castile, s. XIII[1]; transcr. H. Anglés; discussed above, p. 103)

Fowe - les in þe frith, þe fis - ses in

þe flod: and I mon wa - xe wod, mu!ch sorw I

wal - ke with for beste of bon and blod.

10 *Foweles in the frith* (England, s. XIII[2]; transcr. A. Hughes; discussed above, pp. 144-5)

1. Hie vor do wir kyn - der wa - ren

Und die tzit was in den ia - ren.

Daz wir lie - fen of die we - sen

Her von ie - nen wi - der tzuo de - sen:

Da wir un - der stun - den Fi - ol wun - den.

Da sicht man nu ryn - der be - sen.

11 Der wilde Alexander, *Hie vor dô wir kinder wâren* (Southern Germany or Switzerland, s. XIII²; transcr. F. Gennrich, text from MS. J; discussed above, pp. 78–81)

Bryd one bre - re, brid, brid, one bre - re, Kynd is co - me of

love, love to cra - ve. Blith - ful biryd on me thu — re - - we,

Or greyth, lef, greyth thu me — my gra - ve.

12 *Bryd one brere* (England, *c.* 1300; transcr. John Stevens; discussed above, pp. 145–6)

SELECT BIBLIOGRAPHY

(1) GENERAL

COLLECTIONS AND SERIES

AH	G. M. Dreves/C. Blume/H. M. Bannister, *Analecta Hymnica Medii Aevi* (55 vols., 1886–1922)
Ajuda	C. Michaëlis de Vasconcellos, *Cancioneiro da Ajuda* (2 vols., 1904)
Amigo	J. J. Nunes, *Cantigas d'amigo* (3 vols., 1928)
Amor	J. J. Nunes, *Cantigas d'amor* (1932)
Arundel	W. Meyer, *Die Arundel Sammlung mittellateinischer Lieder*, Abhandlungen der kgl. Gesellschaft der Wissenschaften, Göttingen, XI (1909), 2
ASPR	*The Anglo-Saxon Poetic Records* (6 vols., 1931–42)
CB	A. Hilka/O. Schumann/B. Bischoff, *Carmina Burana* (1930 ff.)
CC	K. Strecker, *Die Cambridger Lieder/Carmina Cantabrigiensia* (1926)
CFMA	Les Classiques Français du Moyen Age
Chrestomathie	K. Bartsch/E. Koschwitz, *Chrestomathie Provençale* (6th ed., 1904)
Dichtungen	F. Maurer, *Die religiösen Dichtungen des 11. und 12. Jahrhunderts* (3 vols., 1964–70)
DLD	C. von Kraus, *Deutsche Liederdichter des 13. Jahrhunderts* (2 vols., 1952–8)
EL	C. Brown, *English Lyrics of the XIIIth Century* (1932)
Escarnho	M. Rodrigues Lapa, *Cantigas d'escarnho e de mal dizer* (2nd ed., 1970)[1]
Giocosi	M. Marti, *Poeti giocosi del tempo di Dante* (1956)

1. The numbering of the songs in the first edition of *Escarnho* is retained in the references below. Nos. 1–133 are identical in the two editions; 134–63 in the first become 135–64 in the second; 164–394 become 166–396; 395–428 become 398–431.

Kharjas G   E. García Gómez, *Las jarchas romances de la serie árabe en su marco* (2nd ed., 1975)

Kharjas H   K. Heger, *Die bisher veröffentlichten Harǧas und ihre Deutungen* (1960)

Kharjas S   S. M. Stern, *Les chansons moʐarabes* (1953)

Lesebuch   W. Braune/K. Helm, *Althochdeutsches Lesebuch* (11th ed., 1949)

MF   C. von Kraus, *Minnesangs Frühling* (1944)

MGH   Monumenta Germaniae Historica

MLREL   P. Dronke, *Medieval Latin and the Rise of European Love-Lyric*, vol. 2 (2nd ed., 1968): *Medieval Latin Love-Poetry*

Nachlass   F. Gennrich, *Der musikalische Nachlass der Troubadours* (3 vols. 1958 ff.)

Poetae   *Poetae Latini Aevi Carolini* (MGH, 1881 ff.)

Poeti   G. Contini, *Poeti del Duecento* (2 vols., 1960)

Poesia   C. Muscetta/P. Rivalta, *Poesia del Duecento e del Trecento* (1956)

Rimatori   M. Vitale, *Rimatori comico-realistici del Due e Trecento* (2 vols., 1956)

RL   C. Brown, *Religious Lyrics of the XIVth century* (2nd ed., 1952)

Romances   K. Bartsch, *Romances et Pastourelles/Altfranʐösische Romanʐen und Pastourellen* (1870)

Rondeaux   F. Gennrich, *Rondeaux Virelais und Balladen* (2 vols., 1921–7)

SATF   Société des Anciens Textes Français

Scuola   B. Panvini, *Le rime della scuola siciliana* (2 vols., 1962–4)

SL   R. H. Robbins, *Secular Lyrics of the XIVth and XVth Centuries* (1952)

Testi   R. M. Ruggieri, *Testi antichi romanʐi* (2 vols., 1949)

Troubadours   C. A. F. Mahn, *Gedichte der Troubadours in provenʐalischer Sprache* (4 vols., 1856–73)

TTM   F. Gennrich, *Troubadours Trouvères Minne- und Meistergesang* (1951)

SECONDARY LITERATURE

Alonso, D., 'Cancioncillas "de amigo" mozárabes', *Revista de Filologia Española* XXXIII (1949), pp. 297–349

Anglés, H., 'La danza sacra y su música en el templo durante el Medioevo', *Medium Aevum Romanicum* (ed. H. Bihler/A. Noyer-Weidner, 1963) pp. 1–20. *La música de las Cantigas* (3 vols. in 4, 1943–64)

Asensio, E., *Poetica y realidad en el cancionero peninsular de la Edad Media* (1957)

Baehr, R. (Ed.), *Der Provenʐalische Minnesang* (1967)

Bédier, J., 'Les plus anciennes danses françaises', *Revue des Deux Mondes* 1906, pp. 398–424

Bezzola, R. R., *Les origines et la formation de la littérature courtoise en occident* (5 vols., 1944–63).

de Boor, H./Newald, R., *Geschichte der deutschen Literatur*, vol. 1: *770–1170* (4th ed., 1960); vol. 2: *1170–1250* (5th ed., 1962); vol. 3 i: *1250–1350* (1962)

Cecchi, E./Sapegno, N. (Ed.), *Storia della letteratura italiana*, vol. 1: *Le origini e il Duecento* (1965)

Chambers, E. K., *The Medieval Stage* (2 vols., 1903)

da Costa Pimpão, A. J., *História da literatura portuguesa*, vol. 1: *Séculos XII a XV* (1947)

Díaz–Plaja, G. (Ed.), *Historia general de las literaturas hispánicas*, vol. 1: *Desde los orígenes hasta 1400* (1949)

Dobiache–Rojdestvensky, O., *Les poésies des goliards* (1931)

Favati, G., 'Contributo alla determinazione del problema dello stil nuovo', *Studi mediolatini e volgari* IV (1956), pp. 57–70

Fisher, John H. (Ed.), *The Medieval Literature of Western Europe: A Review of Research, Mainly 1930–1960* (1966)

Frank, I., *Trouvères et Minnesänger* (1952)
Répertoire métrique de la poésie des troubadours (2 vols., 1953–7)

Friedrich, H., *Epochen der italienischen Lyrik* (1964)

Frings, T., *Minnesinger und Troubadours* (Deutsche Akademie der Wissenschaften zu Berlin, 1949)

Fromm, H. (Ed.), *Der deutsche Minnesang* (4th ed., 1969)

García Gómez, E. 'La lírica hispano-árabe y la aparición de la lírica románica', *Al-Andalus* XXI (1956), pp. 303–38

Gennrich, F., *Die Kontrafaktur im Liedschaffen des Mittelalters* (1965)

Geschichte der Textüberlieferung, vol. 2: *Überlieferungsgeschichte der mittelalterlichen Literatur* (1964)

Gröber, G., (Ed.), *Grundriss der romanischen Philologie*, vol. 2, i-iii (1897–1902)

Hoepffner, E., *Les troubadours dans leur vie et dans leurs oeuvres* (1955)

Hughes, A. (Ed.), *Early Medieval Music up to 1300* (New Oxford History of Music, vol. 2 (1954)

Jeanroy, A., *La poésie lyrique des troubadours* (2 vols., 1934)

Ludwig, F., in Adler, G. (Ed.), *Handbuch der Musikgeschichte* (1924), pp. 127–228
Repertorium organorum recentioris et motetorum vetustissimi stili, I, i (1910); I, ii and II (Summa Musicae Medii Aevi VII–VIII, 1961–2)

Machabey, A., 'Etudes de musicologie pré-médiévale', *Revue de Musicologie* XVI (1935), pp. 65, 129, 213 ff., XVII (1936), pp. 1 ff.

Menéndez Pidal, R. 'La primitiva lírica europea', *Revista de Filología Española* XLIII (1960) pp. 279 ff.

van Mierlo, J., *De Letterkunde van de Middeleeuwen* (2nd ed., 2 vols., 1949)

Nardi, B., 'Filosofia dell' amore nei rimatori italiani del Duecento e in Dante' *Dante e la cultura medievale* (2nd ed., 1949) pp. 1–92

Norberg, D., *Introduction à l'étude de la versification latine médiévale* (1958)

Raby, F. J. E., *A History of Christian-Latin Poetry* (2nd ed., 1953)
A History of Secular Latin Poetry in the Middle Ages (2nd ed., 2 vols., 1957)

Reese, G., *Music in the Middle Ages* (1940)

de Riquer, M., *Història de la literatura catalana, Part antiga* (2 vols., 1964)

Rodrigues Lapa, M., *Lições de literatura portuguesa: época medieval* (6th ed., 1966)

Salmen, W., *Der fahrende Musiker im europäischen Mittelalter* (1960)

Singer, S., *Die religiöse Lyrik des Mittelalters* (1933)

Spanke, H., *Beziehungen zwischen romanischer und mittellateinischer Lyrik* (1936)
'Tanzmusik in der Kirche des Mittelalters', *Neuphilologische Mitteilungen* XXXI (1930), pp. 143 ff.
'Zum Thema "Mittelalterliche Tanzlieder" ', ibid. XXXIII (1932), pp. 1 ff.

Spitzer, L., 'The Mozarabic Lyric and Theodor Frings' Theories', *Comparative Literature* IV (1952), pp. 1–22
'The Influences of Hebrew and Vernacular Poetry in the Judeo–Italian Elegy', *Twelfth-century Europe and the Foundations of Modern Society* (Ed. M. Clagett/ G. Post/R. Reynolds, 1961) pp. 115–30
'L'amour lointain de Jaufré Rudel', *Romanische Literaturstudien* (1959), pp. 363–417
'The Text and Artistic Value of the Ritmo cassinese', ibid. pp. 425–63
'Il Cantico di Frate Sole', ibid. pp. 464–87

von den Steinen, W., *Notker der Dichter und seine geistige Welt* (2 vols., 1948)

Szövérffy, J., *Die Annalen der lateinischen Hymnendichtung* (2 vols., 1964–5)

Taylor, R. J., *Die Melodien der weltlichen Lieder des Mittelalters* (2 vols., 1964)

ANTHOLOGIES WITH TRANSLATIONS

Abbott, C. C., *Early Medieval French Lyrics* (1932)

Audiau, J./Lavaud, R., *Nouvelle anthologie des troubadours* (1928)

Berry, A., *Florilège des troubadours* (1930)

Cohen, J. M., *The Penguin Book of Spanish Verse* (1956; some medieval lyrics)

Davies, R. T., *Medieval English Lyrics* (1963)

Eberle, J., *Psalterium Profanum* (1962; Latin lyrics with German translation)

Forster, L. W., *The Penguin Book of German Verse* (1957; some medieval lyrics)

Kay, G., *The Penguin Book of Italian Verse* (1958; some medieval lyrics)

Kershaw, N., *Anglo–Saxon and Norse Poems* (1922)

Langosch, K., *Hymnen und Vagantenlieder* (1954)

Mary, A., *La fleur de la poésie française depuis les origines jusqu'à la fin du XVe siècle* (1951)

Nelli, R./Lavaud, R., *Les troubadours*, vol. 2: *Le trésor poétique de l'Occitanie* (1965)

Waddell, H., *Medieval Latin Lyrics* (1929; Penguin Books 1952)

Wehrli, M., *Deutsche Lyrik des Mittelalters* (1955)

Whicher, G., *The Goliard Poets* (1949)

Woledge, B., *The Penguin Book of French Verse*, vol. 1: *To the Fifteenth Century* (1961)

Wolfskehl, K./von der Leyen, F., *Älteste deutsche Dichtungen* (1909; now Insel-Bücherei Nr. 432)

(2) GUIDE TO INDIVIDUAL AUTHORS AND POEMS

Figures with asterisks refer to pages in this book

CATALAN

Twelfth and thirteenth centuries

Catalan troubadours (see PROVENÇAL, 259*):

Guillem de Berguedan (fl. 1143–1192/6).

Guillem de Cabestanh (fl. late 12th).

Guillem de Cervera [Cerveri de Girona] (fl. 1259–85).

For a comprehensive bibliographical guide to the Catalan troubadours, see M. de Riquer, *Història* I, pp. 39, 56–196.

Thirteenth century

Anonymous:

Al yorn del iusivy (the Sibyl's song): R. B. Donovan, *The Liturgical Drama in Medieval Spain* (1958), pp. 197–9.

Augats, seyós qui credets Déu lo Payre (Lament of the Virgin Mary).

Rosa plasent, soleyl de resplandor (Virolay de Madona Sancta Maria).

For these, and a further group of songs to the Virgin Mary, see M. de Riquer, *Història* I, pp. 200–2.

Ramón Lull (1232/5–1315): 72*; *Obres essencials* (2 vols., 1957–60) I, pp. 1271–1348.

DUTCH

Twelfth century

Heinrich von Veldeke (fl. 1170–90): 22*. Heinrich's lyrics, which survive only in German (Alemannic) MSS., have been reconstructed in his native Limburg dialect: T. Frings/G. Schieb, *Heinrich von Veldeke, Die Servatiusbruchstücke und die Lieder* (1947).

Thirteenth century

Hadewijch (fl. mid-13th): 81*; J. van Mierlo (2 vols., 1942); E. Rombauts/ N. De Paepe (1961).

For further bibliography on medieval Dutch lyric, see J. van Mierlo, *De Letterkunde van de Middeleeuwen* (2nd ed., 1949) I, pp. 231–74; II, pp. 7–32.

ENGLISH

Seventh century

Nu scylun hergan hefaenricaes uard (Caedmon's hymn, *c.* 657–80): 37*; ASPR VI, pp. 105–6.

Eighth century

For thaem neidfaerae naenig uuiurthit (Bede's death song, 735): ASPR VI, pp. 107–8.

Tenth century

Leodum is minum swylce him mon lac gife (Wulf and Eadwacer): 91*; ASPR III, pp. 179–80.

Welund him be wurman wræces cunnade (Deor): ASPR III, pp. 178–9.

For other short Anglo-Saxon poems with affinities to lyric (e.g. elegies, prayers), see the section 'Anglo-Saxon Poetry' in *The New Cambridge Bibliography of English Literature*, ed. G. Watson, I (1974), cols. 225 ff.   ASPR gives a complete corpus.

Twelfth century

Saint Godric († 1170): 63*; J. Hall, *Early Middle English* (1920), I, p. 5.

For other twelfth century fragments, see R. M. Wilson, *The Lost Literature of Medieval England* (1952), pp. 171, 174.

c. 1200

Eueriche freman hach to ben hande: EL 57.
Haly Thomas of heoueriche: EL 42.
Theh thet hi can wittes fule-wis: 44*; EL, p. xii.

Thirteenth century

Anonymous:
A substantial corpus is assembled in EL. Some further brief lyrics in R. M. Wilson, op. cit. pp. 177 ff.; J. A. W. Bennett/G. V. Smithers, *Early Middle English Verse and Prose* (2nd ed., 1968), p. 128.

Bryd one brere: 145*, 245*; SL 147.

Thomas de Hales (fl. mid-13th): *A mayde Cristes me bit yorne;* EL 43; B. Dickins/ R. M. Wilson, *Early Middle English Texts* (1951), xx.

Thirteenth to early fourteenth century

The Harley Lyrics: 146*; G. L. Brook (2nd ed., 1956); EL 72–91, RL 6–11. Facsimile of the MS (*c.* 1340): Early English Text Society 255 (1965).

For other brief lyrics and fragments of this period, see R. H. Robbins, *Anglia* 83 (1965), p. 47. For a detailed bibliographical guide, see the section 'Pieces lyrical in impulse or form' (ch. xiii) in J. E. Wells, *A Manual of the Writings in Middle*

English (1916), and in each of the nine *Supplements* (1929–51). This work also gives information about melodies, in the rare instances where these survive. *The New Cambridge Bibliography of English Literature* I, cols. 697 ff., has a fine section 'Middle English Songs and Lyrics'.

FRENCH

Ninth century

Buona pulcella fut Eulalia: 40*; *Testi* 21 (with facsimile).

Twelfth century

Blondel de Nesle (fl. before 1200): L. Wiese (1904).

Le Chastelain de Couci (probably † 1203): 127, 138*; A. Lerond (1964).

Chrétien de Troyes (fl. 1160–90): 126*; W. Förster, *Kristian von Troyes, Wörterbuch* (1914), pp. 205–9.

Conon de Béthune (*c*. 1150–1219): 128*; A. Wallensköld (CFMA, 1921); A. Pauphilet, *Poètes et romanciers du Moyen Age* (1952), pp. 865 ff.

Gace Brulé (fl. 1159–1212): 127*; H. Petersen Dyggve (1951).

Richard Coeur-de-Lion († 1199): 211*; F. Gennrich, *Die Rotruenge* (1925), p. 20.

Thirteenth century

Adam de la Halle (*c*. 1250–*c*. 1288): E. de Coussemaker (1872); R. Berger (1900).

Colin Muset (fl. mid–13th): J. Beck (CFMA, 2nd ed., 1938).

Guiot de Dijon (fl. early 13th): E. Nissen (CFMA, 1928).

Jacques d'Autun (? early 13th): 129*; *Romania* 58 (1932), pp. 341 ff.

Moniot d'Arras (fl. mid–13th): H. Petersen Dygge (1938).

Rutebeuf (fl. 1250–85): E. Faral/J. Bastin (2 vols., 1959–60).

Thibaut de Champagne (1201–52): A. Wallensköld (SATF, 1925).

Anonymous lyrics (twelfth and thirteenth centuries) are contained in the following collections:

K. Bartsch, *Romances et pastourelles/Altfranzösische Romanzen und Pastourellen* (1870).

J. Bédier/P. Aubry, *Les chansons de croisade* (1909).

F. Gennrich, *Rondeaux Virelais und Balladen* (2 vols., 1921–7).

E. Jarnström/A. Langfors, *Recueil de chansons pieuses du XIIIe siècle* (2 vols., 1910–27).

A. Jeanroy/L. Brandin/P. Aubry, *Lais et descorts français du XIIIe siècle* (1901).

A. Jeanroy/A. Langfors, *Chansons satiriques et bachiques* (CFMA, 1921).

A. Jeanroy/A. Langfors, *Recueil général des jeux-partis* (SATF, 2 vols.,1926).

A. Langfors, *Deux recueils de sottes chansons* (1945).

G. Raynaud, *Recueil de motets français* (2 vols., 1881–3).

H. Spanke, *Eine altfranzösische Liedersammlung* (1925).

For further trouvères and anonymous lyrics, see the section 'L'ancien français ch. iv: la poésie lyrique' in R. Bossuat, *Manuel bibliographique de la littérature française du Moyen Âge* (1951), and *Suppléments* (1955, 1961).

Melodies: there is no corpus of trouvère melodies comparable to Gennrich's *Nachlass* for the troubadours. The most complete guide is H. Spanke, *G. Raynauds Bibliographie des altfranzösischen Liedes* I (1955), supplemented by F. Gennrich, *Bibliographie der ältesten französischen und lateinischen Motetten* (1958). F. Gennrich's *Altfranzösische Lieder* (2 vols., 1953–6) and TTM give valuable selections with concise bibliography.

Ninth century   GERMAN

Dat gafregin ih mit firahim (Wessobrunner Gebet, early 9th): 37*; *Lesebuch*, p. 73.

Einan kuning uueiʒ ih (Ludwigslied, 881/2): 39*; *Lesebuch*, p. 118.

Gorio fuor ʒi mahalo (Georgslied, probably 896): *Lesebuch*, p. 114.

Liubene ersaʒta síne grûʒ (satirical quatrain): K. Wolfskehl/F. von der Leyen, *Älteste deutsche Dichtungen*, (Insel) p. 34.

Otfrid († *c.* 870): *Er allen uuóroltkreftin* (*Evangelienharmonie* II, 1); 38*; *Lesebuch*, p. 97.

Ratpert († 890): *Hymn to Saint Gall* (*c.* 880; only Latin transl. survives: *Poetae* V, pp. 536–40).

Tenth century

Nunc almus assis filius (Latin–German, *De Heinrico*, 996–1002): *Lesebuch*, p. 120; CC 19.

Prayers and Psalm 138 in verse (first decade): *Lesebuch*, p. 119.

Unsar trohtîn hât farsalt (Petruslied, first decade): *Lesebuch*, p. 118.

Eleventh century

Suavissima nunna (Latin–German love-dialogue, early 11th): 131*; MLREL II, p. 353; CC 28.

Ezzo: *Nu wil ih iu herron* (*Cantilena de Miraculis Christi*, 1063): 48*; *Dichtungen* 7.

Noker von Zwiefalten: *Nu denchant wîb unde man* (*Memento Mori, c.* 1070); *Dichtungen* 5.

Twelfth century

Anonymous religious:

Ave du vil sconiu maris stella (Mariensequenz aus St. Lambrecht [Seckau]): *Dichtungen* 21.

Ave vil liehtiu maris stella (Mariensequenz aus Muri): *Dichtungen* 20.

Jû in erde (Melker Marienlied): 74*; *Dichtungen* 13.

The other strophic religious poems, some of which are close to lyric, are collected in *Dichtungen*.

Anonymous secular:

Auwê lîp vor allem lîbe: 131*; K. Wolfskehl/F. von der Leyen, *Älteste deutsche Dichtungen*, (Insel) p. 40.

The other anonymous secular lyrics are collected in CB (cf. also F. Lüers, *Die deutschen Lieder der Carmina Burana*, 1922) and in MF i.

Albrecht von Johansdorf (fl. late 12th): MF xiii.

Burggraf von Rietenburg (fl. second half of 12th): 132*; MF v.

Dietmar von Eist: strophes of varying styles and dates are printed under his name in MF vii.

Friedrich von Hausen (*c.* 1155–90): 139*; MF ix.

Heinrich von Veldeke (fl. 1170–90): see Bibliography 250*.

Kaiser Heinrich (1165–97): MF viii.

Kürenberc (fl. mid–12th): 109–118*; MF ii.

Meinloh von Sevelingen (fl. 1170–80): 95*; MF iii.

Twelfth to thirteenth century

Hartmann von Aue (*c.* 1170–*c.* 1215): MF xxi.

Heinrich von Morungen († 1222): 132*, 180*; MF xviii; C. von Kraus (2nd ed. 1950, with modern German translation).

Otto von Botenlauben (fl. 1197–1244): 138*; DLD 41.

Reinmar († before 1210): 136*, 225*; MF xx.

Walther von der Vogelweide (*c.* 1170–*c.* 1230): 23, 135, 201, 224*; K. Lachmann/ C. von Kraus/H. Kuhn (1965); H. Böhm (1955, cpte., with modern German transl.); P. Wapnewski (1962, sel., with modern German transl.).

Wolfram von Eschenbach (*c.* 1170–*c.* 1220): 178*; DLD 69.

Thirteenth century

Anonymous lyrics: DLD 38.

Der wilde Alexander (fl. late 13th): 78*; DLD 1.

Burkhart von Hohenfels (fl. 1212–42): DLD 6.

Gottfried von Neifen (fl. 1234–55): DLD 15.

Heinrich Frauenlob [Heinrich von Meissen] (*c.* 1260–1318): 140*; L. Ettmüller (1843).

Konrad von Würzburg (*c.* 1225–*c.* 1287): 140*; E. Schröder (1959).

Mechthild von Magdeburg (*c.* 1212–*c.* 1280): lyrical interludes in *Das fliessende Licht der Gottheit*; 83*; P. G. Morel (1869).

Neidhart von Reuenthal (*c.* 1180–*c.* 1250): 204*; M. Haupt/E. Wiessner (1923). Songs with melodies: A. T. Hatto/R. J. Taylor (1958, with English transl.); F. Gennrich (1962); E. Rohloff (Abhandlungen der Sächsischen Akademie, 2 vols., 1962).

Süsskind der Jude von Trimberg: 218*; DLD 56.

Tannhäuser (fl. 1230–70): 140*; J. Siebert (1934).

Ulrich von Lichtenstein (c. 1198–c. 1275); DLD 58.

Von Wissenlo (? later 13th): 181*; DLD 68.

For further Minnesinger (twelfth and thirteenth centuries), see MF and DLD. Melodies: only a small proportion of *Minnesang* survives with music. Sometimes a Minnesinger's melody can be deduced because it is a 'contrafactum' (musical adaptation) of a French or Latin song. The best bibliographical guide is R. J. Taylor, *Die Melodien der weltlichen Lieder des Mittelalters* (2 vols., 1964).

ITALIAN

Twelfth century

Raimbaut de Vaqueiras (c. 1155–after 1205): 125*; J. Linskill (1964). Genoese stanzas in *Domna, tant vos ai preiada* (iii, st. 2, 4, 6, 8), an Italian stanza in *Era quan vey verdeyar* (xvi, st. 2). See also Bibliography, p. 255.

c. 1200

Eo, sinjuri, s'eo fabello (Ritmo cassinese): 57*; *Poeti* I, p. 9.

La ienti de Sion plange a lutta (Elegia giudeo–italiana): 58*; *Poeti* I, p. 37.

Salva lo vescovo senato (Ritmo laurenziano): 152*; *Poeti* I, p. 5.

Thirteenth century

Religious lyric:

St Francis of Assisi (1182–1226): *Laudes Creaturarum* [*Cantico di Frate Sole*, probably 1224]: 59*; *Poeti* I, p. 33.

Jacopone da Todi (1236–1306): 59*, 215*; F. Ageno (1953).

Laude of Cortona: F. Liuzzi, *La lauda e i primordi della melodia italiana* (2 vols., 1935); *Poeti* II, pp. 11–59 (a selection).

Rayna possentissima (*Lauda*, Bologna): *Poeti* II, p. 9.

The Sicilian school:

Cielo d'Alcamo: *Rosa fresca aulentissima* (*Contrasto*, between 1231 and 1250): 155*; *Scuola* xv; *Poeti* I, p. 177.

Giacomino Pugliese (fl. first half 13th): 156*; *Scuola* xvi.

Giacomo da Lentini [il Notaro] (fl. 1233–40): 152*; *Scuola* i; *Poeti* I, pp. 49–90.

Guido delle Colonne (fl. 1243–87): *Scuola* iv; *Poeti* I, pp. 94–110.

Rinaldo d'Aquino (c. 1200/10–c. 1280): 156*; *Scuola* vii.

For the other poets and poetry of the Sicilian school, *Scuola* gives a complete corpus (with the exceptions explained in the Introduction, I, pp. xlix–l).

Tuscan and Northern:

Bonagiunta Orbicciani (fl. 1242–57): 157*; A. Parducci/G. Zaccagnini, *Rimatori Siculo-Toscani del Dugento* (1915); *Poeti* I, pp. 257–82 (a selection).

Cecco Angiolieri (c. 1260–c. 1312): 161*; *Giocosi*, pp. 113–250; *Rimatori* vi.

Chiaro Davanzati († 1304): A. Menichetti (1965).

Compiuta Donzella (? mid-13th): *Poeti* I, pp. 433–8.

Folgore di San Gimignano (*c.* 1270–*c.* 1330): *Giocosi*, pp. 355–93; *Rimatori* xiv.

Guittone d'Arezzo (*c.* 1235–94): 156*; F. Egidi (1940); *Poeti* I, pp. 189–255 (a selection).

Rustico Filippi (1230/40–*c.* 1290): *Giocosi*, pp. 29–91; *Rimatori* i.

For further courtly poets see *Poeti* I, pp. 283 ff.; *Giocosi* and *Rimatori* give a corpus of the comic and realistic poets. For anonymous and popular lyrics, see *Poeti* II, pp. 713 ff.

Dolce stil novo and Dante:

Cino da Pistoia (*c.* 1270–1337): G. Zaccagnini (1925); *Poeti* II, pp. 629–90 (a selection).

Guido Cavalcanti-(*c.* 1255–1300): 158*; G. Favati (1957); *Poeti* II, pp. 487–567.

Guido Guinizelli (1230/40–1276): 156, 160*; *Poeti* II, pp. 447–85.

For the other *stilnovisti*, see *Poeti* II, pp. 569 ff.

Dante Alighieri (1265–1321): 157, 161*; editions of the *Rime*: G. Contini (3rd ed. 1965); K. Foster/P. Boyde (2 vols., 1967, with English transl.).

Melodies: no music survives for lyrics of the age of Dante or earlier, except for a group of thirteenth-century *Laude* from Cortona. These melodies are printed in F. Liuzzi's *La Lauda* (cited above), I, pp. 256–479; cf. also II, pp. 96 ff. (a melody for one of Jacopone's *Laude*).

LATIN

Eighth to tenth centuries

Anonymous:

The hymns and sequences of this period are set out with extensive bibliography in J. Szövérffy, *Annalen* I, ch. vi–ix. The most important collections of texts are in AH 2, 14, 27, 50, 51, 53.

The anonymous rhythmic poetry, secular and sacred, often intended for singing, can be found in *Poetae*, especially IV 2.

Gottschalk (*c.* 805–69): 32, 34–6*; *Poetae* III, pp. 725–38; VI, pp. 86–106.

Notker (*c.* 840–912): 41–4, 47*; W. von den Steinen (2 vols., 1948; Editio minor, with five melodies, 1960).

Paulinus of Aquileia (*c.* 750–802): *Poetae* I, pp. 131–48.

Eleventh century

Anonymous:

The Cambridge Songs (mid-eleventh century MS., including some songs from earlier centuries): 29, 92*; K. Strecker, CC (1926).

MLREL II, pp. 334–60.

Fulbert of Chartres (*c.* 960–1029): for his hymns, see Szövérffy's *Annalen* I, pp. 353–7; among secular lyrics, Fulbert is possibly author of CC 10 and 42.

Gottschalk of Limburg († 1098): AH 50, 264–86; 53, 167.

Hermann of Reichenau (1013–54): 44*; AH 44, 227; 50, 239–41, 243, 247; possibly 244–6.

St Peter Damian (1007–72): 47*; M. Lokrantz (1964).

For further hymns and sequences in this century, see Szövérffy's *Annalen* I, ch. x; for further secular lyrics, F. J. E. Raby's *Secular Latin Poetry* I, ch. vii–ix.

Twelfth century

Adam of St Victor (fl. 1150): E. Misset/P. Aubry (texts with music, 1900); F. Wellner (2nd ed., 1955). Many of the attributions remain uncertain.

Archpoet (*c.* 1130–*c.* 1167): 21*, 217*; H. Watenphul/H. Krefeld (1958).

Hilary the Englishman (fl. 1140): J. J. Champollion-Figeac (1838); J. B. Fuller (1929).

Hugh Primas of Orleans (1095–1160): 215*; secular lyrics, W. Meyer, Nachrichten der Gesellschaft der Wissenschaften, Göttingen 1907; possibly also the sacred sequence *Laudes crucis attollamus*, AH 54, 120.

Nicolas of Clairvaux (fl. 1140–70): J. F. Benton, *Traditio* 18 (1962), pp. 149–63 (sequences, with melodies).

Peter Abelard (1079–1142): 52*; G. M. Dreves (1891); AH 48; J. Szövérffy (2 vols., 1975). *Planctus*: W. Meyer, *Gesammelte Abhandlungen* I (1905), pp. 340–74; G. Vecchi (1951, with some melodies); P. Dronke, *Poetic Individuality in the Middle Ages* (1970): *Planctus* I, IV, VI (with melody): pp. 121–3, 146, 203–9.

Peter of Blois (*c.* 1135–*c.* 1205): 213*; *Patrologia Latina* 207, cols. 1127–36, *Olim militaveram* and five other lyrics printed as one long poem: *Qui habet aures audiat*, 1129; *In nova fert animus*, 1131; *Quid hic agis, anima*, 1131; *Quis aquam tuo capiti*, 1132; *Quod amicus suggerit*, 1133. To these must almost certainly be added CB 29–31, CB 63, and AH 21, 165 (cf. CB *Kommentar*, pp. 47–9), lyrics in *Arundel* (1–17, 20, 28), and probably some twenty-two further songs: cf. P. Dronke, *Mediaeval Studies* XXXVIII (1976), pp. 185–235 (with new ed. of five of Peter's songs).

Walter of Châtillon (*c.* 1135–after 1184): 64*, 200*; K. Strecker (2 vols., 1925–9); for other possible attributions, see A. Wilmart, *Revue Bénédictine* 49 (1937), pp. 121–69, 322–65.

Anonymous twelfth and thirteenth century lyrics:

Carmina Burana: 83*, 192*; the text volumes of CB have now been completed (CB I 3, 1970). Facsimile: *Veröffentlichungen mittelalterlicher Musikhandschriften*, vol. ix.

Firenze, Laurenziana Plut. XXIX 1: many of the texts in AH 20 and 21; facsimile, *Veröffentlichungen mittelalterlicher Musikhandschriften*, vols. x–xi.

Montpellier, Bibliothèque de l'Ecole de Médicine H 196; cpte. texts (Latin and French), music and facsimile: Y. Rokseth, *Polyphonies du XIIIe siècle* (4 vols., 1935–48).

From various MSS: MLREL II, pp. 361–400, 411–16.

Thirteenth century

Gil de Zamora († *c.* 1300): bibl. in Szövérffy's *Annalen* II, pp. 279–83).

John of Hoveden († 1275): F. J. E. Raby (1939).

John Pecham († 1292): 63*; AH 5, 1; 31, 105; 50, 390–7.

Philip the Chancellor († 1236): 55*; the canon of Philip's songs is not yet fully established; bibl. in *Annalen* II, pp. 192–202; cf. also CB *Kommentar*, p. 53.

St Thomas Aquinas (1224/5–1274): AH 50, 385–9; cf. also *Annalen* II, pp. 246–54.

For a bibliographical guide to further secular lyric: Raby's *Secular Latin Poetry* II, ch. xiii–xiv, Appendix iii. To further authors and collections of religious lyric: Szövérffy's *Annalen* II, i. Abschnitt 1–20, ii. Abschnitt A1–20.

Melodies: a small, well-chosen selection of melodies is included in G. Vecchi, *Poesia latina medievale* (2nd ed., 1958). A corpus of monodic music has been begun by B. Stäblein: *Monumenta Monodica Medii Aevi* (vol. 1, 1956). The Institute of Medieval Music (Brooklyn, N.Y.) is publishing important MSS: *Veröffentlichungen mittelalterlicher Musikhandschriften/Publications of Medieval Musical Manuscripts* (1957 ff.). For further bibliography, see *Early Medieval Music up to 1300* (Ed. Dom A. Hughes), pp. 410–17. The encyclopaedia *Musik in Geschichte und Gegenwart* (Ed. F. Blume, 1949 ff.) gives lavish bibliography for specific topics (e.g. under *Ars Antiqua, Conductus, Motette, Sequenz, Tropus*).

PORTUGUESE

Thirteenth century (individual dates mostly uncertain)

Afonso [Alfonso] X, 'el Sabio', King of Castile (1221–84): 70, 222*; *Cantigas de Santa Maria*: W. Mettmann (3 vols., 1959–64); (with music and fascimile) H. Anglés, *La música de las Cantigas* (3 vols. in 4, 1943–64). Other songs: *Amor* 25–27; *Escarnho* 1–35, 149, 303, 419, 427.

Airas Nunes: 194*; *Amigo* 256–9; *Amor* 138–43; *Escarnho* 68–72.

Denis, King of Portugal [grandson of Alfonso] (1261–1325); 148*; H. R. Lang (1894); *Amigo* 1–55; *Amor* 28–100; *Escarnho* 88–97.

Joan Airas de Santiago: 148*; *Amigo* 279–325; *Amor* 172–91; *Escarnho* 175–85, 246.

Joan [Garcia] de Guilhade: 150*; O. Nobiling (1907); *Ajuda* 228–39, 454–6; *Amigo* 176–96; *Amor* 116; *Escarnho* 201–17.

Joan Zorro: 194*; C. Ferreira da Cunha (1949); *Amigo* 380–90.

Juião Bolseiro: 183*; *Amigo* 394–408; *Amor* 218; *Escarnho* 249, 300.

Martin Codax: 103*, 244*; C. Ferreira da Cunha (1956); *Amigo* 491–7.

Martin Padrozelos: 104*; *Amigo* 451–9.

Mendinho: 102*; *Amigo* 252.

Nuno Fernandez Torneol: 182*; *Ajuda* 70–81, 402; *Amigo* 75–82; *Escarnho* 301.

Paai Gomez Charinho: C. Ferreira da Cunha (1945); *Ajuda* 246–56; *Amigo* 220–5; *Amor* 117–25; *Escarnho* 302–3.

Paai Soarez de Taveiroos: 148*; *Ajuda* 31–39, 396–7; *Amigo* 72–74; *Escarnho* 299.

Pero da Ponte: 150*, 219*; *Ajuda* 288–92, 459–66; *Amigo* 238–44; *Escarnho* 53, 340–70.

Pero Garcia Burgalès: 151*, 220*; *Ajuda* 82–110, 403–9; *Amigo* 83–84; *Escarnho* 372–85.

Pero Meogo: 103*; *Amigo* 411–19.

Roi Queimado: 150*, 220*; *Ajuda* 129–43, 413–14; *Amigo* 147–50; *Escarnho* 415–18.

The lyrics of other trovadores, and anonymous lyrics, can be found in the four great collected editions, *Ajuda*, *Amigo*, *Amor* and *Escarnho*, which together constitute a virtually complete corpus. Of the principal MSS. of secular lyric, there are diplomatic editions of the *Cancioneiro da Ajuda* (H. H. Carter, 1941) and of the *Cancioneiro Vaticano* (E. Monaci, 1875), and a critical edition of the *Cancioneiro da Biblioteca Nacional* (E. P. and J. P. Machado, 1949 ff.).

Melodies: apart from Afonso's *Cantigas* (see above), only six melodies, for songs by Martin Codax, survive. These also have been edited by H. Anglés, *La música* III, ii, pp. 53–57, together with four deduced melodies.

PROVENÇAL

Tenth century

Phebi claro nondum orto iubare (with Provençal refrain); 170*; *Testi* 3 (with facsimile); melody: G. Vecchi, *Poesia latina medievale* pl. x.

Eleventh century

Be deu hoi mais finir nostra razos; *Testi* 28 (with facsimile); *Nachlass* 3.

Mei amic e mei fiel: 50*; *Chrestomathie*, col. 19; *Nachlass* 1.

O Maria, Deu maire: *Chrestomathie*, col. 19; *Nachlass* 2.

Twelfth century

Arnaut Daniel (fl. 1180–95): 125*; G. Toja (1961); *Nachlass* 90–1.

Arnaut de Mareuil (fl. 1195): R. C. Johnston (1935); *Nachlass* 49–54.

Béatrice de Die [Beatriz de Dia] (fl. late 12th): 105*; G. Kussler-Ratyé, *Archivum Romanicum* I (1917), pp. 161–82; *Nachlass* 38.

Bernart Marti (fl. mid-12th): E. Hoepffner (CFMA, 1929).

Bernart de Ventadour (fl. 1147–70): 121*; C. Appel (1915); S. G. Nichols Jr., and others (1962); M. Lazar (1966); *Nachlass* 16–34, 291.

Bertran de Born (fl. 1159–95, † 1215): 210*; C. Appel (1932); *Nachlass* 39, 292–4.

Cercamon (fl. 1137–49): A. Jeanroy (CFMA, 1922).

Folquet de Marseille (fl. 1178–95, † 1231): S. Stronski (1910); *Nachlass* 77–89.

Gaucelm Faidit (fl. 1172–1203): J. Mouzat (1965); *Nachlass* 103–16.

Guillaume IX, Duc d'Aquitaine (1071–1126): 109*; A. Jeanroy (CFMA, 2nd ed., 1927); *Nachlass* 7, 287.

Guillem de Berguedan (fl. 1138–92): A. Keller (1849); further bibl. in M. de Riquer, *Historia* I, pp. 74–94.

Guillem de Cabestanh (fl. 1212): A. Langfors (CFMA, 1924).

Guiraut de Borneil (fl. 1162–99): 176*; A. Kolsen (2 vols., 1910); *Nachlass* 56–9.

Jaufre Rudel (fl. 1125–48): 119*; A. Jeanroy (CFMA, 2nd ed., 1924); M. Casella (1945); *Nachlass* 12–15.

Marcabru (fl. 1130–49): 208*; J. M. L. Dejeanne (1909). For corrections and editions of single poems since then, see F. Pirot, *Le Moyen Age* 73 (1967) pp. 87–126. *Nachlass* 8–11, 288–90.

The Monk of Montaudon (fl. 1193–1210); R. Lavaud, *Les troubadours cantaliens* vol. 2 (1910).

Peire d'Auvergne (fl. 1149–68); 123*; A. Del Monte (1955); *Nachlass* 35–6.

Peire Vidal (fl. 1183–1204): 125*; d'A. S. Avalle (2 vols., 1960); *Nachlass* 60–72.

Raimbaut d'Orange (c. 1147–73): 124*; W. T. Pattison (1952); *Nachlass* 37.

Raimbaut de Vaqueiras (fl. 1180–1205): 125*; J. Linskill (1964); *Nachlass* 96–102.

Rigaut de Barbezieux (fl. 1141–60): A. Varvaro (1960); M. Braccini (1960); *Nachlass* 170–3.

Thirteenth century

Aimeric de Peguilhan (fl. 1190–1221): W. P. Shepard/F. M. Chambers (1950); *Nachlass* 177–82.

Cadenet (fl. first third of 13th): 176*; C. Appel (1920); *Nachlass* 183, 298.

Guillem de Cervera [Cerveri de Girona] (fl. 1259–85): M. de Riquer (1947).

Guillem Montanhagol (fl. 1233–68): P. T. Ricketts (1964).

Guiraut Riquier (fl. 1254–92): *Troubadours* IV, pp. 1–100, 233–54; U. Mölk (1962); *Nachlass* 193–240.

Lanfranc Cigala (fl. 1235–57): F. Branciforti (1954).

Peire Cardenal (fl. 1205–72:) 56*; R. Lavaud (1957); *Nachlass* 185–7.

Peirol (fl. 1188–1222): S. C. Aston (1953); *Nachlass* 117–33.

Raimon de Miraval (fl. 1191–1229): L. W. Topsfield (1971); *Nachlass* 137–58.

Sordello (fl. 1220–69): M. Boni (1954); *Nachlass* 299.

Nearly all the editions of individual troubadours referred to above also contain a translation into a modern language. For a comprehensive bibliography of named troubadours, as well as of anonymous lyrics, see I. Frank, *Répertoire métrique de la poésie des troubadours*, vol. 2 (1957).

Melodies: F. Gennrich's *Nachlass* gives a complete corpus of the surviving melodies, and extensive musical bibliography.

Eleventh and twelfth centuries

Mozarabic *kharjas*: 86*, 172*; S. M. Stern (1953); K. Heger (1960); E. García
Gómez (2nd ed., 1975).

Chronology (cf. *Kharjas H*, pp. 54–55): nine of the Spanish *kharjas* occur in
muwashshahs whose authors can be placed with certainty in the eleventh century;
the great majority (at least thirty-five) occur in *muwashshahs* of the first half of
the twelfth, which saw the height of the genre. The earliest *muwashshah* preserving a Spanish *kharja* is a Hebrew one (*Kharjas S, H, G* 18) composed
before 1042. The last, which uses a much older *kharja*, is a *muwashshah* (*Kharjas
S, H* 38b, *G* XXIb) by the Arabic poet Ibn Luyun (1282–1349).

BIBLIOGRAPHIC SUPPLEMENT 1966–77

The principles by which editions and studies have been selected for this supplement are indicated in the Postscript, p. 231. The basic choice of material is from the years 1968–76; it was possible to include a few still more recent entries, as well as some for 1966–7 that enlarge the original selection. Some works that have appeared in a new edition since 1966 have been updated in the earlier bibliography (pp. 246–61) and are not cited again here.

I have kept the bibliographic information as succinct as possible, but occasionally I include the place of publication, or the title of a series, where this may help to locate a work more speedily. Where a *Festschrift* by various scholars, or a volume of collected essays by one scholar, contains several pieces that are of interest for medieval lyric, I have, to save space, listed the volume rather than individual items.

For those who require a more complete coverage of particular areas of medieval lyric, the following regular bibliographies are recommended. The journal *Germanistik*, which has appeared quarterly since 1960, has three regular sections devoted to periods of medieval German literature. Among annual publications, the *Bibliographie der französischen Literaturwissenschaft* (since 1945) includes under 'Moyen-Age' a section 'Poésie lyrique, Questions de métrique', the *Bibliographie der deutschen Literaturwissenschaft* (also since 1945) one on 'Mittelalter', with several relevant sub-sections. *The Year's Work in English Studies* (since 1919) includes work on lyric in its Old and Middle English sections; *The Year's Work in Modern Language Studies* (since 1931) includes regular—annual or biennial—treatments of medieval Catalan, Dutch, French, German, Italian, Latin, Portuguese, Provençal, and Spanish. These languages, as well as medieval English, are also covered in the annual bibliography of the American Modern Language Association's journal, *PMLA* (with international coverage since 1956). The *Cahiers de civilisation médiévale* have a regular (now annual) bibliography, listed under topics, for work on the earlier Middle Ages. The bibliography of the *Revue d'histoire ecclésiastique* (annual since 1900) includes some important entries concerning medieval religious lyric; the *Répertoire international de la littérature musicale* (since 1966) contains annual sections on medieval music. Finally, work on lyric in the medieval Romance languages is covered very fully (at the time of writing, up to 1968) in the bibliographic supplements of the *Zeitschrift für romanische Philologie*, which began a century ago.

GENERAL

Anderson, G. A. 'Motets of the 13th Century Manuscript La Clayette', *Musica Disciplina* 27 (1973): 11–40; 28 (1974): 5–37.

'Notre Dame Latin Double Motets ca. 1215–1250', *ibid.* 25 (1971): 35–98.

'Notre Dame and Related Conductus: A Catalogue Raisonné', *Miscellanea Musicologica* 6 (1972): 153–229; 7 (1975): 1–81.

'Notre Dame Bilingual Motets', *ibid.* 3 (1968): 50–144.

'A Small Collection of Notre Dame Motets', *Journal of the American Musicological Society* 22 (1969): 157–96.

Anglès, H. *Historia de la música medieval en Navarra* (1970).

Scripta Musicologica (3 vols., Storia e Letteratura 1975).

Auerbach, E. *Gesammelte Aufsätze zur romanischen Philologie* (Bern–München, 1967).

Bec, P. 'Genres et régistres dans la lyrique médiévale des XIIᵉ et XIIIᵉ siècles', *Revue de linguistique romane* 38 (1974): 26–39.

'Le type lyrique des *chansons de femme* dans la poésie du moyen âge', in *Mélanges offerts à Edmond-René Labande* (Poitiers, 1974): 13–24.

Becker, Ph. A. *Zur romanischen Literaturgeschichte* (Bern–München, 1967).

Boutière, J. *Mélanges de philologie romane dédiés à la mémoire de Jean Boutière* (2 vols., Liège, 1971).

Bronzini, B. *Filia, visne nubere? Un tema di poesia popolare* (Roma, 1967).

Clausen, A. M. *Le origini della poesia lirica in Provenza e in Italia* (Revue romane, no. spécial 7, 1976).

Colledge, E. (ed.) *Richard Ledrede: The Latin Poems* (Toronto–Leiden, 1974).

Delbouille, M. 'A propos des origines de la lyrique romane', *Marche Romane* 20 (1970): 13–27.

Deroy, J. 'A l'entrade del tens clar—Veris ad imperia', *Mélanges Christine Mohrmann* (Spectrum: Utrecht, 1973): 191–204.

Deyermond, A. D. 'Lyric Traditions in Non-Lyrical Genres', *Studies in Honor of Lloyd A. Kasten* (Madison, 1975): 39–52.

Dronke, P. 'The Lament of Jephtha's Daughter: Themes, Traditions, Originality', *Studi medievali*, 3a serie, 12 (1971): 819–63 (written in collaboration with M. Alexiou).

'Learned Lyric and Popular Ballad in the Early Middle Ages', *Studi medievali*, 3a serie, 17 (1976): 1–40.

'Peter of Blois and Poetry at the Court of Henry II', *Mediaeval Studies* 38 (1976): 185–235.

Poetic Individuality in the Middle Ages (1970).

'Tradition and Innovation in Medieval Western Colour-Imagery', *Eranos-Jahrbuch* 41 (1972): 51–107.

'Two Thirteenth Century Religious Lyrics', *Chaucer and Middle English Studies in honour of Rossell Hope Robbins* (1974): 392–406.

Evans, P. *The Early Trope Repertory of Saint Martial de Limoges* (Princeton Studies in Music 2, 1970).

Falck, R. 'Rondellus, Canon and related Types before 1300', *Journal of the American Musicological Society* 25 (1972): 38–57.

Ferrante, J. M. *Woman as Image in Medieval Literature from the Twelfth Century to Dante* (1975).

Ferrante, J. M. & Economou, G. D. (ed.) *In Pursuit of Perfection: Courtly Love in Medieval Literature* (1975).

Françon, M. 'La structure du rondeau', *Medium Aevum* 44 (1975): 54–9.

Gewehr, W. 'Der Topos "Augen des Herzens" ', *Deutsche Vierteljahrsschrift für Literaturgeschichte und Geisteswissenschaft* 46 (1972): 626–49.

Goldin, F. (ed.) *German and Italian Lyrics of the Middle Ages* (1973).
Lyrics of the Troubadours and Trouvères (1973).
The Mirror of Narcissus in the Courtly Lyric (1967).

Greene, R. L. (ed.) *The Lyrics of the Red Book of Ossory* (Oxford, 1974).
Grundriss der Romanischen Literaturen des Mittelalters (ed. H. R. Jauss *et al.*, Heidelberg, 1968 sqq.): VI *La littérature didactique, allégorique et satirique* (2 vols., 1968–70); I *Généralités* (1973).

Halbach, K. H. ' "Klassizität" um 1200 . . .', *Festschrift G. Storz* (1973): 87–113.

d'Heur, J.-M. 'Des descorts occitans et des descordos galicien-portugais', *Zeitschrift für romanische Philologie* 84 (1968): 323–39.

'Le motif du vent . . .', *ibid.*, 88 (1972): 69–104.

Troubadours d'oc et troubadours galiciens-portugais (Paris, 1973).

Hughes, A. *Medieval Music: the Sixth Liberal Art* (Toronto Medieval Bibliographies 4, 1974).

Husmann, H. *Speculum musicae artis: Festgabe für Heinrich Husmann*, ed. H. Becker, R. Gerlach (1970).

Jakobson, R. *Questions de poétique* (1973).

Jammers, E. *Schrift, Ordnung, Gestalt* (Neue Heidelberger Studien zur Musikwissenschaft 1, 1969).

Jansen, R. K. 'Randbemerkungen zum ersten Troubadour und ersten Minnesänger', *Deutsche Vierteljahrsschrift* 48 (1974): 767–71.

Killy, W. *Elemente der Lyrik* (1972).

Kittel, M. 'Humility in Old Provençal and Early Italian Poetry', *Romance Philology* 27 (1973): 158–71.

Klein, K. W. *The Partisan Voice. A Study of the Political Lyric in France and Germany, 1180–1230* (The Hague, 1971).

Le Gentil, P. *Mélanges de langue et de littérature médiévales offerts à Pierre Le Gentil* (1974).

Lejeune, R. *Mélanges offerts à Rita Lejeune* (2 vols., Gembloux, 1969).

Lida de Malkiel, M. R. 'La dama como obra maestra de Dios', *Romance Philology* 28 (1974–5): 267–324.

Lipphardt, W. 'Die liturgische Funktion deutscher Kirchenlieder . . . des Mittelalters', *Zeitschrift für katholische Theologie* 94 (1972): 158–98.

Machabey, A. 'Comment déterminer l'authenticité d'une chanson médiévale?', *Mélanges offerts à René Crozet* (Poitiers, 1966): 2, 915–20.

Metzner, E. E. *Zur frühesten Geschichte der europäischen Balladendichtung* (1972).

Mohr, W. 'Die Natur im mittelalterlichen Liede', *Festschrift W. Kohlschmidt* (Bern, 1969): 45–63.

Mosaic VIII, 4: On the Rise of the Vernacular Literatures in the Middle Ages (Univ. of Manitoba Press, 1975).

Newman, F. X. (ed.) *The Meaning of Courtly Love* (1968).

Nichols, S. G. 'The Medieval Lyric and its Public', *Mediaevalia et Humanistica* n.s. 3 (1972): 133–53.

Orenstein, H. *Die Refrainformen im Chansonnier de l'Arsenal* (Musicological Studies 19, 1970).

Peters, U. 'Cour d'amour—Minnehof', *Zeitschrift für deutsches Altertum* 101 (1972): 117–33.
'Niederes Rittertum oder hoher Adel?', *Euphorion* 67 (1973): 244–60.

de Poerck, G. 'Le MS. Paris Latin 1139', *Scriptorium* 23 (1969): 298–312.

Porte, J. (ed.) *Encyclopédie des musiques sacrées*, vol. 2 (1969).

Räkel, H. H. S. 'Drei Lieder zum dritten Kreuzzug', *Deutsche Vierteljahrsschrift für Literaturgeschichte und Geisteswissenschaft* 47 (1973): 508–50.

Ranawake, S. *Höfische Strophenkunst* (Münchener Texte und Untersuchungen, 1975).

Reaney, G. *Manuscripts of Polyphonic Music: 11th–early 14th Century* (München–Duisburg, 1966).

Roncaglia, A. (ed.) *Antologia delle letterature medievali d'oc e d'oïl* (2nd ed., Milano, 1973).
'De quibusdam provincialibus translatis in lingua nostra', in *Studi in onore di N. Sapegno* II (1975): 1–36.

Rostaing, C. *Mélanges . . . Charles Rostaing* (2 vols., Liège, 1974).

Ruhe, D. *Le Dieu d'Amours avec son Paradis* (München, 1974).

Saíz, P. *Personae and Poiesis. The poet and the poem in medieval love lyric* (The Hague, 1976).

Saville, J. *The Medieval Erotic Alba: Structure as Meaning* (New York, 1972).

Schlumbohm, C. *Jocus und Amor: Liebesdiskussionen . . .* (Hamburg, 1974).

Sesini, U. *Musicologia e filologia: raccolta di studi* (1968).

Stemmler, T. (ed.) *The Latin Hymns of Richard Ledrede* (Mannheim, 1975).

Viscardi, A. *Le letterature d'oc e d'oïl* (2nd ed., 1976).
Ricerche e interpretazioni mediolatine e romanze (Milano, 1970).

van der Werf, H. *The chansons of the troubadours and trouvères* (Utrecht, 1972).

Worstbrock, F. J. 'Rhetorische Formtypen der mittelalterlichen Lyrik', *Deutsche Vierteljahrsschrift für Literaturgeschichte und Geisteswissenschaft* 49 (1975): 8–31.

Ziltener, W. *Repertorium der Gleichnisse und bildhaften Vergleiche der okzitanischen und französischen Versliteratur des Mittelalters* (Bern, 1972 ff.).
Studien zur bildungsgeschichtlichen Eigenart der höfischen Dichtung (Bern, 1972).

Zink, M. *La pastourelle. Poésie et folklore au Moyen Age* (Paris–Montréal, 1972).

Zumthor, P. *Essai de poétique médiévale* (1972).

CATALAN

Guillem de Berguedà, ed. M. de Riquer (2 vols., Poblet, 1971).

Marshall, J. H. (ed.) *The Razos de trobar of Raimon Vidal and Associated Texts* (1972).

Pi de Cabanyes, O. 'Dos poemas i una crisi: Lo Desconhort i el Cant de Ramon', *Miscellanea Barcinonensia* 28 (1971).

Pirot, F. *Recherches sur les connaissances littéraires des troubadours occitans et catalans des XIIe et XIIIe siècles* (Barcelona, 1972).

de Riquer, M. *Literatura catalana medieval* (1972).
'El trovador Huguet de Mataplana', *Studia Hispanica in Honorem R. Lapesa* I (1972): 455–94.

DUTCH

De Paepe, N. *Hadewijch, Strofische Gedichten. Een studie van de minne* . . . (Gent, 1967).
Hadewijch, Strofische Gedichten, een Keuze; Grondige studie van een Middelnederlandse auteur (2 vols., Gent–Leuven, 1972).
(ed.) *Ik zag nooit zo roden mond. Middeleeuwse liefdespoëzie* (Leiden, n.d.).

Gerritsen, W. P. 'Kritische kanttekeningen bij de inleiding tot Heeroma's editie van het Gruuthuse-liedboek', *Nieuwe Taalgids* 62 (1969): 187–215.

Guest, T. M. *Some Aspects of Hadewijch's Poetic Form in the 'Strofische Gedichten'* (The Hague, 1975).

Heeroma, D. and Lindenburg, C. W. H. (ed.) *Liederen en gedichten uit het Gruuthuse-Handschrift, Eerste deel* (Leiden, 1966).

Kaplowitt, S. J. 'Heinrich von Veldeke's Song Cycle of "Hohe Minne" ', *Seminar* 11 (1975): 125–40.

King, P. K. *Dawn Poetry in the Netherlands* (Amsterdam, 1971).

Obbema, P. F. J. *Die Gheestelicke Melody* (1975).
'Het einde van de Zuster van Gansoirde', *Nieuwe Taalgids* 65 (1975): 181–90.

Sinnema, R. *Heinrik van Veldeke* (New York, 1972).

de Smet, G. A. R. (ed.) *Heinríc van Veldeken* (Antwerp–Utrecht, 1971).

Vellekoop, K. *et al.* (ed.) *Het Antwerps Liedboek* (2 vols., Amsterdam, 1972).

ENGLISH

Bennett, J. A. W. and Smithers, G. V. (ed.) *Early Middle English Verse and Prose* (2nd ed., 1968).

Davidson, C. 'Erotic "Women's Songs" in Anglo-Saxon England', *Neophilologus* 59 (1975): 451–62.

Gneuss, H. *Hymnar und Hymnen im englischen Mittelalter* (1968).

Gray, D. *Themes and Images in the Medieval English Religious Lyric* (1972).
(ed.) *A Selection of Religious Lyrics* (1975).

Hartung, A. E. (ed.) *A Manual of the Writings in Middle English* (*1050–1500*)
(1967 ff.): III (1972) sect. vii 'Dialogues, Debates and Catechisms'; V
(1975) sect. xiii 'Poems dealing with contemporary conditions'.

Luria, M. S. and Hoffman, R. L. (ed.) *Middle English Lyrics* (New York, 1974).

Oliver, R. *Poems without Names* (Berkeley, 1970).

Reiss, E. *The Art of the Middle English Lyric* (Athens, Ga., 1972).

Rogers, W. E. *Image and Abstraction. Six Middle English Religious Lyrics*
(Anglistica 18, 1972).

Silverstein, Th. (ed.) *Medieval English Lyrics* (1971).

Sisam, C. (ed.) *The Oxford Book of Medieval English Verse* (1970).

Stemmler, T. (ed.) *Medieval English Love-Lyrics* (Tübingen, 1970).

'More English Texts from MS. Cambridge UL Ii.III.8', *Anglia* 93 (1975): 1–16.
'Textologische Probleme mittelenglischer Dichtung', *Mannheimer Berichte* 8
(1974): 245–8.
'The Vernacular Snatches in the Red Book of Ossory', *Anglia* 95 (1977): 122–9.

Weber, S. A. *Theology and Poetry in the Middle English Lyric* (Columbus, 1969).

Wenzel, S. 'The Moor Maiden—a Contemporary View', *Speculum* 49 (1974):
69–74.
'Unrecorded Middle English Verses', *Anglia* 92 (1974): 55–78.

Woolf, R. *The English Religious Lyric in the Middle Ages* (1968).

FRENCH

Adam de la Halle *The Chansons*, ed. J. H. Marshall (Manchester, 1971).

The Lyric Works, ed. N. E. Wilkins (Corpus Mensurabilis Musicae 44, 1967).

Archibald, J. K. (ed.) 'La chanson de captivité du roi Richard', *Cahiers d'études
médiévales* I (1974): 149–58.

Baumgartner, E. 'Remarques sur les pièces lyriques du Tristan en prose', in
Etudes . . . offertes à Félix Lecoy (Paris, 1973): 19–25.

Bec, P. 'L'aube française Gaite de la Tor', *Cahiers de civilisation médiévale* 16
(1973): 17–33.

van den Boogaard, N. H. J. 'Les chansons attribuées à Wilart de Corbie',
Neophilologus 55 (1971): 123–41.
Rondeaux et refrains du XIIe siècle au début du XIVe (1969).

Bulst, W. 'Buona pulcella fut Eulalia', in *Festschrift Bernhard Bischoff* (1971):
207–17

Frappier, J. *Amour courtois et Table Ronde* (Genève, 1973).

Gillebert de Berneville, ed. M. d'Hartog (Paris, 1974).

Guiette, R. *D'une poésie formelle en France au Moyen Age* (1972).

Guillaume le Viner *Les poésies*, ed. P. Ménard (Genève, 1971).

Jehan Erart *Les poésies*, ed. T. Newcombe (Genève, 1972).

Jonin, P. 'Le refrain dans les chansons de toile', *Romania* 96 (1975): 209–44.

'Les types féminins dans les chansons de toile', *Romania* 91 (1970): 433–66.

Kooijman, J. (ed.) *Trouvères lorrains* (Nancy, 1974).

Lavis, G. *L'expression de l'affectivité dans la poésie lyrique française du moyen âge* (Paris, 1972).

Mölk, U. and Wolfzettel, F. *Répertoire métrique de la poésie lyrique française des origines à 1350* (München, 1972).

Newcombe, T. 'Les poésies du trouvère Raoul de Beauvais', *Romania* 93 (1972): 317–36.

Payen, J. C. (ed.) *Histoire littéraire de la France I: Des origines à 1492* (1974). 'Sens et structure d'une chanson courtoise', *Cahiers de civilisation médiévale* 12 (1969): 243–52.

Pollmann, L. *Die Liebe in der hochmittelalterlichen Literatur Frankreichs* (Analecta Romanica, 1966).

Regalado, N. F. *Poetic Patterns in Rutebeuf* (Yale Romanic Studies, 1970).

Rivière, J. C. (ed.) *Pastourelles* (3 vols., Textes Littéraires Français 1974–6).

Rosenberg, S. N. 'The Chanson of Jacques d'Autun', *Romania* 96 (1975): 552–60.

Serper, A. *La manière satirique de Rutebeuf* (Napoli, 1972).

Yllera, A. 'Ensayo de estilistica medieval: Rutebeuf, Goliardo y "syntaxier" ', *Filología moderna* 49 (1973): 65–102.

Zai, M.-C. (ed.) *Les Chansons courtoises de Chrétien de Troyes* (Bern–Frankfurt, 1974).

Zumthor, P. *Langue, texte, énigme* (1975).

GERMAN

Annolied, Das, ed. and tr. E. Nellmann (Reclam, 1975).

Ashcroft, J. 'Crabbed Age and Youth: the Self-stylisations of Reinmar and Walther', *German Life and Letters* 28 (1975): 187–99. 'Parodie und Maskenspiel bei Walther', *Euphorion* 69 (1975): 197–218.

Bertau, K. *Deutsche Literatur im europäischen Mittelalter* (2 vols., München, 1972–3).

Beyschlag, S. (ed.) *Walther von der Vogelweide* (Wege der Forschung, 1971).

Blamires, D. '*Pherierlin* in der Wilde Alexander's *Kindheitslied*', *Medium Aevum* 45 (1976): 269–76.

Böhmer, M. *Untersuchungen zur mittelhochdeutschen Kreuzzugslyrik* (Roma 1968).

Brandes, K. *Heinrich von Morungen: Zyklische Liedergruppen* (1975). *Friderich von Hûsen*, ed. D. G. Mowatt (1971).

Frings, Th. 'Ein Morungenportrait', *Beiträge zur Geschichte der deutschen Sprache und Literatur* (Halle) 88 (1967): 91–9. 'Namenlose Lieder', *ibid.*, 307–28.

Glier, I. 'Diener zweier Herrinnen: Zu Ulrichs von Lichtenstein Frauendienst', in *The Epic and Medieval Society*, ed. H. Scholler (Tübingen, 1977) 290–306.

'Der Minneleich im späten 13. Jahrhundert', in *Werk—Typ—Situation* (ed. I. Glier *et al.*, 1969): 161–83.

Grimminger, R. *Poetik des frühen Minnesangs* (Münchener Texte und Untersuchungen 27, 1969).

Halbach, K. H. ' "Humanitätsklassik" des Stauferzeitalters in der Lyrik Walthers von der Vogelweide', *Festschrift K. Ziegler* (1968): 13–35.
Walther von der Vogelweide (3rd ed., 1973).

Heger, H. (ed.) *Mondsee-Wiener Liederhandschrift* (Facsimile, Graz, 1968).

Heinrich von Morungen *Lieder*, ed. and tr. H. Tervooren (Reclam, 1975).

Herzog, U. 'Minneideal und Wirklichkeit. Zum "Frauendienst" des Ulrich von Lichtenstein', *Deutsche Vierteljahrsschrift* 49 (1975): 502–19.

Hinmann, M. M. 'Minne in a New Mode: Walther and the Literary Tradition' *Deutsche Vierteljahrsschrift* 48 (1974): 249–63.

Hofmann, W. *Die Minnefeinde in der deutschen Liebesdichtung des 12. und 13. Jahrhunderts* (Coburg, 1974).

Janota, J. *Studien zu Funktion und Typus des deutschen geistlichen Liedes im Mittelalter* (Münchener Texte und Untersuchungen 23, 1968).

Jungbluth, G. (ed.) *Interpretationen mittelhochdeutscher Lyrik* (1969).

Kaiser, G. *Beiträge zu den Liedern des Minnesängers Rubin* (1969).

Kartschoke, D. *Altdeusche Bibeldichtung* (Sammlung Metzler, 1975).

Kircher, A. *Dichter und Konvention. Zum gesellschaftlichen Realitätsproblem der deutschen Lyrik um 1200* (1973).

Knoop, U. *Das mittelhochdeutsche Tagelied* (Marburger Beiträge, 1976).

Kuhn, H. 'Minnesang als Aufführungsform', *Festschrift K. Zielger* (1968): 1–12.
Text und Theorie (Stuttgart, 1969).

Laubner, H. *Studien zum geistlichen Sinngehalt des Adjektivs im Werk Mechthilds von Magdeburg* (1975).

Lea, E. 'Erziehen—im Wert erhöhen—Gemeinschaft in Liebe', *Beiträge zur Geschichte der deutschen Sprache und Literatur* (Halle) 89 (1968): 255–81.
'Die Sprache Lyrischer Grundgefüge', *ibid.*, 90 (1969): 305–79.

Lea, E. and Frings, Th. 'Nachtrag und Bestätigung', *ibid.* 89 (1968): 282–9.

McLintock, D. R. 'Walther's Mädchenlieder', *Oxford German Studies* 3 (1968): 30–43.

Maurer, F. *Die 'Pseudoreimare'* (Abhandlungen der Heidelberger Akademie, 1966).
'Sprachliche und musikalische Bauformen des deutschen Minnesangs um 1200', *Poetica* 1 (1967): 462–82.
'Zu Text und Form der "Elegie" Walthers von der Vogelweide', in *Festschrift Karl Bischoff* (1975): 390–9.
(ed.) *Die religiösen Dichtungen des 11. und 12. Jahrhunderts*, vol. 3 (1970).

Mohr, W. 'Altersdichtung Walthers von der Vogelweide', *Sprachkunst* 2 (1971): 329–56.
'Spiegelungen des Tagelieds', *Festschrift H. de Boor* (Tübingen, 1971): 287–304.

Moser, H. (ed.) *Mittelhochdeutsche Spruchdichtung* (Wege der Forschung, 1972).

Moser, H. and Müller-Blattau, J. (ed.) *Deutsche Lieder des Mittelalters* (1968).

Müller, U. (ed.) *Kreuzzugsdichtung* (Tübingen, 1969).
Politische Lyrik des deutschen Mittelalters. Texte I (Göppingen, 1972).
Untersuchungen zur politischen Lyrik des deutschen Mittelalters (Göppingen, 1974).
Neidhart von Reuenthal *Die Lieder*, ed. S. Beyschlag (Darmstadt, 1975).

Ohlenroth, D. *Sprechsituation und Sprecheridentität . . . im frühen deutschen Minnesang* (Göppingen, 1975).

Ohly, F. 'Du bist mein, ich bin dein . . .', *Festschrift Werner Schröder* (Berlin, 1974): 371–415.

Pickerodt-Uthleb, E. *Die Jenaer Liederhandschrift* (1975).

Ploss, E. 'Der Beginn politischer Dichtung in deutscher Sprache', *Zeitschrift für deutsche Philologie* 86 (1969): 1–18.

Renk, H.-E. *Der Manessekreis, seine Dichter und die Manessische Handschrift* (Stuttgart, 1974).

Ruh, K. and Schröder, W. (ed.) *Beiträge zur weltlichen und geistlichen Lyrik* (1973).

Sayce, O. (ed.) *Poets of the Minnesang* (1967).

Schröder, F. R. 'Heinrich von Morungen', *Germanisch-Romanische Monats-schrift* N.F. 18 (1968): 337–48.

Schupp, V. 'Er hât tûsent man betoeret', *Poetica* 6 (1974): 38–59.

Schwietering, J. *Philologische Schriften* (München, 1968).

Seiffert, L. 'Hartmann von Aue and his Lyric Poetry', *Oxford German Studies* 3 (1968): 1–29.

Simon, E. *Neidhart von Reuenthal: Geschichte der Forschung und Bibliographie* (Harvard Germanic Studies 4, 1968).
Neidhart von Reuenthal (Twayne's World Authors, 1975).

Stadler, H. 'Rudolf von Fenis and his Sources', *Oxford German Studies* 8 (1974): 5–19.

Taylor, R. J. (ed.) *The Art of the Minnesinger* (2 vols., Cardiff, 1968).

Tervooren, H. *Bibliographie zum Minnesang und zu den Dichtern aus 'Des Minnesangs Frühling'* (1969).

Touber, A. H. *Deutsche Strophenformen des Mittelalters* (1975).

Wachinger, B. *Sängerkrieg* (Münchener Texte und Untersuchungen 42, 1973).

Walther von der Vogelweide *Die politischen Lieder*, ed. F. Maurer (3rd ed., 1972).
Sprüche, Lieder, der Leich, ed. and tr. P. Stapf (1972).

Wapnewski, P. *Waz ist minne. Studien zur mittelhochdeutschen Lyrik* (1975).

Wenzel, H. *Frauendienst und Gottesdienst. Studien zur Minne-Ideologie* (1974).

Wolf, A. 'Komik und Parodie . . . zu Ulrichs von Lichtenstein "Fraudienst" ', *Amsterdamer Beiträge zur älteren Germanistik* 10: (1976): 73–102.

Wolfram von Eschenbach *Die Lyrik*, ed. P. Wapnewski (1972).
Zeitschrift für deutsche Philologie 87 (1968), Sonderheft: Mittelhochdeutsche Lyrik.

Zeitschrift für deutsche Philologie 90 (1971), Sonderheft: Neue Arbeiten zum mittelalterlichen Lied.

ITALIAN

Baldelli, I. *Dante e i poeti fiorentini del Duecento* (1968).

Bettarini, A. B. 'Le rime di Meo dei Tolomei e di Musica da Siena', *Studi di Filologia Italiana* 32 (1974): 31–98.

Bettarini, R. (ed.) *Dante da Maiano, Rime* (Firenze, 1969).
Jacopone e il Laudario Urbinate (Firenze, 1969).

Bigongiari, P. *Capitoli di una storia della poesia italiana* (1968).

Bizziccari, A. 'L'amore mistico nel canzoniere di Jacopone da Todi', *Italica* 45 (1968): 1–27.

Boyde, P. *Dante's Style in his Lyric Poetry* (1971).

Cecco Angiolieri *Rime*, ed. G. Cavalli (1975).

Contini, G. *Letteratura italiana delle origini* (1970).

Elwert, W. Th. *Italienische Metrik* (1968).
Studien zu den romanischen Sprachen und Literaturen, vols. 1 (1968); 3 (1970); 4 (1971).

Favati, G. 'Cino de' Sinibaldi da Pistoia poeta', in *Letteratura e critica. Studi in onore di Natalino Sapegno* I (Roma, 1974) 149–78.
Inchiesta sul dolce stil nuovo (Firenze, 1975).

Fiorino, A. *Metri e temi della scuola siciliana* (1969).

Folena, G. 'Cultura poetica dei primi fiorentini', *Giornale storico della letteratura italiana* 147 (1970): 1–42.

Fubini, M. *Metrica e poesia. I: Dal Duecento al Petrarca* (2nd ed., 1970)

Hainsworth, P. R. J. 'Artifice in "Pir men cori alligrari" ', *Italian Studies* 29 (1974): 12–27.

Jacopone da Todi *Laude*, ed. F. Mancini (Bari, 1974).

Margueron, C. 'Immagini, metafore e miti nelle Rime . . . di Guittone d'Arezzo', *Lettere Italiane* 25 (1973): 461–90.
Recherches sur Guittone d'Arezzo (1966).

Marti, M. *Storia dello stil nuovo* (2 vols., 1973).
(ed.) *Poeti del Dolci stil nuovo* (1969).

Minetti, F. F. *Sondaggi guittoniani* (1974).

Mölk, U. 'Le sonnet "Amor è un desio" ', *Cahiers de civilisation médiévale* 14 (1971): 329–39.

Monteverdi, A. 'Giacomo da Lentini e Cielo d'Alcamo', *Cultura Neolatina* 27 (1967): 263–84.

Onesto da Bologna *Le rime*, ed. S. Orlando (Firenze, 1974).

Pagani, W. *Repertorio tematico della scuola poetica siciliana* (1968).

Possiedi, P. 'Con quella spada ond'elli ancise Dido', *Modern Language Notes* 89 (1974): 13–34.

Ruggeri, S. 'Materiali per uno studio sul "Cantico di Frate Sole" ', *Rivista delle Biblioteche* 43 (1975): 60–102.

Savona, E. *Repertorio tematico del Dolce stil nuovo* (1973).

Varanini, G. (ed). *Laude Dugentesche* (Padova, 1972).

LATIN

Arias y Arias, R. *La poesía de los goliardos* (1970).

Autenrieth, J. 'Einige Bemerkungen zu den Gedichten im Hortus deliciarum Herrads von Landsberg', *Festschrift Bernhard Bischoff* (1971): 307–21.

Beatie, B. A. 'Macaronic Poetry in the Carmina Burana', *Vivarium* 5 (1967): 16–24.

Behrends, F. (ed.) *The Letters and Poems of Fulbert of Chartres* (1976).

Bulst, W. *Carmina Leodensia* (Heidelberg Akademie, Sitzungsberichte, 1975).

Carmina Burana. Die Lieder der Benediktbeurer Handschrift in vollständiger deutscher Übertragung (München, 1975).

Carmina Burana I 3: Die Trink- und Spielerlieder—Die geistlichen Dramen— Nachträge (ed. O. Schumann †, B. Bischoff, 1970).

Corpus Troporum I, ed. R. Jonsson; II, ed. O. Marcusson (Stockholm, 1975–6).

Díaz y Díaz, M. C. *De Isidoro al Siglo XI* (Barcelona, 1976).

Dronke, P. 'The Composition of Hildegard of Bingen's *Symphonia*', *Sacris Erudiri* 19 (1969–70): 381–93.

'Poetic Meaning in the Carmina Burana', *Mittellateinisches Jahrbuch* 10 (1974–5): 116–37.

Frings, Th. 'Ein mittellateinisches Frauenlied . . .', *Beiträge zur romanischen Philologie* 7 (1968): 311–18.

García-Villoslada, R. *La poesía rítmica de los goliardos medievales* (1975).

Herde, R. 'Das Hohelied in der lateinischen Literatur des Mittelalters', *Studi medievali*, 3a serie, 8 (1967): 957–1073.

Hildegard von Bingen *Lieder*, ed. P. Barth, M. I. Ritscher, J. Schmidt-Görg (Salzburg, 1969); Supplement: M. I. Ritscher, *Kritischer Bericht* (Salzburg, 1969).

Könsgen, E. 'Bemerkungen und Ergänzungen zur Edition der . . . Ripollsammlung', *Mittellateinisches Jahrbuch* 12 (1977): 82–91.

Latzke, Th. 'Die Carmina erotica der Ripoll-Sammlung', *Mittellateinisches Jahrbuch* 10 (1974–5): 138–201.

'Zu Könsgens Bemerkungen . . .' *ibid.*, 12 (1977): 92–6.

'Das Verwahrungsgedicht . . .' *ibid.*, 11 (1976): 151–76.

Monumenta Monodica Medii Aevi, ed. B. Stäblein (Kassel-Basel, 1956 ff.) II Die Gesänge des altrömischen Graduale (1970); III Introitus-Tropen I (1970); VII Alleluia-Melodien I (1968).

von Moos, P. 'Gottschalk's Gedicht *O mi custos*—eine confessio', *Frühmittelalterliche Studien* 4 (1970): 201–30; 5 (1971): 317–58.

Moralejo, J. L. 'El Cancionero erótico de Ripoll en el marco de la lírica mediolatina', *Prohemio* 4 (1973): 107–41.

'Notas al texto de los "Carmina Erotica Rivipullensia"', *Studi medievali*, 3a serie, 16 (1975): 877–86.

Naumann, H. 'Gab es eine Vagantendichtung?', *Der altsprachliche Unterricht* 12 (1969): 69–105.

Offermans, W. *Die Wirkung Ovids auf die literarische Sprache der lateinischen Liebesdichtung des 11. und 12. Jahrhunderts* (Beiheft zum Mittellateinischen Jahrbuch 3, 1970).

Rico, F. 'Las letras latinas del siglo XII en Galicia, León y Castilia', *Abaco* 2 (1969) 9–91.

Robertson, D. W. J., Jr 'Two Poems from the *Carmina Burana*', *American Benedictine Review* 27 (1976): 36–60.

Schaller, D. 'Bemerkungen zum Schlussband der kritischen Edition der "Carmina Burana"', *Mittellateinisches Jahrbuch* 10 (1974–5): 106–15.

Schüppert, H. *Kirchenkritik in der lateinischen Lyrik des 12. und 13. Jahrhunderts* (Medium Aevum, 1972).

Spitzmuller, H. (ed.) *Poésie latine chrétienne du moyen âge* (Bruxelles, 1972).

Spreckelmeyer, G. *Das Kreuzzugslied des lateinischen Mittelalters* (1974).

von den Steinen, W. *Ein Dichterbuch des Mittelalters* (Bern, 1974).
'Die Planctus Abaelards—Jephthas Tochter', *Mittellateinisches Jahrbuch* 4 (1967): 122–44.

Steiner, R. 'The Prosulae of the MS. Paris B.N. lat. 1118', *Journal of the American Musicological Society* 22 (1969): 367–93.

Sticca, S. 'The Literary Genesis of the Planctus Mariae', *Classica et Mediaevalia* 27 (1966): 296–319.

Szövérffy, J. 'Iberian Hymnody', *Classical Folia* 25 (1971): 9–136.
Weltliche Dichtungen des lateinischen Mittelalters I (Berlin, 1970).

Traill, D. 'The Addressee and Interpretation of Walahfrid's "Metrum Sapphicum"', *Medievalia et Humanistica* N.S. 2 (1971): 69–82.

Waddell, H. *More Latin Lyrics, From Virgil to Milton* (1976).

Walther, H. *Initia carminum ac versuum medii aevi posterioris Latinorum*, (2nd ed., Göttingen, 1969).

Weinrich, L. 'Peter Abaelard as Musician', *Musical Quarterly* 55 (1969): 295–312.

Worstbrock, F. J. 'Zu Gedichten Walthers von Châtillon und seiner "Schule"', *Zeitschrift für deutsches Altertum* 101 (1972): 200–7.

PORTUGUESE

Alegria, J. A. *A Problemática musical das Cantigas de Amigo* (Lisboa, 1968).

Ayras Carpancho ed. V. Minervini, *Annali dell'Istituto Orientale di Napoli, Sezione Romanica* 16 (1974): 21–113.

Cancioneiro português da Biblioteca Vaticana (Cód. 4803) Facsímil (Lisboa, 1973).

Lanciani, G. 'Ayras Veaz o il trovatore dimezzato', *Cultura Neolatina* 34 (1974): 99–116.

Martin Moya *Le poesie*, ed. L. Stegagno Picchio (Roma, 1968).

Panunzio, S. 'Per una lettura del canzoniere amoroso di Roy Queimado', *Studi mediolatini e volgari* 19 (1971): 181–209.

Pedr' Amigo de Sevilha ed. G. Marroni, *Annal idell'Istituto Orientale di Napoli, Sezione Romanica* 10 (1968): 189–339.

Pero Meogo *O cancioneiro*, ed. X. L. Méndez Ferrín (Vigo, 1966).

Pero da Ponte *Poesie*, ed. S. Panunzio (Bari, 1967).

Reckert, S. *Lyra Minima: structure and symbol in Iberian traditional verse* (1970).

Reckert, S. *et al. Do Cancioneiro de Amigo* (Lisboa, 1976).

Rico, F. 'Otra lectura de la "Cantiga da garvaia" ', *Studia Hispanica in Honorem R. Lapesa* I (1972): 443–53.

Rodrigues Lapa, M. (ed.) *Cantigas d'escarnho e de mal dizer* (2nd ed., 1970).

Scholberg, K. R. *Sátira e invectiva en la España medieval* (1971).

Tavani, G. *Poesia del Duecento nella penisola iberica* (1969).

'Problèmes de la poésie lyrique galégo-portugaise', *Colóquio/Letras* (Jan. 1974): 45–56.

Repertorio metrico della lirica galego-portoghese (1967).

Vilhena, M. C. 'O carácter abstracto das Cantigas de Amor', *Ocidente* 81 (1971): 133–51.

PROVENÇAL

Actes du V^eCongrès International de Langue et Littérature d'Oc et d'Etudes Franco-Provençales (Nice, 1974).

Actes du VIe Congrès . . . (2 vols., Montpellier, 1971).

Bec, P. 'La douleur et son univers poétique chez Bernart de Ventadour', *Cahiers de civilisation médiévale* 11 (1968): 545–71; 12 (1969): 25–33.

Nouvelle anthologie de la lyrique occitane au moyen âge (Avignon, 1970).

(ed.) *Présence des troubadours (Annales de l'Institut d'Etudes Occitanes*, 4e série, II 5, 1970).

Berengar de Palazol ed. T. Newcombe, *Nottingham Medieval Studies* 15 (1971): 54–95.

Bogin, M. *The Women Troubadours* (1976).

Bondanella, P. E. 'The Theory of the Gothic Lyric and the Case of Bernart de Ventadorn', *Neuphilologische Mitteilungen* 74 (1973): 369–81.

Camproux, C. 'Cardenal et Rutebeuf poètes satiriques', *Revue des langues romanes* 79 (1971): 3–28.

Histoire de la littérature occitane (2nd ed., 1971).

Chambers, F. M. *Proper Names in the Lyrics of the Troubadours* (1971).

Condren, E. I. 'The Troubadour and his Labor of Love', *Mediaeval Studies* 34 (1972): 174–95.

Cropp, G. *Le vocabulaire courtois des troubadours de l'époque classique* (Genève, 1975).

Davenson, H. (H.-I. Marrou), *Les troubadours* (2nd ed., 1971).

Dumitrescu, M. 'Eble II de Ventadorn et Guillaume IX d'Aquitaine', *Cahiers de civilisation médiévale* 11 (1968): 379–412.

'Les premiers troubadours connus et les origines de la poésie provençale', *ibid.*, 9 (1966): 345–54.

Estevan da Guarda ed. W. Pagani, *Studi Mediolatini e Volgari* 19 (1971): 51–179.

Fantazzi, C. 'Marcabru's *Pastourelle*', *Studies in Philology* 71 (1974): 385–403.

Gay-Crosier, R. *Religious Elements in the Secular Lyrics of the Troubadours* (1971).

Guglielmo IX d'Aquitaine *Poesie*, ed. N. Pasero (1973).

Hamlin, F. R., Ricketts, P. T., Hathaway, J. *Introduction à l'étude de l'ancien provençal* (Genève, 1967).

Jernigan, C. 'The Song of the Nail and the Uncle: Arnaut Daniel's Sestina', *Studies in Philology* 71 (1974): 127–51.

Köhler, E. 'Trobar clus: discussione aperta', *Cultura Neolatina* 30 (1970): 300–14.
'La pastourelle dans la poésie des troubadours', in *Etudes . . . offertes à Félix Lecoy* (Paris, 1973): 279–92.

Lawner, L. 'Tot es niens', *Cultura Neolatina* 31 (1971): 155–70.

Leube-Fey, C. *Bild und Funktion der 'dompna' in der Lyrik der Troubadors* (Studia Romanica 21, 1971).

Limentani, A. 'A la fontana del vergier', *Annali di Ca' Foscari* 11 (1972): 361–80.

Majorano, M. 'Lingua e ideologia nel canzoniere di Jaufre Rudel', *Annali dell'Istituto Univ. Orientale di Napoli*, Sez. Romanica 16 (1974): 159–201.

Marshall, J. H. *The Transmission of Troubadour Poetry* (1975).

Méjean S. (ed). *La chanson satirique provençale au Moyen Age* (1971).

Mölk, U. *Trobar clus, Trobar leu. Studien zur Dichtungstheorie der Troubadours* (1968).

Neumeister, S. *Das Spiel mit der höfischen Liebe. Das altprovenzalische Partimen* (1969).

Oroz Arizcuren, F. J. *La lírica religiosa en la literatura provenzal antigua* (Pamplona, 1972).

Paden, W. D., Jr 'The Troubadours' Lady', *Studies in Philology* 72 (1975): 28–50.

Pagani, W. 'Per un'interpretazione di *A la fontana del vergier*', *Studi Mediolatini e Volgari* 20 (1972): 169–74.

Paterson, L. M. *Troubadours and Eloquence* (1975).

Payen, J.-C. ' "Peregris": De l'"amor de lonh" au congé courtois', *Cahiers de civilisation médiévale* 17 (1974): 247–55.

Peire Rogier *The Poems*, ed. D. E. T. Nicholson (1976).

Pellegrini, S. 'Appunti su Marcabruno', *Studi Mediolatini e Volgari* 20 (1972): 175–9.
'Frammento inedito di canzoniere provenzale', *ibid.*, 15–16 (1968): 89–99.

Pirot, F. 'A la fontana del vergier du troubadour Marcabru', in *Mélanges Paul Imbs* (Strasbourg 1973): 621–42.
' "L'idéologie" des troubadours', *Moyen Age* 74 (1968): 301–31.

Press, A. R. (ed.) *Anthology of Troubadour Lyric Poetry* (Edinburgh, 1971).
'The adulterous nature of Fin' Amors: a re-examination', *Forum for Modern Language Studies* 6 (1970): 324–41.

Raimon de Miraval *Les poésies*, ed. L. T. Topsfield (1971).

Raimon de las Salas ed. F. M. Chambers, in *Essays in Honor of L. F. Solano* (1971): 29–51.

Regan, M. S. 'Amador and Chantador . . .', *Philological Quarterly* 53 (1974): 10–28.

Rieger, D. *Gattungen und Gattungsbezeichnungen der Trobadorlyrik* (Tübingen, 1976).
'Die trobairitz in Italien', *Cultura Neolatina* 31 (1971): 205–23.
'Zur Stellung des Tagelieds in der Trobadorlyrik', *Zeitschrift für romanische Philologie* 37 (1971): 223–32.
Der 'vers de dreyt nien' Wilhelms IX . . .', Heidelberger Akademie der Wissenschaften, Sitzb. 1975, no. 3.

de Riquer, M. *Los trovadores. Historia literaria y textos* (3 vols., Barcelona, 1975).

Roncaglia, A. [Notes on four recent Marcabru studies], *Cultura Neolatina* 33 (1973): 379–83.
'Trobar clus: discussione aperta', *Cultura Neolatina* 29 (1969): 5–55.

Serper, A. 'Guiraut de Borneil, le "gant" . . .', *Revue des langues romanes* 80 (1974): 93–106.

Simonelli, M. P. *Lirica moralistica nell'Occitania del secolo XII: Bernart de Venzac* (1975).

Spampinato, M. 'Per un esame strutturale della lingua poetica dei trovatori', *Filologia e Letteratura* 16 (1970): 39–76.

Topsfield, L. T. *Troubadours and Love* (1975).

SPANISH

Deyermond, A. D. *Historia de la literatura española I: La Edad Media* (1974).

Fernandez Alonso, M. R. *Una visión de la muerte en la lírica española* (1971).

Frenk Alatorre, M. *Las jarchas mozárabes y los comienzos de la lírica románica* (Colegio de México, 1975).

Gangutia Elícegui, E. 'Poesía griega "de amigo" y poesía arabigo-española' *Emerita* 40: (1972): 329–96.

Gonzalo de Berceo *Obras completas*, ed. B. Dutton (3 vols., London, 1967–75).

Monroe, J. T. 'Formulaic Diction and the Common Origins of Romance Lyric Traditions', *Hispanic Review* 43 (1975): 341–50.
'Two New Bilingual "Harğas" ', *ibid.*, 42 (1974): 243–64.
(ed.) *Hispano-Arabic Poetry: a Student Anthology* (1974).

Rico, F. 'Corraquín Sancho, Roldán y Oliveros: un cantar paralelístico castellano del siglo XII', in *Homenaje a la memoria de Don Antonio Rodríguez-Moñino* (1975): 537–64.

Sánchez Romeralo, A. *El villancico* (1969).

Solá-Solé, J. M. (ed.) *Corpus de poesía mozárabe: Las harğas andalusíes* (1973).

Stern, S. M. *Hispano-Arabic Strophic Poetry* (Oxford, 1974).

Torner, E. M. *Lírica hispánica. Relaciones entre lo popular y lo culto* (1966).

REFERENCES TO WORKS CITED

Figures with asterisks refer to pages in this book

CHAPTER 1

13* The Syrian cabaret-hostess: *Appendix Vergiliana, Copa* vv. 1–3. 14* Quintilian: *De institutione oratoria* I, 12, 3. Suetonius: *Galba* xiii. 15* St John Chrysostom: *Patrologia Graeca* 55, 156–7. Lactantius: *Divinae institutiones* VI, 20. 16* Gregory of Tours: *Historia Francorum* II, 12. 17* *Widsith*: vv. 50–57, 75–77, 88–108, 135–43 (ASPR III, p. 151). 19* Cuthbert: *Epistolae Selectae* (MGH, A. Tangl) I, pp. 250–2. 22* Heinrich von Veldeke: *Eneasroman* vv. 13184 ff. *Dit de la maaille*: A. Jubinal, *Jongleurs et trouvères* (1835), p. 103. 23* *I have my land*: Walther (Lachmann/Kraus/Kuhn) 28, 31. 24* *Horn: The Romance of Horn* (M. K. Pope, 1955) vv. 2830–45. 27* The earliest musical manuscript: Paris Bibliothèque Nationale lat. 1154 (described by H. Spanke, *Studi medievali*, n.s. IV, pp. 288 ff.). Adam of Bremen: *Gesta* III, 38. 28* Sextus Amarcius (K. Manitius, 1969): *Sermones*, I v, 392 ff. 29* Three of the four lyrics: CC 14, 12, and 10. On the seven love-songs in the CC, see MLREL I, pp. 271–81.

For references to music and musicians in this chapter, I am particularly indebted to the studies of A. Machabey and W. Salmen cited above pp. 248–9*. Guenther Wille's *Musica Romana* (1967) appeared too late for me to use.

CHAPTER 2

33* *Hic ignis*: W. Bulst, *Hymni Latini Antiquissimi LXXV Psalmi III* (1956), p. 46. *Exsultet: Liber Usualis Missae et Officii* (1937), p. 740. 34* Venantius Fortunatus (MGH, F. Leo): *Salve festa dies*, extracts from III, 9, adapted for processional use; *Vexilla regis*, II, 6; *Pange lingua*, II, 2. *Ut quid iubes*: the partial text in *Poetae* III, p. 732, has now been completed by B. Bischoff, *Medium Aevum Vivum* (Ed. D. Schaller/H. R. Jauss, 1960), p. 68. Melody: E. de Coussemaker, *Histoire de l'harmonie au Moyen Age* (1852), pl. v. 36* *Porrige dextram: Poetae* III, p. 726. 37* *Dat gafregin ih*: *Lesebuch*, pp. 73–74, adopting Kögel's completion of v. 3 and Grimm's of v. 4; *Völuspá* (Poetic *Edda*), st. 3. 38* Otfrid: *Lesebuch*, p. 97. 40* *Eulalia: Testi* 21. Latin *Eulalia*: P. von Winterfeld, *Zeitschrift für deutsches Altertum* XLV, pp. 133–47. 41* *A ladder stretching*: Notker, W. von den Steinen II, p. 90. 42* Perpetua: *Passio SS. Perpetuae et Felicitatis* iv and x.

45* Hermann of Reichenau: AH 44, 227. 48* Peter Damian: M. Lokrantz, pp. 91, 93. 49* Ezzo: *Dichtungen* I, pp. 289, 301. 50* *Mei amic: Chrestomathie*, col. 19. Melody: *Nachlass* 1. 52*–53* Abelard, hymns: AH 48, 169–70 and 177–8. 54* *Lament of Dinah*: W. Meyer, *Gesammelte Abhandlungen* I (1905), pp. 366–7. 55* Philip, hymns: AH 50, 363; AH 21, 14; CB 131 (melody: H. Husmann, *Die mittelalterliche Mehrstimmigkeit*, p. 34); CB 34, st. 3 (I adopt the spellings and the reading 'rex' from the Codex Buranus, fol. 5v). 56* Peire Cardenal: R. Lavaud lxxx. 58* *Ritmo cassinese*: *Poeti* I, p. 9. *Elegia giudeo-italiana*: *Poeti* I, p. 37. 59* St Francis: *Poeti* I, p. 33. 59*–61* Jacopone: *Poeti* II, pp. 116, 148 (vv. 329–38); F. Ageno (1953) lxxv; *Poeti* II, p. 119. 62* *Stabat mater*: AH 54, 201. 63* St Godric: J. Hall, *Early Middle English* I, p. 5. 64* *Nou goth sonne*: EL 1. Walter of Châtillon: K. Strecker (1925) 4. 65* *Whyt was hys nakede brest*: RL 1 (cf. notes p. 241). I have based my text on three versions, and slightly normalised spelling. The earliest MS. of this poem is *c.* 1230. 66* *Hey a-pon a dune*: EL 64. 67* *In that blisful*: EL 4; Latin: AH 8, 58. Judas: EL 25; K. Sisam, *Fourteenth Century Verse and Prose*, p. 168. 69* *Wen the turuf*: EL 30. *At a sprynge-wel*: RL 130. 70* *Gold and al*: RL 71. 72* '*Ay, Madre de Deus*': *Cantigas* xciv (W. Mettmann I, p. 268). 73*–74* Ramon Lull: *Obres essencials* I, pp. 1308–28, 1301–2. 75* *Song to Mary* (*Melker Marienlied*): *Dichtungen* I, p. 361. 76* *Columba aspexit*: Nassauische Landesbibliothek MS. 2, fol. 476 r-v (facsimile, J. Gmelch, 1913). 78* *Long ago*: DLD 1, v; melody, TTM, p. 56. 81* Hadewijch: E. Rombauts–N. De Paepe 10 (p. 88). 83*–85* Mechthild: P. G. Morel I, 13; VII, 40; I 44; III, 3; II, 3.

CHAPTER 3

88* Joseph Bédier 'Danses' (247*). 90* Theodor Frings: *Minnesinger und Trouba-dours*, Deutsche Akademie der Wissenschaften zu Berlin, 1949. Pompeii: *Corpus Inscriptionum Latinarum* IV 2060; 3117; 8878; 5092. 91* *Wulf and Eadwacer*, ASPR III, p. 179. 92* *Levis exsurgit Zephirus*: CC 40. 94* *Du bist mîn*: MF 3, 1. *Gruonet der walt*: CB 149. 95* *Mich dunket*: MF 3, 18. *Mir erwelten*: MF 13, 27. 96* *Siet soi*: *Romances*, p. 16 (l. 3, *em.* P.D.). 97* *Bele Aielis*: *Romances*, p. 209. *Bele Yolanȝ*: *Romances*, p. 10. 100* *Lévati dalla porta*: *Poesia*, p. 104. 102* Mendinho: *Amigo* 252. 103* Martin Codax: *Amigo* 494; melody, H. Anglés, *La música de las Cantigas* III, 2, p. 54. 104* Pero Meogo: *Amigo* 414. 105* Martin Padrozelos: *Amigo* 456. Béatrice de Die: A. Berry, *Florilège des troubadours*, p. 272 (cf. also G. Kussler-Ratyé, *Archivum Romanicum* I, 1917, p. 173). 107* *Jherusalem*: J. Bédier/P. Aubry, *Les chansons de croisade*, p. 278.

CHAPTER 4

110* *Comrades, I'll make a song*: Guillaume IX (A. Jeanroy) i. 112* *Who is my love*: Jeanroy iv, st. 5–6. Kürenberc: MF 8, 9 (on the last lines, see F. R. Schröder, *Beiträge Tübingen* 1956, p. 345). 113* *I stood*: MF 8, 1 and 9, 29 (I accept the common view that these form one poem). *I nurtured a falcon*: MF 9, 33. 114* *A falcon is perched*: V. Karadžić, *Srpske narodne pjesme* V 500. I am grateful to Mr K. S. Pavlowitch for assistance with the translation. 115* *Women and falcons*: MF 10, 17. *What good*: Jeanroy viii, st. 4. *In the sweetness*: Jeanroy x. 117* *Loveliest lady*: MF 9, 21. *As the morning star*: MF 10, 1. 118* *I'll make a song*: Jeanroy v. *To reject*: MF 7, 1. 119*–20* Jaufre Rudel (A. Jeanroy): ii, st. 2; iii, st. 3, 6; iv, st. 2; a parodistic song: vi; *Lanquan li jorn*: v. 121–4* Bernart de Venta-dour (C. Appel): 31, st. 3, 6–7; 39, st. 3–7; 15, st. 5; 2, st. 4; 29, st. 7; 23, st. 4, 6–7; 6, st. 7. 125* Arnaut Daniel (G. Toja): ix, st. 5; xv. 126* Raimbaut de Vaqueiras:

J. Linskill xviii, st. 6. 127* Gace Brulé: H. Petersen Dyggve xxv, st. 3; spelling as normalised by B. Woledge (see Bibliography 245*). Chastelain de Couci: A. Lerond i, st. 4, 6; melody, J. Bédier/P. Aubry, *Les chansons de croisade*, p. 308. 128* Conon de Béthune: A. Pauphilet, pp. 869–70. 129* Jacques d'Autun: A. Langfors, *Romania* LVIII (1932) pp. 341–5. 131* *Auwê lîp*: K. Wolfskehl/F. von der Leyen, *Älteste deutsche Dichtungen* p. 40. (The MS München Clm 536, fol. 136r, has *nemen*, 'accept', for *minnen* in l. 4). 132* Burggraf von Rietenburg: MF 19, 17. Heinrich von Morungen: MF 139, 19. 134* *Si hât mich verwunt*: MF 141, 37. 136–8* Walther (Lachmann/Kraus/Kuhn): 53, 25, st. 3, 5; 72, 31, st. 4–5; 47, 36, st. 4; 62, 6, st. 4. 138* Otto von Botenlauben: DLD 41, xii. Friedrich von Hausen: MF 45, 37. 140* Heinrich Frauenlob: L. Ettmüller, p. 246. 141* *Annualis mea:* CB 168. 144* *I am all bereft*: v. *infra*, p. 280; *Foweles in the frith*: EL 8; with melody, A. Hughes, *Early Medieval Music*, p. 343. 145* *Bryd one brere*: SL 147; melody, John Stevens (see above, p. 245)*. 146* *Levedy of alle londe*: *Harley Lyrics* (G. L. Brook) 5, st. 2. 147* *So longe ic have, lavedi*: R. H. Robbins, *Anglia* 83 (1965), p. 47. *Mercy me graunt*: SL 139. 148* King Denis: *Amor* 73. 149* *Como morreu*: *Ajuda* 35. 150* *If I were able to unlove*: Pero da Ponte, *Ajuda* 289. *For the little*: Joan de Guilhade, *Ajuda* 239. *If I meet my death*: Roí Queimado, *Ajuda* 143. 151* *Joana, I said*: *Ajuda* 104. 152* *Meravigliosamente*: *Poeti* I, p. 55. 154* *Lo viso mi fa andare*: *Scuola* I, p. 50. 155* *Contrasto*: *Poeti* I, p. 177. 156* *Vedut 'ho la lucente*: *Poeti* II, p. 469. 158* *Al cor gentil*: *Poeti* II, p. 460. *Donna me prega*: *Poeti* II, p. 522. 160* *Whoever has seen Lucia*: *Poeti* II, p. 479. 161* *'Becchina, love!'*: *Poeti* II, p. 372. 162* Dante: *Rime* (G. Contini) 46.

CHAPTER 5

168* *The cock has crowed*: A. Waley, *The Book of Songs* (1937), p. 37. 169* Meleager: *Anthologia Graeca (Palatina)* V, 172. Chaucer: *Troilus and Criseyde* III st. 204. 170* *When Phoebus's bright beam*: *Testi* 3. Melody: G. Vecchi, *Poesia latina medievale* pl. x. 171* *O you who guard*: G. Vecchi, *op. cit.* p. 146. Melody *ibid.* pl. iii. *Bjarkamál: Heimskringla*, Óláfs saga helga ch. 208 (*Íslenzk Fornrit* XXVII, p. 361). Prudentius: *Cathemerinon* i, vv. 5 ff. 173* *Cantant omnes volucres*: MLREL II, p. 352. *Quan lo rossinhols*: A. Berry, *Florilège des troubadours* p. 2; 174* *En un vergier*: *ibid.* p. 4. 176* *Glorious king*: (with melody) TTM, p. 14. Anonymous alba: *Ab la genser que sia*, *Troubadours* I, p. 102; M. de Riquer, *Las albas provençales* (1944) ii. Cadenet: C. Appel, p. 80; melody: *Nachlass* 183. 177* *Ich sich den morgensterne*: CB 183a. *Sláfst du*: MF 39, 18. 178–9* Wolfram: DLD 69, iv (the palinode); ii (*Sîne klâwen*). 180* Heinrich von Morungen: MF 143, 22. 182* Von Wissenlo: DLD 68, i. *Gaite de la tor*: (with melody) P. Aubry, *Trouvères et troubadours*, pp. 89–94. *Quant voi l'aube*: B. Woledge, *The Penguin Book of French Verse* I, p. 89. *Entre moi et mon ami*: *ibid.* p. 88. Torneol: *Amigo* 75. 183* Juião Bolseiro: *Amigo* 394. 184* *Pàrtite, amore, adeo*: *Poesia*, p. 122.

CHAPTER 6

186* *Tuba clarifica*: B. Thorsberg, *Etudes sur l'hymnologie moçarabe* (1962), p. 137. 188* *bella 'n tresca*: *Chanson de Sainte Foy* (P. Alfaric/E. Hoepffner, 2 vols., 1926) v. 14. 189* *Swaz hie gât umbe*: CB 167a (literally, the first line is not a question but introduces a statement). *Dance round the fiddlers*: CB 165, st. 3. 190* *Come to me*: CC 49 (cf. MLREL I, p. 274). *Est il paradis*: *Rondeaux* I, p. 83. 191* *E·lla mia donna*: *Poeti* I, p. 777. 192* Baude dela Kakerie: F. Gennrich, *Altfranzösische Lieder*

II 51 (with melody); J. Bédier, 'Danses' (247*) pp. 412–19. *The time of joy*: CB 179. 194* Joan Zorro: *Amigo* 390. 195* *Maiden in the mor lay*: SL 18. 196* *A l'entrada*: (with melody) TTM, p. 22. 200* *In un boschetto*: Poeti II, p. 555. 201* *Nemt, frowe*: Walther (Lachmann/Kraus/Kuhn) 74, 20. 204* *An old woman*: Neidhart (M. Haupt/E. Wiessner) 4, 31, st. 3. 205* *Sinc ein guldîn huon*: *ibid*. 40, 1; (with melody) TTM, p. 54.

CHAPTER 7

208* Marcabru: J. M. L. Dejeanne, xl. Corrections by K. Lewent, *Zeitschrift für romanische Philologie* 37 (1913), pp. 445–6. 211* Bertran de Born: C. Appel, 37. 212* *Ja nus hons pris*: (with melody) F. Gennrich, *Die Rotruenge* (1925), p. 20. 214* *Quis aquam tuo capiti*: text from the Bodleian MSS. Add. A 44, fol. 66r, and Lat. Misc. d. 6, fol. 60v (which reads *dum regem*); *Patrologia Latina* 207, 1132. 215* *Que farai, fra Iacovone*: Poeti II, p. 97. 218* Süsskind: DLD 56, v. 219* *I've always heard*: Escarnho 366. 220* *Do you want your daughter*: Escarnho 365. *Maria Péreȝ*: Escarnho 356. *In his songs*: Escarnho 380. 221* *Lord God*: Escarnho 381. *Maria Negra*: Escarnho 384. 223* *Non me posso*: Escarnho 10. 225–7* Walther (Lachmann/Kraus/Kuhn): 34, 4; 83, 1; 66, 21.

In the original edition of *The Medieval Lyric*, the first English song cited on p. 144 was translated from the text Carleton Brown had established in 1932 (EL, p. xii), which has remained standard ever since. In 1974 some of Brown's readings were questioned, however, by Theo Stemmler (*Mannheimer Berichte* 8, p. 247). The fine accompanying photograph that Stemmler published—in several places more legible than the MS itself, which I collated afresh recently—will show readers the exceptional difficulties involved in establishing a reliable text of this song. Further work with an ultra-violet lamp, or special photographic techniques, may bring complete success, though it is also possible that parts of the text are far more faded today than they were in 1932 and may never be fully recoverable.

Stemmler suggested some important modifications of Brown's text. In the first line, for Brown's '[þe]h þet hi can wittes fule-wis', he proposes 'ic am witles, ful awis' (Brown's two opening words having been erased by the copyist); in the ninth, in place of 'mon non', he proposes 'moni mon'. In both these cases, Stemmler's reconstruction makes the line mean the exact opposite of what it meant in Brown! In the eighth line he corrects Brown's unattested word 'þriminde' to 'þriuiinde' (though here the meaning remains unchanged).

I have accepted Stemmler's corrections in so far as they alter the sense, and have modified my translation accordingly. But on examining the MS, while 'witles', 'þriuiinde' and 'moni mon' are undoubtedly correct readings, I was persuaded that the first line reads thus:

ic añ witles fuli wis

('fuli' might conceivably be 'fula'; about the word-division there can be no doubt). A new text of the lyric must naturally emend 'añ' to 'am' and alter the word-division to 'ful iwis'.

Stemmler in his article does not discuss the remainder of Brown's text. I would query several other readings, though these concern forms rather than sense (e.g. in 6 I read 'stan', not 'ston', in 9 'bildes', not 'bildeð'). I cannot decipher the concluding line with any confidence. But one other new reading, which seems to me certain, is important for its implications: where Brown (and presumably

Stemmler also) read 'bliþe for to *boe / ned* efter mi deað me longgeð', I believe the MS reads:

    . . . bliþe for to been ed efter (etc.)

If Brown's interpretation remains correct, the word-division in the MS ('to been ed' for 'to bee / ned') is so bizarre that, if we recall the copyist's earlier 'fuli wis' (for 'ful iwis') as well as his erroneous 'ic an̄' for 'ic am', the conclusion seems unavoidable, these lines are not an autograph, 'written in pencil apparently because their author had no thought of preserving them', as Brown (p. xiii) argued, but a copy by a careless scribe. And if they are a copy, it seems likely that our earliest extant Middle English love-lyric, copied 'shortly after 1200' (ibid. p. xii), still belongs to the twelfth century rather than the early thirteenth.

INDEX